THE REBELLIOUS LIFE OF
MRS. ROSA PARKS

Center Point
Large Print

**This Large Print Book carries the
Seal of Approval of N.A.V.H.**

THE
REBELLIOUS LIFE
OF
MRS. ROSA PARKS

Jeanne Theoharis

CENTER POINT LARGE PRINT
THORNDIKE, MAINE

This Center Point Large Print edition
is published in the year 2013 by arrangement with
Beacon Press.

The text of this Large Print edition is unabridged.
In other aspects, this book may vary
from the original edition.
Printed in the United States of America
on permanent paper.
Set in 16-point Times New Roman type.

ISBN: 978-1-61173-676-2

Library of Congress Cataloging-in-Publication Data

Theoharis, Jeanne.
   The rebellious life of Mrs. Rosa Parks / Jeanne Theoharis. — Center point
large print edition.
      pages cm
   Originally published: 2012.
   ISBN 978-1-61173-676-2 (library binding : alk. paper)
   1. Parks, Rosa, 1913–2005.
      2. African American women civil rights workers—
         Alabama—Montgomery—Biography.
      3. Civil rights workers—Alabama—Montgomery—Biography.
      4. African Americans—Civil rights—Alabama—Montgomery—
         History—20th century.
      5. Segregation in transportation—Alabama—Montgomery—
         History—20th century. 6. Montgomery (Ala.)—Race relations.
      7. Montgomery (Ala.)—Biography. I. Title.
   F334.M753P3883 2013
   323.092—dc23
   [B]
                                                    2012045317

CONTENTS

INTRODUCTION

National Honor/Public Mythology
The Passing of Rosa Parks

ON OCTOBER 24, 2005, AFTER nearly seventy years of activism, Rosa Parks died in her home in Detroit at the age of ninety-two. Within days of her death, Representative John Conyers Jr., who had employed Parks for twenty years in his Detroit office, introduced a resolution to have her body lie in honor in the Capitol rotunda. Less than two months after Hurricane Katrina and after years of partisan rancor over the social justice issues most pressing to civil rights activists like Parks, congressional leaders on both sides of the aisle rushed to pay tribute to the "mother of the civil rights movement." Parks would become the first woman and second African American to be granted this honor. "Awesome" was how Willis Edwards, a longtime associate who helped organize the three-state tribute, described the numbers of the people who pulled it together.

Parks's body was first flown to Montgomery for a public viewing and service attended by various dignitaries, including Condoleezza Rice, who affirmed that "without Mrs. Parks, I probably would not be standing here today as Secretary of State." Then her body was flown to Washington,

DC, on a plane commanded by Lou Freeman, one of the first African American chief pilots for a commercial airline. The plane circled Montgomery twice in honor of Parks, with Freeman singing "We Shall Overcome" over the loudspeaker. "There wasn't a dry eye in the plane," recalled Parks's longtime friend, federal Sixth Circuit judge Damon Keith. Her coffin was met in Washington by the National Guard and accompanied to its place of honor in the Capitol rotunda.

Forty thousand Americans came to the Capitol to bear witness to her passing. President and Mrs. Bush laid a wreath on her unadorned cherrywood coffin. "The Capitol Rotunda is one of America's most powerful illustrations of the values of freedom and equality upon which our republic was founded," Senate majority leader Bill Frist, resolution cosponsor, explained to reporters, "and allowing Mrs. Parks to lie in honor here is a testament to the impact of her life on both our nation's history and future." Yet, Frist claimed Parks's stand was "not an intentional attempt to change a nation, but a singular act aimed at restoring the dignity of the individual."

Her body was taken from the Capitol to the Metropolitan African Methodist Episcopal Church for a public memorial before an overflowing crowd. Then her casket was returned to Detroit for another public viewing at the Museum of African

American History. Thousands waited in the rain to pay their respects to one of Detroit's finest. The seven-hour funeral celebration held at Detroit's Greater Grace Temple on November 2 attracted four thousand mourners and a parade of speakers and singers from Bill Clinton to Aretha Franklin. In their tributes, Democratic presidential hopefuls focused on Parks's quietness: Senator Barack Obama praised Parks as a "small, quiet woman whose name will be remembered," while Senator Hillary Clinton spoke of the importance of "quiet Rosa Parks moments." As thousands more waited outside to see the dramatic spectacle, a horse-drawn carriage carried Mrs. Parks's coffin to Woodlawn Cemetery, where she was buried next to her husband and mother. Six weeks later, President Bush signed a bill ordering a permanent statue of Parks placed in the U.S. Capitol, the first ever of an African American, explaining, "By refusing to give in, Rosa Parks showed that one candle can light the darkness. . . . Like so many institutionalized evils, once the ugliness of these laws was held up to the light, they could not stand . . . and as a result, the cruelty and humiliation of the Jim Crow laws are now a thing of the past."

Parks's passing presented an opportunity to honor a civil rights legend and to foreground the pivotal but not fully recognized work of movement women. Many sought to commemorate her commitment to racial justice and pay tribute to her courage and public service. Tens of thousands of Americans took off work and journeyed long distances to Montgomery, DC, and Detroit to bear witness to her life and pay their respects. Across the nation, people erected alternate memorials to Mrs. Parks in homes, churches, auditoriums, and public spaces of their com-munities. The streets of Detroit were packed with people who, denied a place in the church, still wanted to honor her legacy. Awed by the numbers of people touched by Parks's passing, friends and colleagues saw this national honor as a way to lift up the legacy of this great race woman.

Despite those powerful visions and labors, the woman who emerged in the public tribute bore only a fuzzy resemblance to Rosa Louise Parks. Described by the *New York Times* as the "acci-dental matriarch of the civil rights movement," the Rosa Parks who surfaced in the deluge of public commentary was, in nearly every account, characterized as "quiet." "Humble," "dignified," and "soft-spoken," she was "not angry" and "never raised her voice." Her public contribution as the "mother of the movement" was repeatedly defined by one solitary act on the bus on a long-ago December day and linked to her quietness. Held up as a national heroine but stripped of her lifelong history of activism and anger at American injustice, the Parks who emerged was a self-sacrificing mother figure for a nation who would use her death for a ritual of national redemption. In this story, the civil rights movement demonstrated the power and resilience of American democracy. Birthed from the act of a simple Montgomery seamstress, a nonviolent struggle built by ordinary people had corrected the aberration of Southern racism without overthrowing the government or engaging in a bloody revolution.

This narrative of national redemption entailed rewriting the history of the black freedom struggle along with Parks's own rich political history—disregarding her and others' work in Montgomery that had tilled the ground for decades for a mass movement to flower following her 1955 bus stand. It ignored her forty years of political work in Detroit *after* the boycott, as well as the substance of her political philosophy, a philosophy that had commonalties with Malcolm X, Queen Mother Moore, and Ella Baker, as well as Martin Luther King Jr. The 2005 memorial celebrated Parks the individual rather than a community coming together in struggle. Reduced to one act of conscience made obvious, the long history of activism that laid the groundwork for her decision, the immense risk of her bus stand, and her labors over the 382-day boycott went largely unheralded, the happy ending replayed over and over. Her sacrifice and lifetime of political service were largely backgrounded.

Buses were crucial to the pageantry of the event and trailed her coffin around the country. Sixty Parks family members and dignitaries traveled from Montgomery to DC aboard three Metro buses draped in black bunting. In DC, a vintage bus also dressed in black, along with other city buses, followed the hearse to the public memorial at the Metropolitan African Methodist Episcopal Church. The procession to and from the Capitol rotunda included an empty vintage 1957 bus. The Henry Ford Museum in Dearborn, Michigan, offered free admission the day of her funeral so visitors could see the actual bus "where it all began."

Parks's body also served an important function, brought from Detroit to Montgomery to Washington, DC, and then back to Detroit for everyone to witness. Her body became necessary for these public rites, a sort of public communion where Americans would visit her coffin and be sanctified. This personal moment with Parks's body became not simply a private moment of grief and honor but also a public act of celebrating a nation that would celebrate her. Having her casket on view in the Capitol honored Parks as a national dignitary while reminding mourners that their experience was sponsored by the federal government. Look how far the nation has come, the events tacitly announced, look at what a great nation we are. A woman who had been denied a seat on the bus fifty years earlier was now lying in the Capitol. Instead of using the opportunity to illuminate and address current social inequity, the public spectacle provided an opportunity for the nation to lay to rest a national heroine *and* its own history of racism.

This national honor for Rosa Parks served to obscure the present injustices facing the nation. Less than two months after the shame of the federal government's inaction during Hurricane Katrina, the public memorial for Parks provided a way to paper over those devastating images from New Orleans. Burying the history of American racism was politically useful and increasingly urgent. Parks's body brought national absolution at a moment when government negligence and the economic and racial inequities laid bare during Katrina threatened to disrupt the idea of a color-blind America. Additionally, in the midst of a years-long war where the Pentagon had forbidden the photographing of coffins returning from Iraq and Afghanistan, Parks's coffin was to be the one that would be seen and honored.

Friends and colleagues noted the irony of such a misappropriation. Many bemoaned the fact that some of the speakers at the memorials didn't really know Mrs. Parks, while many friends and longtime political associates weren't invited to participate. Some refused to go or even to watch, seeing this as an affront to the woman they had admired, while others felt troubled but attended nevertheless. Still others used the events to pay tribute to the greatness of the woman they had known. Regardless, they saw the nation squandering the opportunity to recommit itself to the task of social justice to which Parks had dedicated her life.

The public memorial promoted an inspirational fable: a long-suffering, gentle heroine challenged backward Southern villainy with the help of a faceless chorus of black boycotters and catapulted a courageous new leader, Martin Luther King Jr. into national leadership. Mrs. Parks was honored as midwife—not a leader or thinker or long-time activist—of a struggle that had long run its course. This fable is a romantic one, promoting the idea that without any preparation (political or psychic) or subsequent work a person can make great change with a single act, suffer no lasting consequences, and one day be heralded as a hero. It is also gendered, holding up a caricature of a quiet seamstress who demurely kept her seat and implicitly castigating other women, other black women, for being poor or loud or angry and therefore not appropriate for national recognition. Parks's memorialization promoted an improbable children's story of social change—one not-angry woman sat down and the country was galvanized—that erased the long history of collective action against racial injustice and the widespread opposition to the black freedom movement, which for decades treated Parks's extensive political activities as "un-American."

This fable—of an accidental midwife without a larger politics—has made Parks a household name but trapped her in the elementary school curriculum, rendering her uninteresting to many young people. The variety of struggles that Parks took part in, the ongoing nature of the campaign against racial injustice, the connections between Northern and Southern racism that she recognized, and the variety of Northern and Southern movements in which she engaged have been given short shrift in her iconization. Parks's act was separated from a community of people who prepared the way for her action, expanded her stand into a movement, and continued with her in the struggle for justice in the decades that followed.

This limited view of Parks has extended to the historical scholarship as well. Despite the wealth of children's books on Parks, Douglas Brinkley's pocket-sized, un-footnoted biography *Rosa Parks: A Life* and Parks's own young-adult-focused autobiography with Jim Haskins, *Rosa Parks: My Story*, are the only more detailed treatments of her life and politics. With biographies of Abraham Lincoln numbering over a hundred and of Martin Luther King in the dozens, the lack of a scholarly monograph on Parks is notable. The trend among scholars in recent years has been to de-center Parks in the story of the early civil rights movement, focusing on the role of other activists in Montgomery; on other people, like Claudette Colvin, who had also refused to give up their seats; and on other places than Montgomery that helped give rise to a mass movement. While this has provided a much more substantive account of the boycott and the roots of the civil rights movement, Rosa Parks continues to be hidden in plain sight, celebrated and paradoxically relegated to be a hero for children.

When I began this project, people often stared at me blankly—another book on Rosa Parks? Surely there was already a substantive biography. Others assumed that the mythology of the simple, tired seamstress had long since been revealed and repudiated. Many felt confident we already knew her story—*she was the NAACP secretary who'd attended Highlander Folk School and hadn't even been the first arrested for refusing to move,* they quickly recited. Some even claimed that if Rosa Parks had supported other movements, "don't you think we would know that already."

For my part, I had spent more than a decade documenting the untold stories of the civil rights movement in the North. This work had sought to complicate many of the false oppositions embedded in popular understandings of the movement: North versus South, civil rights versus Black Power, nonviolence versus self-defense, pre-1955 and post. When Rosa Parks died in 2005, I, like many others, was captivated and then horrified by the national spectacle made of her death. I gave a talk on its caricature of her and, by extension, its misrepresentation of the civil rights movement, decrying the funeral's homage to a post-racial America and ill-fitting tribute to the depth of Parks's political work. Asked to turn the talk into an article, I felt humbled and chastened. Here in the story of perhaps the most iconic heroine of the civil rights movement lay all the themes I had written about for years. And yet I kept bumping up against the gaps in the histories of her. It became clear how little we actually knew about Rosa Parks.

If we follow the actual Rosa Parks—see her decades of community activism before the boycott; take notice of the determination, terror, and loneliness of her bus stand and her steadfast work during the year of the boycott; and see her political work continue for decades following the boycott's end—we encounter a much different "mother of the civil rights movement." This book begins with the development of Parks's self-respect and fierce determination as a young person, inculcated by her mother and grandparents; her schooling at Miss White's Montgomery Industrial

School for Girls; and her marriage to Raymond Parks, "the first real activist I ever met." It follows her decades of political work before the boycott, as she and a small cadre of activists pressed to document white brutality and legal malfeasance, challenge segregation, and increase black voter registration, finding little success but determined to press on. It demonstrates that her bus arrest was part of a much longer history of bus resistance in the city by a seasoned activist frustrated with the vehemence of white resistance and the lack of a unified black movement who well understood the cost of such stands but "had been pushed as far as she could be pushed." The community's reaction that followed astonished her. And thus chapter 4 shows how a 382-day boycott resulted from collective community action, organization, and tenacity, as Parks and many other black Montgomerians worked to create and maintain the bus protest for more than a year.

The second half of the book picks up Parks's story after the boycott. It shows the enduring cost of her bus stand for her and her family, and the decade of death threats, red-baiting, economic insecurity, and health issues that followed her arrest. Forced to leave Montgomery for Detroit, her life in the North—"the promised land that wasn't"—is a palpable reminder that racial inequality was a national plague, not a Southern malady. Parks's activism did not end in the South nor did it stop with the passage of the Civil and Voting Rights acts. And so the last chapters of the book illustrate the interconnections between the civil rights and Black Power movements, North and South, as Parks joined new and old comrades to oppose Northern segregation, cultivate independent black political power, impart black history, challenge police brutality and government persecution, and oppose U.S. involvement in Vietnam.

One of the greatest distortions of the Parks fable has been the ways it made her meek and missed her lifetime of progressive politics and the resolute political sensibility that identified Malcolm X as her personal hero. The many strands of black protest and radicalism ran through her life. Parks's grandfather had been a follower of Marcus Garvey. She'd gotten her political start as a newlywed when her husband, Raymond, worked to free the Scottsboro boys, and she spent a decade with E. D. Nixon helping transform Montgomery's NAACP into a more activist chapter. She attended Highlander Folk School to figure out how to build a local movement for desegregation and helped maintain—not simply spark—the 382-day Montgomery bus boycott. Arriving in Detroit in 1957, she spent more than half of her life fighting racial injustice in the Jim Crow North and was hired by the newly elected congressman John Conyers in 1965 to be part of his Detroit staff. Parks's long-standing political commitments to self-defense, black history, criminal justice, and black political and community empowerment intersected with key aspects of the Black Power movement, and she took part in numerous events in the late 1960s and 1970s. Indeed, the reach of Parks's political life embodies the breadth of the struggle for racial justice in America over the twentieth century and the scope of the roles that women played.

Finding and hearing Rosa Parks has not been easy. The idea of the "quiet" Rosa Parks has obscured much of what she said and did. It has made it all too easy to be satisfied with a narrow sense of her contributions, which rest on a gendered caricature of a quiet NAACP secretary who kept her seat on the bus. Despite a voluminous number of articles about and interviews with her, most reporters asked similar questions. They tended to see her without hearing her, without listening for the political sensibility of the real actor behind the idea of Rosa Parks. Mrs. Parks's words were slow and measured, and interviewers often missed what she was actually saying, impatiently plowing ahead with the story they wanted to tell. The history of the boycott, of what led up to it and what happened during it, has become the stuff of legend—and numerous mistakes and mis-impressions have been canonized in the historical record, creating another set of blinders. Memories fade, distort, and bend—and the invaluable oral histories of the period offer different, sometimes contradictory accounts of the boycott and its pre-history. Moreover, as her friends and colleagues make amply clear, Mrs. Parks never volunteered information that wasn't directly asked for. She was a political activist and a Southern black woman—both of which called for the judicious use of stories, the masking of unpleasant or unnecessary details, and the tendency to background the individual to put forth the interests of the group. Her political activism was born in the viciousness of the 1930s Jim Crow South and the anti-Communist hysteria that attended it—and this would indelibly shape how she obscured her own political sensibility and activities. While maintaining her activism over decades, she remained circumspect about it. Finally, for the second half of her life, Rosa Parks yearned for privacy and found her fame hard to bear, yet she simultaneously believed in her responsibility to continue telling the story of the movement as a way to keep it going. Wanting the history of black struggle to be preserved but disliking the spotlight, she often sought to endure the interviews, rather than use them to tell a different story.

Thus, identifying her frame of these events—her philosophy and narrative voice—has required listening around the margins of those scores of interviews to excavate a more substantive account of what was happening and how she saw it. She chose her words with care, and so, particularly in the sections related to her bus stand and the boycott, I have stitched together many, many quotes from dozens of interviews so that we might hear her insights and understand the events as she saw them. The black press has proven invaluable to this work, providing some record of her activities, particularly in the years after she left Montgomery. In addition to combing the archives for mentions of her activities, letters, meeting records, newsletters, and other documents, I have interviewed many of her friends, family, and political associates to round out this picture.

Unfortunately, many of Parks's personal effects—dresses, awards, sewing basket, eyeglasses, and papers—have been caught up in an extended legal dispute over her estate between the Rosa and Raymond Parks Institute, which she cofounded with Elaine Steele, and her family. This led a Michigan probate judge to give Guernsey's, a celebrity auction house in New York City, the responsibility of selling all of it, with the profits to be distributed between her institute and family. Guernsey's has been attempting to sell the Rosa Parks Archive for five years, steadfastly unwilling to let any scholar make even a cursory examination. The auction house prepared an inventory of materials, a sixty-four-page list and companion sampling of interesting documents—a task that would be unthinkable without a scholar to contextualize the significance of the documents if Parks was considered a serious political thinker like Thomas Jefferson or Martin Luther King Jr.

The legacy of Rosa Parks over the past decade has been besieged by controversies around profit, control, and the use of her image. This treatment is at odds with how Parks lived and her commitment to the preservation and dissemination of African American history. Parks had donated the "first" installment of her papers to Wayne State University in 1976. "I do hope that my contribution can be made use of," she told a Wayne student reporter. Yet a vast trove of her papers, letters, and other ephemera sits in a storage facility in Manhattan, of use to no one, priced at $6 million to $10 million. Institutions such as Wayne State University, Alabama State University, and the New York Public Library's Schomburg Center for Research in Black Culture would be logical homes for Parks's papers, but they cannot compete in such an auction. And so Parks's ideas and life's work sit idly in a New York warehouse, waiting to be purchased. When that archive is finally opened to researchers, a far more nuanced and detailed record of Parks's political ties and perspectives will be available, no doubt deepening and challenging aspects of this book.

All of this provides certain challenges for a biographer. In attempting to find Rosa Parks I have tried to go beyond the symbol to excavate the political actor, to hear her amidst the bells and whistles. Although I believe I have come to understand some of her political sensibility and to contextualize its roots and historical landscape, there is much still unknown. This is fundamentally a political biography; it does not fully capture her community of friends and family ties, her faith and church life, her marriage, her daily activities. That is a task for others.

What I have endeavored to do is to begin the job of going behind the icon of Rosa Parks to excavate and examine the scope of her political life. In the process, I have used her history to retell and reexamine the span of the black freedom struggle, and to critique the many mythologies that surround much of the popular history of the civil rights movement. Rosa Parks's life is already employed to tell a story of the United States. And so what I do here is tell a different story—showing the much broader truths about race in America, the struggle for black freedom, and the nature of individual courage to be gained from a fuller accounting of her life, a "life history of being rebellious" as she put it. It is a story with far greater lessons on how we might work for social justice today—how a person makes change in a moment and over a lifetime, and what is entailed in the struggle for justice.

A word on naming: I refer to Rosa Parks throughout the book both as Parks and Mrs. Parks. Most people, even young schoolchildren, recognize the name "Rosa Parks." Using Parks and Mrs. Parks—less familiar ways of naming her—signals the need to look at her more carefully. I predominantly use "Parks" (despite the fact that this was how she and others referred to her husband) to follow the custom in scholarly biographies of referring to the subject by her last name. But I interchange this with "Mrs. Parks," the title a form of respect that white people of the era routinely denied black women and the way many people who respected her referred to her. Using the honorific, then, does more than assert Parks's marital and family status; it also adds a degree of dignity, distance, and formality to mark that she is not fully ours as a nation to appropriate. And through the title's juxtaposition of "Mrs. Rosa Parks" and "rebellious," I hope to get at the complex and significant ways she moved through the world.

It is a rare gift as a scholar to get to deconstruct

the popular narrative and demythologize an historical figure, and, in the process, discover a more impressive and substantive person underneath. I have been greatly fortunate in this task. Rosa Parks's political history spans most of the twentieth century, providing an exceptional glimpse into the scope and steadfastness of the struggle for racial justice in America over the past century.

CHAPTER ONE

"A Life History of Being Rebellious"
The Early Years of Rosa McCauley Parks

WHEN ASKED WHAT GAVE HER the strength and commitment to refuse segregation, Parks credited her mother and grandfather "for giving me the spirit of freedom . . . that I should not feel because of my race or color, inferior to any person. That I should do my very best to be a respectable person, to respect myself, to expect respect from others, and to learn what I possibly could for self improvement." This learned sense of rectitude and race pride made Rosa Parks a woman who insisted on respect and found ways over the course of her life to fight for justice and freedom.

Parks's life reveals "a life history of being rebellious," as she liked to explain it. She also learned that society did not take kindly to black rebels. Survival thus necessitated "treading the tightrope of Jim Crow," a complex daily negotiation. From an early age, respectability for Parks meant not just the image she presented to the world but the respect she expected—and would demand—from society around her.

Nevertheless, Parks long struggled with the idea of recounting her life story—approached to do one since the boycott began. On a scrap of paper written in the late 1950s, she wondered "Is it worthwhile to reveal the intimacies of the past life? Would the people be sympathetic or disillusioned when the facts of my life are told?" On another scrap from this period, she notes, "Hurt, harm and danger. The dark closet of my mind. So much to remember." For the second half of her adult life, Parks was bombarded with interviews. This continual questioning weighed heavily on her, particularly having to tell and retell painful incidents. In 1980, she asked a reporter, "Have you ever been hurt and a place tries to heal a little bit, and then you just pull that scab off it over and over again? So some things I don't mention and some things I do. . . . there's plenty I have never told." At two substantive junctures—the writing of her autobiography with civil rights colleague and children's book author Jim Haskins and her collaboration with celebrated historian Douglas Brinkley on his Penguin Lives short biography—she safeguarded a modicum of privacy, limiting which aspects of her political and personal biography she reported. The fear of people being disillusioned may have still weighed on her decades later.

Born on February 4, 1913, in Tuskegee, Alabama, "halfway between the Emancipation Proclamation and the new era of freedom," Rosa Louise McCauley was named for her mother's mother, Rose, and her father's mother, Louisa. Her audacity and political sensibility emerged early, influenced by her mother's firm determination. "Instead of saying, 'Yes sir,'" Rosa recalled, her mother "was always saying 'No, you won't do this.'" Given the racial climate of early twentieth-century Alabama, saying no required a deep sense of courage. Elaine Steele, Rosa's longtime friend and caretaker, made a similar observation about Rosa: "She can very quietly say 'no' or 'I prefer not,' and you know instinctively that that is the bottom line."

Rosa's mother, Leona Edwards, had been born on April 2, 1887, in Pine Level, Alabama, and attended Payne University in Selma, though she didn't earn a degree. Leona became a schoolteacher and met Rosa's father, James McCauley, a skilled carpenter and stonemason. James, who had been born in Abbeville, Alabama, the second of twelve children born to Anderson and Louisa McCauley, built houses and did masonry work. Rosa's parents were accomplished and driven, and that motivation transferred to their children.

James and Leona married on April 12, 1912, in Pine Level. Leona, who quit teaching when she became pregnant, was unprepared for being a parent and felt isolated and lonely. "She always talked about how unhappy she was," Rosa recalled. Rosa was a frail infant and required a great deal of care. James's brother Robert had come to stay with them, and James left often to find work. Alone and with little financial support, Leona first lived with her in-laws and then moved into her parents' home in Pine Level when Rosa was two.

For stability and access to education for their children, Leona wanted James to find work at Tuskegee Institute but he resisted. James's vocation as a skilled craftsman and his wandering eye took him in search of work across the South and on to New York and Ohio. This left Leona on her own to raise Rosa and her younger brother Sylvester, who was born two and half years after Rosa, on August 20, 1915. Except for a visit when she was five, Rosa did not see her father while she was growing up; he "wasn't stable enough to settle for a long time in one place." After she became an adult, her father reached out to make amends. "I kept thinking of writing you and still putting it off," he wrote her in 1950. "It was in view of the fact that I was over shadowed. With open shame that I and I alone allowled [*sic*] the Evil spirit to lead me completely out of myself for these many years in grose [*sic*] desertion of a good wife and two of the sweetest children ever lived." So Rosa Parks was raised by a single mother—in a home full of love with her grandparents, great-grandfather, mother, and brother.

Because the Pine Level school had a teacher,

Leona McCauley got a job teaching in the village of Spring Hill and was gone during the week, leaving the children in her parents' care. This was hard on Rosa. She once argued with her grandmother, who wanted to punish Sylvester, telling her not to "whip brother and I said he's just a little baby and he doesn't have no mamma and no papa either."

Her grandparents had been enslaved. The product of a union between his mother and the slave owner's son, Rosa's grandfather had "no discernible features of black people," but Sylvester Edwards was a committed race man. Because he had been regularly beaten and nearly starved as a slave boy, he had, according to Rosa, a "somewhat belligerent attitude towards white people" and "liked to laugh at whites behind their backs." He took advantage of his light skin to say and do things that would "embarrass and agitate white people." He didn't let his daughters work in white houses or want his grandchildren playing with white children—and took pleasure in resisting the racial customs of the day.

At six, Rosa saw black soldiers returning from World War I, acting "as if they deserved equal rights because they had served their country" and being shown that this was not the case. Indeed, the summer of 1919 became known as Red Summer, as whites rioted and reasserted their power and position in the wake of the changes brought by the war. A staunch believer in self-defense, Rosa's grandfather became a supporter of Marcus Garvey and his pan-Africanist Universal Negro Improvement Association. Though often associated with New York and the urban North, Garvey had a large and supple base of supporters in the rural South, who were drawn to his bold message of economic self-sufficiency, black-nationalist pride, and self-determination. Klan violence worsened in Pine Level after World War I. They burned churches, and, as Rosa remembered, "people were often flogged or found dead." Garvey's message resonated even more. In the face of this growing violence, Sylvester Edwards would often sit out at night on the porch with his rifle. Rosa recalled that he almost dared the Klan to come onto their property because he was ready to meet them head on. She stayed awake with him some nights, keeping vigil with him. "I wanted to see him kill a Ku Kluxer," she explained. Sometimes they would sleep with their clothes on in fear of being attacked in their sleep.

According to Garvey historian Mary Rolinson, Marcus Garvey came to Alabama in November 1923, meeting with ministers in Birmingham and giving an address in Tuskegee. Parks's grand-father attended a meeting "but he was rejected because of his white appearance. That ended our talking about our going to Africa. . . . [T]hey wouldn't accept him and I can remember that very well." Rosa's grandfather, who was disabled from arthritis, died when she was ten.

Steeped in political thought from an early age, Rosa's family exposed her to a sense of black pride. From an early age, she knew "we were not free." Her mother admired Booker T. Washington and George Washington Carver. A schoolteacher by profession, Leona McCauley taught Rosa her alphabet and figures before she went to school. "In fact I don't even remember [a time] when I didn't read," Parks explained. She extolled her mother's skill and commitment to education: "she believed in teaching anybody . . . and she *could* teach them."

Rosa would grow to be a lifelong devoted reader, but this also exposed her to racist texts. Her early introduction to the philosophy of white supremacy came around age eight when she stumbled upon William Gallo Schell's *Is the Negro a Beast? A Reply to Chas. Carroll's Book Entitled "The Negro a Beast"; Proving That the Negro Is Human from Biblical, Scientific, and Historical Standpoints*. While seeking to counter the argument that black people were akin to beasts and therefore only fit for slavery, Schell's 1901 book still maintained the idea of black inferiority. After reading the book, Rosa felt "awful" as she realized that black people were "not considered complete human beings." "When

I learned that we, my family, were Negroes, it caused me to think that throughout my life I'd have to prove myself as something other than a beast." The impact of the book on young Rosa was immense and devastating as she "didn't have any idea that there would ever be a way to protest this." Thus, her discovery of black history in high school was transformative: "I read everything I could, first in school and then later in magazines."

The revelation of black history would indelibly shape Rosa McCauley Parks's life. She saw the history of black survival, accomplishment, and rebellion as the ultimate weapon against white supremacy. To imagine rebellion was not crazy, a comforting lesson to the adolescent Rosa. As an adult, Parks articulated the ways that the segregated education black children like her received "educate[d] the Negro into believing that he is happier segregated, discriminated against, mistreated and humiliated. Such a good job of brainwashing was done on the Negro that a militant Negro was almost a freak of nature to them, many times ridiculed by others of his group." Education for liberation, reclaiming the history of black resistance, would thus become a driving passion of her adult life. Like other black families, the Edwards family regarded education as a precious commodity that could not be taken away no matter the unequal or dehumanizing treatment. Rosa read voraciously and, upon becoming a public figure, would do everything she could to promote and preserve black history.

The school for black children in Pine Level consisted of "a meager one-room, unpainted shack with wooden shutters and no windows" for children from first through sixth grade and operated on a shortened calendar to allow for agricultural work. Black children attended school for five or six months compared to the nine months for white children. Rosa realized "that we went to a different school than the white children and that the school we went to was not as good as theirs." When Rosa was very young, the town built a new school for white children: "a nice brick building . . . built with public money, including taxes paid by both whites and blacks. Black people had to build and heat their own schools without the help of the town or county or state." The school bus, publicly financed for white children, was not available for black children, so Rosa watched the bus pass by as she walked. This educational inequity laid the foundation for economic inequality, trapping black people in the worst jobs. "We could not compete," Rosa Parks explained as an adult, "so when we had to finally leave school to take a job with poor education we could only get menial work to do for the most part."

Her experiences growing up in a deeply

segregated community dovetailed with those of other black children growing up in the South at this time. "Like millions of black children, before me and after me, I wondered if 'White' water tasted different from 'Colored' water. I wanted to know if 'White' water was white and if 'Colored' water came in different colors. It took me a while to understand that there was no difference in the water." From a young age, Rosa McCauley questioned and saw the ways "coming up in a segregated society does something to you—not only to the oppressed but also to the oppressor."

Like many black children, Rosa picked cotton as a child from "can to can't"—from sunup until after it set. She recalled the ways the boss would ride his horse across the plantation "to see how his niggers were working to bring in the harvest for his wealth and comfort." The material comforts of black subjugation for white families were apparent. As small children, they would sometimes chant while they played, "White folks in the parlor eatin' cold ice cream. Niggers in the back yard eatin' cold collard greens." Rosa's grandparents were in poor health, and due to financial struggles, she sometimes went without shoes. The McCauley family kept a regular garden and a number of fruit trees to supplement their small earnings and have enough to eat.

Rosa Parks's faith also emerged early on. Church was one of the "events that I could look forward to," she explained. A lifelong member of the African Methodist Episcopal Church, she gravitated to the hymns and prayers that filled the weekly service, moved by a God who sought justice on earth. She learned a theology of liberation that affirmed the equality of all people, laid forth a Christian responsibility to act, and provided sustenance to struggle against injustice. "And that's sort of in my family background, too. The Lord's power within me to do what I have done."

Often sick with chronic tonsillitis, Rosa McCauley missed a lot of school and grew up with few friends. When she was nine, her mother was finally able to afford a tonsillectomy. Rosa's mother traveled throughout the county teaching at black church schools. Rosa described the precarious nature of Leona McCauley's work, as black schools often came under attack from white vigilantes. "Many times the children would want to take their books and belongings home in order that they wouldn't be burned during the night by the KKK. However, the particular building that she used as a school house was never burned or molested in any way. But because it happened in other areas near by, there was always the threat that it might happen to us." Then, for three years, Leona McCauley served as the teacher in the school Rosa attended.

At home, the McCauleys discussed the history

of slavery, the situation of blacks in Alabama, and how "to survive, not getting into trouble by confrontation with white people who were not friendly to us." Rosa's family sought to teach her a controlled anger, a survival strategy that balanced compliance and militancy. One of the lessons Leona McCauley imparted that lodged in young Rosa's head was how "slaves had to fool the white people into thinking that they were happy. The white people would get angry if the slaves acted unhappy. They would also treat the slaves better if they thought the slaves liked white people." As she became aware of the terms of white supremacy, the fact that acting happy produced better treatment stuck in her throat. She longed for ways to contest this treatment. She also well understood the punishment for resistance. Recollecting her life growing up in an interview in the late 1960s, Parks, wondered "how we have reached where we are, without things being worse. The only explanation I may have is that the most docile and accepting among us were permitted to survive. Occasionally there would be some who would retaliate, take a violent way of trying to express the resentment at being mistreated. He was called a bad nigger and was just killed outright and made an example of." A young Rosa McCauley, much like a young Malcolm X, struggled with this miseducation, with how to express discontent and still survive.

These were rough times to be black in Alabama. Daily interactions required a constant process of negotiation. Rosa McCauley on occasion stood up for herself and her younger brother: "Maybe the habit of protecting my little brother helped me learn to protect myself." One childhood friend recalled, "Nobody ever bossed Rosa around and got away with it." One time, a white young man named Franklin began taunting Rosa and Sylvester. "I picked up a brick," she recalled, "and dared him to hit me. He thought better of the idea and went away."

When she heard about this, Rosa's grandmother reprimanded her, saying she was "too highstrung" and would be lynched before the age of twenty. "You didn't retaliate if they did something to you," her grandmother admonished her.

"I got very upset about that," Rosa recalled. "I felt that I was very much in my rights to try to defend myself if I could." Her grandmother told her not to talk "biggety to white folks." Sobbing, Rosa felt as if her beloved grandmother had "aligned with the hostile white race against me," and told her, "I would be lynched rather than be run over by them. They could get the rope ready for me any time they wanted to do their lynching." Rosa's grandmother was trying to teach her a lesson about the cost and terms of survival. And Rosa would constantly have to balance these two forces: militancy could get a person killed and yet resistance, however dangerous, pushed back on the oppression and at times made it diminish.

The most specific description of this brick incident comes in a series of notes she wrote on the back of NAACP stationery during the boycott, most likely for a public appearance she was making. Seeking to contextualize her bus stand within her experiences as a young person with a brick, Parks wrote, "While my neck was spared of the lynch rope and my body was never riddled by bullets or dragged by an auto, I felt that I was lynched many times in mind and spirit. I grew up in a world of white power used most cruelly and cunningly to suppress poor helpless black people." The adult Rosa Parks often noted the impact growing up amidst this brutality and oppression had upon her.

Rosa's mother held firm to her desire that her daughter would receive a serious education. Because there was no more schooling available to black children after the sixth grade, she enrolled eleven-year-old Rosa at Miss White's Montgomery Industrial School for Girls in Montgomery and sent her to live with an aunt. In 1922, a year or two before Rosa was sent to Miss White's School, Leona Edwards married forty-six-year-old James Carlie, a timber cutter fourteen years her senior in Montgomery. Never did Rosa Parks publicly mention her mother's second husband; and her cousin Barbara

Alexander had "never heard of any other man . . . it was never mentioned in the family." Leona and Jim Carlie appear to have been married at least eight years, and the 1930 census lists Rosa and Sylvester living with them.

Miss White's school embodied Leona McCauley's advice to her daughter to "take advantage of the opportunities, no matter how few they were." However, this schooling required a tremendous financial sacrifice by Rosa's mother. After her first semester, Rosa received a scholarship to the school and would dust, sweep, and clean the classrooms after school. Run by white women for black girls, Miss White's School adhered to the philosophy of industrial education and the domestic arts most prominently espoused by Booker T. Washington. Parks estimated about "300 or more" young women attended Miss White's. Booker T. Washington himself praised the work of the school for "doing good, practical work in that city." The white teachers emphasized the domestic arts—cooking, sewing, and taking care of the sick—in part because these were jobs open to black women. There was an emphasis on home economics. Rosa McCauley learned to use a sewing machine (they hadn't had one at the rural school she attended) and gained the sewing skills that would serve as a source of income and personal pride throughout her life—"although I didn't feel like I wanted to sew for a living." She also learned stenography and office skills.

Teaching young black girls to be proper Christian women along with tutoring them in academic subjects such as English, science, and geography, the school stressed the dignity of all people. Teachers outlined the freedoms set forth in the Constitution, and the responsibilities of all citizens. Parks learned she "was a person with dignity and self-respect, and I should not set my sights lower than anybody else just because I was black. We were taught to be ambitious and to believe that we could do what we wanted in life," reinforcing the message of pride she'd learned at home.

The lessons learned at Miss White's impacted Parks's schoolmates. Johnnie Carr became a life-long activist and joined the NAACP. Students were taught, as Carr explained, "that the color of your skin, the texture of your hair had nothing to do with your character." Another classmate, Mary Fair Burks, attended college and graduate school and became a professor, later founding the Women's Political Council, the organization that instigated the bus boycott. Both credited Miss White's school for instilling in them and other students a firm pride and resolve.

Her classmates viewed Rosa McCauley as a reserved young woman and model student who eschewed attention and was a bit of a Goody

Two-shoes and a rule follower. Burks recalled a "quiet, self-composed girl who did not seek to outshine anyone in the classroom but was always prepared . . . never out of uniform, nor did she ever go on the boys' side as some of us did." Miss White was a strict disciplinarian with a tight moral code: no dancing, movies, makeup, jewelry, short hair, or alcohol. Carr recalled that Rosa was one of the few students who didn't dance, characterizing her as "a straight Christian arrow."

Rosa also had a feisty side. One day, when she was coming home from school with her cousins who went to the public school, a white boy on roller skates tried to push her off the sidewalk. Rosa turned around and pushed him back. The boy's mother threatened her with jail. "So I told her that he had pushed me and that I didn't want to be pushed, seeing that I wasn't bothering him at all." Rosa noticed that standing up for herself with the boy's mother meant that the woman and her son "didn't bother me any further." Fearing her daughter's boldness could get her in trouble, Leona McCauley moved Rosa in with other cousins so she would not have to walk through white neighborhoods to get to school. "A lot of times white youngsters would approach us," Parks remembered, "and threaten us in some way. We'd have to talk sort of rough to them so that we didn't come to blows." Despite her shyness, Rosa

McCauley wasn't afraid to confront white kids when the situation called for it.

Around this time, her sixteen-year-old cousin Howard beat up a white kid and was spirited out of state for his own safety. Some white men came looking for him and almost took her cousin Thomas. Rosa witnessed this, and the experience, according to her cousin Carolyn, seared her. "Why do they treat us the way they treat us?" she grieved.

The school closed after Rosa completed the eighth grade. Miss White along with many of the teachers had grown elderly, and the Klan and other segregationists disapproved of their mission. "I guess running a school for black girls wasn't a very attractive thing for white people to do," Parks later noted. Some white people feared—and rightly so—that such a school would produce empowered young women. Local whites shunned Miss White and the other teachers for their work with black students. "She and the other teachers were completely isolated and not recognized in any way by the white community," remembered Rosa. And the school was the victim of arson.

Still, Miss White was no race radical. She never hired black women teachers, even graduates from the school. And Rosa recalled once, when the topic of slavery came up, Miss White said "if there had not been slavery, and our ancestors had not been brought from Africa, we would probably still be savages climbing trees, and eating bananas." Rosa said nothing, but the message disturbed her.

Much to her mother's disappointment, the school closed the year before Rosa would have graduated, so Rosa completed her last year at Booker T. Washington Junior High School. She was constrained by family responsibilities and the limited economic and educational options that many young black women confronted in the 1920s and 1930s. Because Montgomery did not provide high schools for black students, she attended the laboratory school at Alabama State College. Enjoying the school, Rosa was a serious student. One friend teased her about this seriousness in a letter: "I bet anything the boys in your class can't get their lessons for looking at you. . . . You say you are only in love with books, but you can't fool me. You mean with books & boys too."

Rosa's mother wanted her daughter to teach, though Rosa felt "the schools were just too segregated and oppressive." Like other civil rights luminaries such as Ida B. Wells and Ella Baker, Rosa McCauley didn't want to repeat her mother's experience teaching in a segregated school system. "The humiliation and intimidation they'd have to take from the board of education and the officials just didn't appeal to me then."

She wanted to be a nurse or a social worker and "help people to be relieved of suffering."

Despite her professional ambitions, Rosa had to drop out in the eleventh grade to care for her sick grandmother. The family had little money for tuition, and her mother was also in poor health. "She wasn't a very strong woman" and suffered from disabling migraines, so Parks did "all that she could . . . to make things light as I could for her [mother]." Rosa was "not happy" about dropping out, but "I did not complain; it was just something that had to be done." Throughout her life, Rosa balanced family care responsibilities with her political goals and personal aspirations—cutting back on her political activities time and again to caretake, only to reemerge and continue with her own political goals.

This was the Great Depression, and jobs were scarce. Rosa bore her lot the best she could, working on the family farm and laboring as a domestic in white people's homes. She made about four dollars a week as a domestic, working seven full days and often at night as well. Doing domestic work was not only physically and psychically demanding, but it exposed black women to sexual harassment and assault—perils she documented in a short story. In this first-person account, one evening she looked after the baby while her employers went out. Having just put the baby down, she welcomed a bit of relaxation before the family returned. "Sam," a black man who also worked at the house, came to the back door and said he had lost his coat. Rosa let him in and went to look for the coat. She was then greeted by a white neighbor, "Mr. Charlie," and realized that the purpose of Sam's visit was to bring Mr. Charlie into the house to give him access to Rosa. Mr. Charlie poured himself a glass of whiskey and attempted to put his arm around her waist. Rosa recoiled in fear and disgust. Mr. Charlie said not to worry, that he liked her and had money to give her. The small Rosa was no match for the heavyset Mr. Charlie and was trapped. Sam had set her up, and she felt tricked and betrayed by him, "stripped naked of every shred of decency . . . a commodity from Negro to white man."

Terrified, her mind turned to Psalm 27: "The lord is my light and my salvation—whom shall I fear?" Recalling her great-grandmother's abuse at the hands of her white master, Rosa found her fear replaced by a "steel determination to stand completely alone against this formidable foe." She resolved that she would never "yield to this white man's bestiality." He might kill her or rape her, but she vowed to put up a fight. As she kept moving around the living room, trying to stay an arm's length from him, Parks coolly began haranguing Mr. Charlie about the "white man's inhuman treatment of the Negro. How I hated all white people, especially him. I said I would never stoop so low as to have anything to do with him. . . . I asked him if the white women were not good enough for him, and it was too bad if something was wrong with them."

On and on she went, determined to resist Mr. Charlie's advances. "I taunted him about the supposed white supremacy. The white man's law drawing the color line of segregation. I would stay within the law—on my side of the line." Standing up for herself as a respectable young woman, she informed him she wouldn't engage sexually with anyone she couldn't marry, noting that interracial marriage was illegal in Alabama. When Mr. Charlie replied that color didn't matter to him and that he had gotten permission from Sam to be with her, she informed him that Sam didn't own her. She hated Sam as much as she hated Mr. Charlie. Mr. Charlie repeatedly offered her money and then volunteered to set her up with Sam. Rosa stated there was nothing he could do to get her consent—that "if he wanted to kill me and rape a dead body, he was welcome but he would have to kill me first." The story finishes with Rosa sitting down and reading the paper, trying to ignore Mr. Charlie while he sits across from her. "I said he couldn't pay me or fool me, or frighten me. At long last Mr. Charlie got the idea that I meant no, very definitely no." With no clear-cut conclusion to the story, it is not evident what transpired.

The only account of this incident is found in Parks's own hand, written sometime in the late 1950s or 1960s. She did not include it in her autobiography, in any of the oral histories she gave in the 1960s or 1970s, or in the interviews for Douglas Brinkley's biography of her. There are elements in the story that indisputably correspond to Parks's life; her great-grandmother had been sexually abused by her slave master, Parks herself did domestic work, Psalm 27 was a favorite, and she was a longtime believer in self-defense (and "telling people what you would do to them"). Whether fully or partially true, the piece is a remarkable elucidation of Parks's political philosophy.

Marking the danger of sexual violence that black women faced working in white homes, the story confirmed the importance of resistance and the narrator's refusal to be cowed. "He need not think that because he was a low-down dirty dog of a white man and I was a poor defenseless, helpless colored girl, that he could run over me." That Parks calls the man "Mr. Charlie" (a term used in this period by black people to put down white people and their arbitrary power) and the black man Sam (possibly for Sambo) suggests that Parks wrote this as an allegory to suggest larger themes of domination and resistance. It may be that, given that more than twenty-five years had passed before she wrote this down, she augmented what she said to Charlie that evening with all the points that she had wished to make as she resisted his advances. It may be that this incident was fictionalized or a composite of experiences, or that the incident happened but the ending turned out differently.

Right around the time of this incident, in the spring of 1931, a friend introduced her to the politically active Raymond Parks. Initially Rosa wasn't romantically interested because Raymond was more light-skinned than Rosa preferred and because she had had "some unhappy romantic experiences." Raymond could "pass for white except he didn't have white people's hair." Born in Wedowee, a small town in Randolph County, Alabama, on February 12, 1903, Raymond hadn't attended school. There were few other blacks where his family lived, and the school for blacks "was too far away for him to get there." Raymond taught himself how to read with the help of his mother. And like Rosa, he took care of his ailing mother and grandparents. When he was about ten, his grandfather and grandmother became ill. According to Rosa, Raymond's childhood was difficult, growing up in a town surrounded by hostile white people and bearing heavy family responsibilities: "He had to do what he could, try to work to help them, cook for them . . . he didn't have shoes, didn't have food much of the time." After his mother died, he moved in with a cousin and at the age of twenty-one was finally able to go to school, attending Tuskegee and ultimately picking up the barber trade. An avid reader of the black press as well as writers such as Langston Hughes and James Weldon Johnson, Raymond Parks kept well abreast of the issues of the day. Many who met him assumed he had a college education, and his barber chair was often a space for wide-ranging political discussions.

After meeting Rosa for the first time, Raymond came looking for her house. The first person he asked for her whereabouts wouldn't tell him, perhaps "because he was so fair . . . they might have thought he was a member of the opposite race." Then he stopped at the McCauley residence to inquire if they knew where he might find this Rosa McCauley. Leona McCauley invited him in "and that's when we got acquainted."

Raymond—whom she called "Parks"—was "the first real activist I ever met." In all the iconography of Rosa Parks, there is little that pictures her romance with Raymond. Among the hundreds of media shots of her, there are very few public photos with him. But love it was. Raymond Parks came back to the McCauley house another time "and this time I wouldn't go out to see him. I went to bed and covered up and wouldn't go out." And he came back again "and after that we started going on rides to different places" and talking about the world. It was the first time, outside of her family, that Rosa had discussed racial issues in depth with someone else. But she was impressed with his boldness. Raymond Parks had his own car, a red Nash with a rumble seat. To be a black man driving his own car in Alabama in the 1930s (not as a driver for a white family) was to be an audacious and proud man, and Raymond was "willing to defy the racists and stand up to the establishment." What impressed her was "that he refused to be intimidated by white people—unlike many blacks, who figured they had no choice but to stay under 'Mr. Charlie's' heel." In light of Rosa's experiences and feelings about white supremacy, these qualities of Raymond's were especially precious.

Fifty years later, writer Cynthia Stokes Brown would recall her first meeting with Rosa Parks in 1980. They had gone into the restroom so Mrs. Parks could freshen up before meeting with reporters. Parks removed her hat and hairpin.

And her braids fell below her waist in a cascade of thick wavy hair that Rapunzel would have envied. When Mrs. Parks saw the astonishment on my face, she chuckled softly, "Well, many of my ancestors were Indians. I never cut my hair because my husband liked it this way.

It's a lot of trouble, and he's been dead a number of years, but I still can't bring myself to cut it."

Alice Walker tells a similar story of attending an event with Parks in Mississippi. They went into the bathroom and Parks took down her hair. Walker was "stunned." As she put back her bun, Parks explained "my hair was something that my husband dearly, dearly loved about me. . . . I never wear it down in public." Aware of the racial politics of hair and appearance, Parks kept her hair long in an act of love and affection (even after Raymond died) but tucked away in a series of braids and buns—maintaining a clear division between her public presentation and her private person.

Raymond talked to Rosa about the Scottsboro case and other racial matters. "I just enjoyed listening to him. I didn't talk a great deal . . . He was a very gentle person, very polite. I didn't know exactly what to say, I guess because I hadn't been [with many boys]." Rosa felt shy and inexperienced, but Raymond had taken an immediate liking to her, and she was attracted to his spirit and strength of character. Raymond, according to Rosa, "expected to be treated as a man"—to get along if possible "but whenever white people accosted him, he always wanted to let them know he could take care of business if he had to. They didn't bother you so much back then if you just spoke right up. But as soon as you acted like you were afraid, they'd have fun with you." Like Rosa's grandfather, Raymond was not afraid to speak back to white people. Like many black people in Alabama, Raymond Parks had a gun and would carry it when necessary. The appreciation for race pride and activism that she had learned at home came to fruition in her relationship with Raymond Parks. He was the love of her life.

They married on December 18, 1932, at her mother's house with a small gathering of family and close friends. Their wedding happened "right in the middle of the campaign to save the Scottsboro Boys." Raymond was actively organizing on behalf of the nine young men aged twelve to nineteen who had wrongfully been convicted and sentenced to death in Scottsboro, Alabama in 1931. These young men had been riding the rails on a train in Alabama and gotten in a scuffle with several young white men also riding for free and forced them from the train. At the next stop, the police boarded the train and arrested the nine black boys. But when two young white women were also discovered stowed away on the train, the charge quickly changed to rape. Less than two weeks after their arrest, eight of them (all but twelve-year-old Roy Wright) had been found guilty and sentenced to death. The eight were scheduled to be executed July 10, 1931. While the NAACP initially stood at arm's length from the case (and most cases in this period involving issues or allegations of sex), the American Communist Party took immediate interest in the case and began organizing to protest the verdicts. The International Legal Defense (ILD) took up the case, and a grassroots movement of Alabamians grew to save the young men.

Raymond Parks sprang into action. "Not many men were activists in those days either, because if it was known that they were meeting, they would be wiped right out. But it didn't bother me being married to Parks. He was doing the same thing before we got married; and I knew how dangerous it was." Every time Raymond went out to a Scottsboro meeting, Rosa wondered if he would come back alive. This organizing was clandestine: "I would stand in front of a certain street light," explained Raymond, "and lean over and tie my shoe a certain way to give a signal as to where we would meet and the day and the time." Raymond told Rosa that for security reasons, everyone in the group was simply known to the others as Larry. One person Raymond did tell Rosa about was "a lady he used to call Captola" [sic]—Capitola Tasker, an Alabama sharecropper, leader in the Share Croppers Union and active in the Communist Party (CP). Capitola and Charles Tasker produced leaflets from their home that CP organizer Al Jackson distributed from his Montgomery barbershop.

For the first years of their partnership, Rosa did more of the worrying about Raymond's safety, given his political activities. Later in their marriage, that would reverse. The committee would meet at odd hours—before daybreak and in the middle of the night. Raymond began holding secret meetings at the Parks's home, which Rosa would sometimes attend. Raymond didn't want her to be active "because it was hard enough if he had to run[;] he couldn't leave me and I couldn't run as fast." She recalled their kitchen table "covered with guns," further testament to the long history of armed self-defense in Southern black communities that historian Timothy Tyson has documented.

Raymond brought food to the Scottsboro boys in jail and told Rosa that he would "never sleep well until they're free." They both attended meetings. As the Scottsboro organizing increased, the police looked for people to intimidate. Two of Raymond's associates had been killed a few weeks earlier. One day, two cops on motorcycles drove back and forth in front of the Parks home. Rosa and a friend were sitting out on the porch swing. "I was so frightened, . . . I was shaking so much that I was making the swing tremble." Raymond made it safely back home, coming in through the back door. She was enormously relieved. "At least they didn't get him that time."

Raymond was a longtime member of the Montgomery branch of the National Association for the Advancement of Colored People (NAACP). Begun in 1909 after a vicious lynching in Springfield, Illinois, the NAACP sought to realize the rights guaranteed to black people in the Thirteenth, Fourteenth, and Fifteenth amendments. By the 1930s, and in particular in the wake of local organizing around the Scottsboro case, the organization started to build a grassroots base. Raymond attended branch meetings but in time grew disillusioned with the organization's cautiousness and elitism. According to historian Dorothy Autrey, the Montgomery branch was middle-class dominated and lacked effective leadership in the 1930s.

Black left activist Esther Cooper Jackson recalls meeting Raymond in the early 1940s. Esther Cooper Jackson and her husband, the American Communist Party leader James Jackson, had just moved to Birmingham and Esther began working with the Southern Negro Youth Congress. Her impression was that Raymond Parks was one of the "more advanced political activists in the union movement." Decades later, after Rosa Parks became famous, Cooper Jackson would tell friends of meeting Raymond and describe his activism. They would be surprised, some remarking that they "didn't even know she had a husband." Raymond Parks's politics helped provide fertile soil over the years for Rosa's to grow. According to scholar and former SNCC activist Gwen Patton, he was a "revolutionary in his own right," who decisively impacted Rosa's political development.

On Raymond's urging, Rosa followed her desire to return to school and earned her high school degree in 1933. In 1940, according to Parks, "only 7 of every 100 black people had a high school diploma," and she was extremely proud of the accomplishment. She never attended college, even though it was one of her "greatest desires." Parks struggled to find work commensurate with her skills and education. Office work and secretarial jobs were almost nonexistent for black women in the South. While 8,491 whites were employed in 1940 as typists or stenographers in Alabama, only 140 black people had these jobs. Rosa thus scrounged to find employment—as a nurse's assistant at Saint Margaret's Hospital, as a presser at a tailor shop, and, during World War II, at Maxwell Air Force Base.

Rosa hated the ways some black people kowtowed to white authority. One time, while seeing some friends off at the train station, she was threatened and pushed by a white policeman. Another black woman was also treated rudely by the same officer but responded by flirting with him. "To me she showed a lack of respect for herself as a woman, and especially as a black woman." Parks hated the ways black women had to use their sexuality to protect themselves from white power. She increasingly looked for outlets to contest that disrespect and to encourage others to do the same. Her own activist sensibility was growing.

CHAPTER TWO

"It Was Very Difficult to Keep Going When All Our Work Seemed to Be in Vain"
The Civil Rights Movement before the Bus Boycott

IN DECEMBER 1943, ROSA PARKS decided to go to a meeting of the Montgomery NAACP. Raymond had been an active member of the branch in the 1930s but had grown disenchanted with its cautiousness and elitism, which led some to look down on working-class men like himself, and had long since stopped going. Rosa initially had thought the NAACP was an organization open only to men. She had wanted to attend meetings with Raymond but he had initially discouraged her participation, saying it was too dangerous, particularly in the years around the Scottsboro case. But in 1943, she saw a picture in a black newspaper of Mrs. Johnnie Carr, her former classmate from Miss White's School, attending an NAACP meeting. Parks had grown increasingly frustrated with the paradoxes of American democracy, further highlighted by U.S. participation in World War II. Black people like her brother were serving in the army to defend the United States and its freedoms but not granted that equality and freedom at home. "I had always been taught that this was America, the land of the free and the home of the brave. . . . I felt that it should be actual, in action rather than just something we hear and talk about."

Carr had also been active in the Scottsboro case, raising money for the young men's defense and then joining the NAACP. Parks attended the December meeting, but Carr had not come that day. As the only woman there among a dozen men, Mrs. Parks was asked to take notes and then, because it was election day, to serve as branch secretary. "Too timid to say no," she was then elected secretary of the chapter. She and Carr were typically the only women at the meetings. Her mother would follow her lead, becoming one of just a few women to actively join the local branch, though many Montgomery women were members of the national NAACP. Parks shortly met E. D. Nixon, a Pullman porter active in the Brotherhood of Sleeping Car Porters and the NAACP who was spearheading a campaign to get blacks in Montgomery to attempt to register to vote. Nixon's wife, Arlet, sometimes came to meetings as well.

Working with a handful of committed local leaders in Montgomery, Rosa Parks joined the cadre of Montgomery activists that would lay the groundwork for the civil rights movement in the decade before the *Brown* decision. This decade of activism is often glossed over in standard accounts of the civil rights movement because it stands at odds with a more triumphalist narrative of civil rights. This was a difficult, dangerous, and ultimately demoralizing period for civil rights activists, as a growing black militancy stemming in part from the experiences of World War II met unyielding and increasingly aggres-sive white resistance and violence. Civil rights activism was often a lonely venture for people like Parks who toiled in relative obscurity because most of their fellow citizens, white and black, steered clear of the dangers of civil rights advocacy. The fortitude and faith it took to be an activist in Alabama in this decade is too often overshadowed by the events of the late 1950s and 1960s.

Popular narratives of the civil rights era often move briskly through the 1940s and early 1950s. The power and drama of the mass movement that emerged in the late 1950s and early 1960s—the boycotts and sit-ins, Freedom Rides and voter registration campaigns—are more alluring, the legislative and community successes more clear. And so it becomes all too easy not to linger in this earlier decade and rush ahead to the good parts. But there was nothing inevitable about the mass movement of the mid-1950s and early 1960s, which would not have been possible without this arduous spadework.

To be an activist for racial justice in the 1940s

meant working without any indication that your efforts would be realized in your lifetime. It meant struggling against the fear and nihilism that white supremacy produced in order to continue tilling the soil for a mass movement to be able to flower. For a person like Rosa Parks, whose stand on the bus would come to be seen as ushering in a glorious new chapter of civil rights history, it first meant imagining that there could be a story, finding others who agreed, and then painstakingly writing it, word by word, for more than a decade to get to the good part.

The first real meeting between Rosa Parks and E. D. Nixon—a partnership that would change the course of American history—took place at Parks's apartment. Nixon came to her home to speak to her about registering to vote and, seeing her interest, left a book on the subject for her to read. So began a working collaboration that would span more than a decade.

Born July 12, 1899, Edgar Daniel Nixon grew up just outside Montgomery in a family of eight kids. Nixon's father was an itinerant preacher, and his mother died when he was a boy. Leaving home at the age of fourteen and largely self-taught, Nixon went to school for "only about 18 months in my entire life." He worked a variety of hard physical jobs till he landed a job working in baggage for the Pullman Company, eventually earning a promotion to Pullman porter. Reminiscent of the antebellum South, the Pullman Company only hired black men to serve customers on overnight trains. Because the work was steady and the pay regular, the job was a sought-after position within the black community, though it required porters to attend meticulously to passenger needs, plumping pillows, taking orders, making the ride comfortable for white— and only white—passengers. For Nixon, at this juncture in his life, it was "the best thing in the world that ever happened to me." A fiercely determined man, Nixon used the job to improve his reading and writing skills, partly by reading the newspapers and books people left on the train. He wrote down all the words he did not know in a small notebook and looked them up when he got back to his room.

His first trip to St. Louis as a Pullman porter was transformative. He explained,

> I was dumbfounded when I got up there and found black and white sitting down at the same table eating in the station. It had a heck of an impact on me. Here you have been conditioned traditionally to "This is the way of life," and all your life that's all you have known . . . and then all at once you see something like black and white eating together and it's just like water that's been backed up in a dam, and it

breaks out and flows over. By the time I got back to Montgomery at the end of that first four-day run, I had started to think, "What can I do to help eliminate some of this?"

In 1928, Nixon went to a meeting with labor leader A. Phillip Randolph, who was helping the porters organize a union. Randolph's speech had a decisive impact on him. "It was like a light. Most eloquent man I ever heard. He done more to bring me in the fight than anybody." Nixon joined the Brotherhood of Sleeping Car Porters, a militant group of porters trying to organize and get recognized as the union. When he returned to Montgomery, his boss told him he'd heard that Nixon had attended a Brotherhood meeting and that was not allowed. Nixon had prepared his reply: "Before I joined it I thought about what lawyer I was gonna get to handle my case. Anybody mess with my job, I'm gonna drag 'em into court." Nixon was bluffing but his boss backed down.

Nixon's courage and political sensibility—a "Gandhi with guns," according to Harrison Wofford, special assistant for civil rights to President John F. Kennedy—informed his lifelong conviction that racial inequality should be challenged directly. And with Rosa Parks at his side, he would confront the old leadership of

Montgomery's NAACP chapter, running for and winning the position of Montgomery branch president in 1945. Nixon, according to Parks, was "the first person beside my husband and my immediate family and my mother to really impress upon me the freedom that was ours and [that] we had to take a stand to at least let it be known that we want to be free regardless of the conditions under which we were living." Like her accounts of getting to know Raymond, Rosa's descriptions of the bold Mr. Nixon reflected how liberating she found meeting other race activists. Some people dismissed Nixon because he lacked formal education and class respectability. But Rosa Parks saw his substance. "In ways that matter . . . he was truly sophisticated."

After a period of renewed activism in the late 1930s that stemmed in part from the organizing around the Scottsboro case, the Montgomery NAACP had seen a precipitous drop in membership in 1940, losing 90 percent of its members. Through the work of local activists like Nixon and Parks and outside support from NAACP visionaries like Ella Baker, the membership rolls picked back up over the course of the 1940s. The branch primarily focused on legal cases, in an effort to challenge white brutality and legal lynching in the state. The chapter had also begun a campaign for voter registration. Only thirty-one black people were registered to vote in

Montgomery out of several thousand. The application for voter registration required potential voters to identify their employer, their business and educational background, and any drug and alcohol use and pledge not to "give aid and comfort to the enemies of the United States Government or the government of the State of Alabama." This exposed potential black registrants to direct retribution from that employer.

It also required a person to state whether she had "previously applied for and been denied registration as a voter," providing another mechanism for denial. In order to register, potential voters, if they did not own property, were required to take a test. The registrar determined the questions on the tests, and often black people would be given more difficult tests than whites. Even people with PhDs and other advanced degrees had difficulty because the questions asked of black would-be registrants were obscure and nitpicking. People were "real discouraged," according to Parks, because the voter registration board was "so hostile." "If they didn't come right out and be abusive," Parks observed, "they would act as if you just weren't supposed to be there even talking about registering to vote." Customarily, a white person would have to vouch for each black person who wanted to register to vote. Even when black people succeeded in registering, their names would be printed in the newspaper (inviting possible retaliation). In addition, a successful registrant would be forced to pay poll taxes for each of the past years they had been eligible to register—a hefty sum for working-class families.

Nixon had organized the Montgomery Voters' League in 1940. In 1944, he assembled a group of 750 black people to go down to the courthouse and ask to register to vote. Rosa had to work, but her mother and cousin joined the group—and did succeed in getting registered. Nixon had called on the help of Arthur Madison, a Harlem lawyer who had grown up in Alabama. Viewed as a troublemaker by police, Madison was jailed for his attempts to register black voters and ultimately disbarred in Alabama. Parks was appalled by the ways the Montgomery NAACP did not stand up for Madison.

From 1943 to 1945, Rosa tried numerous times to register to vote "under hazardous conditions" and was repeatedly denied. Refusing to be cowed, the Parks family held Voters' League meetings at their apartment—and Rosa exhorted her fellow Montgomerians to register, despite the enormous poll taxes and the unfair registration tests. She wanted to build an independent group of black voters "without having to go to a white person and be vouched for." On Parks's second try, two young white women were also registering to vote. They asked the registrar "to give them the answers and she, of course, indicated that she would be helpful." In her presence, the registrar told the young women to wait a few moments, with the implication that she would help them after Parks left. In order to cover up the diversion of blacks, the registrar's office rarely served whites and blacks at the same time. "They didn't have to give you a reason" for denial, recalled Parks, and would usually simply inform blacks that they did not pass.

On her third attempt, "pretty sure" she passed the test and having tired of the registrar's chicanery, she hand-copied all the questions so she could use them to bring suit against the voter registration board. The registrar noticed what Parks had done. She soon received a letter certifying her registration. Even when black people succeeded in registering, they had to wait for confirmation in the mail; white people received it immediately on site. She was then forced to pay back poll taxes—$1.50 for each year she had been old enough to vote, $18 in total, a formidable amount of money for a working-class family like the Parkses. Such poll taxes posed a great obstacle for people who succeeded in registering but "hardship or not, almost every Negro finally found some way to get the money and have his name placed on the books." And so Rosa Parks cast her first vote for maverick governor James Folsom in 1945, and she and Raymond joined the crowds cheering his inaugural parade.

Rosa's success was somewhat of an anomaly, and her tenacity in getting registered was a clear hallmark of her determination. Very few black Montgomerians succeeded in registering in this period. Relentlessly segregated, Montgomery in 1951 was 37 percent black in population, but only 3.7 percent of eligible black voters were registered. "There was not even a token representation," Parks recalled.

Raymond tried for years to register and encouraged others to do so. He belonged to a Men's Social Club and tried to get members to pool money for socials to help people pay back poll taxes. But the other club members were not interested, and so he dropped out. He also "tried on his own to interest people in getting registered," according to Rosa, "but it was just considered too dangerous or too risky." Raymond came to disparage his own voter registration attempts, saying, "I was ignorant enough to actually believe that they would let us register and vote after we paid up. After the taxes were paid, those registrars would sit there and ask you 21 questions that even a good white lawyer couldn't answer." Even though a couple of white people offered to vouch for him, he refused to go under those terms. After numerous attempts, he gave up, disheartened. He would not succeed in registering until the family moved to Detroit.

Rosa's brother Sylvester, who had served in the 1318th Medical Detachment Engineering Services Regiment during World War II, returned to Montgomery in December 1945. Despite his military service in both the Pacific and European theaters of the war, he was treated like an "uppity Negro" and could not find work or register to vote. Returning veterans, Rosa explained, "found that they were treated with even more disrespect, especially if they were in uniform. Whites felt that things should remain as they had always been and that the black veterans were getting too sassy. My brother was one who could not take that kind of treatment anymore." Sylvester and his family left Montgomery for Detroit in 1946, never to return. While Detroit was also rife with economic and political inequality, Sylvester found the climate less hostile and ultimately secured work as an auto assembly worker.

Beginning with Scottsboro—and lasting throughout her life—Parks focused on the mistreatment of African Americans under the law. Black men often were tried for "crimes" that not infrequently amounted to having a consensual relationship with a white woman or not being properly submissive. Simultaneously, black people found the law unresponsive to instances of white brutality against them—and black women were particularly vulnerable, as sexual assault by white men went unpunished. Parks and Nixon thus sought to use the law to seek justice for black victims of white violence and to expose the legal lynchings of black people, work that was dangerous and controversial. "Mrs. Parks will tell you this," Nixon explained, "her mother said the white folks was going to lynch us, her and me both. Mrs. Parks and I were in the NAACP when other Negroes were afraid to be seen with us." White minister Robert Graetz underscored how "extraordinarily brave" Parks was in her willingness to be publicly identified with the NAACP in this period. One of Parks's "main duties" as NAACP secretary was to record dozens of cases of violence or unfair treatment against black people, in the hopes of possible redress.

After a twenty-four-year-old black woman was gang raped by six white men at gunpoint near Abbeville, Alabama, in 1944—and authorities made no move to look into the crime—the Montgomery NAACP sent Parks one hundred miles south to assist. Her father hailed from Abbeville, and she still had family there. Taylor, married with a three-year-old daughter, told Parks that she had been walking home from a church meeting when six white men pulled up, forced her into their car at gunpoint, took her to a deserted spot, and raped her. Then they blindfolded her, dropped her off in the middle of town, and threatened to kill her if she said anything.

Nonetheless, Taylor reported the crime to police, who did nothing.

According to historian Danielle McGuire, Parks arrived at Taylor's home and copiously took down her testimony. During their conversation, the police drove by the Taylors' small cabin repeatedly. Finally, the deputy sheriff barged into the Taylor home. Making clear he didn't want "any troublemakers here in Abbeville," he ordered Parks to leave or face arrest. Parks describes her involvement in the Recy Taylor case in a 1988 interview with Jim Haskins somewhat differently: the person who instigated the Montgomery NAACP's involvement in Taylor's case was a white woman named Carolyn Bellin, and it is Bellin, not Parks, who was manhandled by the sheriff in her attempt to visit Taylor. Parks does not mention any run-in she had with the sheriff.

Along with Nixon, Rufus Lewis, and others, Parks worked to draw attention to the case with the Committee for Equal Justice for Mrs. Recy Taylor. The committee used the organizational infrastructure built around the Scottsboro case to reach out to labor unions, African American groups, and women's organizations to pressure Governor Chauncey Sparks to convene a special grand jury. According to McGuire, Parks and Nixon's work "paid off" when the *Pittsburgh Courier* ran an exposé on the case in their

October 28, 1944, issue. A number of key black women on the Left took up the struggle, including Esther Cooper and Audley Moore. Prominent writers and political leaders like Countee Cullen, W. E. B. Du Bois, Langston Hughes, Mary Church Terrell, and Adam Clayton Powell joined the Committee for Equal Justice for Mrs. Recy Taylor. Hundreds of letters poured into Governor Sparks's office from across the country. Postcards and petitions also came from the core group of Montgomery activists, including Rosa and Raymond Parks, E. D. Nixon, and Johnnie Carr.

Disturbed by the mounting campaign, Governor Sparks and other prominent officials in the state worried about "Communist infiltration." They stirred up a backlash against the organizing, trying to paint it as the work of "reds." Given the anti-Communist climate of the time, the committee was increasingly attacked for sedition, and organizers like Cooper Jackson had to leave the state. With increased attention to the case, some of the men confessed to having sex with Taylor but they said it was consensual and Taylor was a prostitute. When it became clear that the men were not going to be indicted, the committee began to focus on other cases. Fearing for Taylor's safety, Nixon and Parks helped Mrs. Taylor and her family move and find work in Montgomery.

Parks and Nixon wanted to make the Montgomery branch a more activist chapter that vigorously stood up for black women and men. In December 1945, Nixon ran for branch president to "return the N.A.A.C.P. to the people as their organization" and get black Montgomerians to "wake up and . . . build it into a powerful organization." This was a class-based call. Nixon and Parks hailed from Montgomery's working-class west side—very different from Robert Matthews, who worked for Pilgrim Insurance.

In order to continue this local organizing, according to McGuire, Parks, Nixon, and Carr distanced themselves from their more radical allies. This did not mean that Parks became an anti-Communist. In fact, over the course of her political career, she would not shy away from working with people and groups, particularly the Highlander Folk School, that came under attack for their "subversive" actions. In the late 1950s, she received letters from Audley Moore, also known as Queen Mother Moore, so her ties from this earlier organizing seem to have continued. In spite of anti-Communist sentiment in the national NAACP by the late 1940s, Parks never publicly disassociated herself from Communists. At the NAACP's annual meeting in 1950, an anti-Communist resolution called for investigating the "ideological composition and trends of the membership" and "expel[ling] any branch . . .

coming under Communist . . . domination." A vocal minority challenged the resolution—and objected to the suspension of suspected Communists from the organization. According to New York tenant leader Lee Lorch, one of the people opposed to the purge was Rosa Parks. Back home in Montgomery, according to white civil rights advocate Virginia Durr, the Montgomery branch didn't "redbait themselves or even pay attention to that kind of thing."

Branch membership in Nixon's first two years as president increased from 861 to 1,600. The organization, under his leadership, pressured the governor to reprieve the death sentences of three black men—Worthy James, John Underwood, and Samuel Taylor—charged with rape. Another case involved a young black serviceman accused of rape by a white nurse on the base who had been unable to find a lawyer to take his case. There were no black attorneys in Montgomery in 1943; even white attorneys were ostracized and punished for taking on black clients, so few would assist. Parks helped pull together the affidavits in these cases and tracked membership rolls. She learned how to type—"it didn't come with your regular tuition in high school"—taking an evening class from a woman she knew to pick up what she could.

Parks's growing activism was given a lift, according to historian Barbara Ransby, after attending an NAACP leadership conference run by veteran organizer Ella Baker in March 1945 in Atlanta and then another in Jacksonville in 1946. A seasoned organizer who saw local activists as key to the work of the organization, Ella Baker was then serving as the NAACP's Director of Branches. Baker shunned the hierarchy and class leanings of many in the organization. In the mid-1940s, Baker sought to develop the NAACP's local chapters and the grassroots leadership within them. She instituted a series of conferences (like the ones Parks attended) to train local leaders in developing ways to attack community problems and encourage them to see local issues as part of larger systemic problems. Baker left the Director of Branches position in 1946, in part because she had grown disappointed by the ways the national office did not adequately support the work and vision of the local chapters. Baker later became branch president of the Harlem NAACP, helped found In Friendship to support the emerging Montgomery protest, served as the first acting executive director of the Southern Christian Leadership Conference (SCLC), and then helped to establish the Student Nonviolent Coordinating Committee (SNCC).

Baker made a powerful impression on Parks. Calling her "beautiful in every way," Rosa Parks noted how "smart and funny and strong" Baker was and wrote to tell the national office how "inspired" she was by the Jacksonville meeting. From then on "whenever she came to Montgomery, [Ella Baker] stayed with me. She was a true friend—a mentor." At a time when Parks's own political activism was increasing and Montgomery's most prominent activists were men, Parks looked to Baker, who was older, with decades of political experience, as a mentor. Civil rights activist Anne Braden noted "the profound effect" Baker had on Parks. Like Baker, Parks was committed to working with young people and saw them as key to promoting a new movement spirit.

Nixon's and Parks's commitment to grassroots organizing and connections to the black poor and working class represented a minority position within Montgomery's NAACP, which was largely dominated by the black professional class. Indeed class differences formed a fissure through Montgomery's black community and made broad-based organizing nearly impossible. The chapter during this period was marked by tension.

In fall 1946, controversy erupted around Nixon's reelection and his management of the branch. Both the vice president and treasurer—whom Nixon characterized as "insurance men"—favored a less confrontational organization and opposed his "dictatorship," complaining to the national office of his misuse of branch funds and "politicking." This power struggle revolved around the intertwined issues of class and militancy. Describing the "superior attitudes" of those opposing the current leadership, Johnnie Carr explained that Nixon's rivals sought to "use the organization for a nice place to sit for one hour, and preside over a meeting, after which no special effort is made to put the organization to work for the masses." Hoping to consolidate his power and encourage a more political membership, Nixon attempted to institute a requirement that all branch leadership be registered voters (a rarity in Montgomery at the time), which the national office rejected. But Nixon also got increasingly defensive and secretive in branch dealings.

The criticisms of Nixon's leadership largely did not extend to Parks, though one letter did mention Mrs. Parks being "too kind" and extolled the need for the branch to have a "man secretary to handle things with a firm hand." The opposing faction did run its own candidate against Parks for the position of secretary—Robert Matthews, who had previously served as both the president and secretary of the branch.

The status divide that ran through the branch separated Nixon and Parks from the Alabama State professors and black businessmen who dominated the active membership. This educational divide would also shape the iconography of Parks after the boycott and the way some members of

Montgomery's black middle class viewed her. She would be held up as a simple heroine, not as a thoughtful and seasoned political strategist in her own right, in part because she lacked the social status, education, and gender that some people believed necessary to be a strategist.

Still, Nixon and Parks were reelected. Parks's work with the branch often consumed her nights and weekends. She typed dozens of letters on an old Underwood in the office, called members and nonmembers to gain support for the NAACP's work, and went door-to-door soliciting volunteers and informing people about the work of the organization. NAACP records suggest that Nixon and Parks attended the NAACP's annual meeting in Washington, DC, in 1947; for the 1948 meeting in Kansas City, Parks was not listed as attending.

By 1947, Parks's stature in civil rights circles had grown. She was selected to serve on the three-person executive committee of the state conference of the NAACP, which recommended that Emory Jackson (of the Birmingham NAACP) step down and E. D. Nixon become state conference head. Nixon ran and was elected president of the Alabama state conference from 1947 to 1949. Though she was shy and generally not one for public speaking, in 1948 Rosa Parks delivered a powerful address at the state convention in Mobile decrying the mistreatment of African American women in the South and criticizing those "feeling proud of their home or the South when Negroes every day are being molested and maltreated. No one should feel proud of a place where Negroes are intimidated." Finishing to thunderous applause, she was then elected the first secretary of the state conference. According to NAACP historian Dorothy Autrey, "Even more than the work of any one branch, the activists of the statewide organization of NAACP branches represented a threat to the Southern society's oppression of blacks."

Nixon and Parks were a powerful team. After Alabama's attorney general publicly claimed federal anti-lynching legislation would only increase lynchings in the state, Nixon went into the office to issue a response—only to find Parks already at work on one. Every year, they wrote letters to Washington to ask for a federal anti-lynching bill. They persisted, but federal anti-lynching legislation never passed Congress. Traveling throughout the state, Rosa Parks sought to document instances of white-on-black brutality in hopes of pursuing legal justice. "Rosa will talk with you" became the understanding throughout Alabama's black communities. This work was tiring, and at times demoralizing because most of the cases Parks documented went nowhere. She issued press releases to the *Montgomery Advertiser* and *Alabama Journal.* She forwarded dozens of reports to the NAACP national office documenting suspicious deaths, rapes of black women by white men, instances of voter intimidation, and other incidents of racial injustice. "It was more a matter of trying to challenge the powers that be," Parks would later write in her autobiography, "and let it be known that we did not wish to continue being treated as second class citizens." She probably also found discouraging the national NAACP's unwillingness to pursue most of these cases.

There were numerous cases of sexual violence against black women. In 1949, Gertrude Perkins was raped by two police officers and forced to commit "unnatural acts." The case drew outrage from Nixon, Parks, Reverend Solomon Seay, and the newly formed Women's Political Council. The police chief initially pursued prosecutions of the officers, but the city commission and mayor did not stand behind him. The mayor blamed the incident on the NAACP, the grand jury dismissed the charges against the officers, and police records were changed to protect the officers who had raped Perkins. Thirteen-year-old Amanda Baker was raped and murdered. Nixon got the governor to agree to an unprecedented $250 reward to find the killer, which the NAACP agreed to match. But Baker's murderer was never apprehended. Faced with these repeated miscarriages of justice, Parks, according to historian Steven Millner, "became quietly embittered by such repeated exposure to the sordid underside of Montgomery's race relations. Mrs. Parks's feelings were seldom shared with others, but with her mother she was able to discuss them in detail." At times, people who came forward with cases would get nervous and refuse to give a written affidavit or testify, fearing for their own lives and jobs. Raymond "got upset" with one minister who had seen a white man shoot a black man but was unwilling to testify to it, but Rosa told him not to be "too hard on him," recognizing the difficulty people had in standing up publicly. "People didn't have any inclination to give up their lives just to try to bring a charge against somebody else."

Nixon found Parks an invaluable grassroots organizer and office manager. Nonetheless, his descriptions of Parks were quite gendered. "She keeps a pencil in her hair all the time," according to Nixon, "every once in a while you see her take it out and mark the old misspelled word. When you get the paper behind her, you know she had it. Because every misspelled word, she'd mark it . . . me and her worked together, traveled over this state together, and I knew that, that she was clean as a pin." Nixon's notions about the proper roles for women did not include them being visible leaders. Parks, at times, confronted him on this. "Women don't need to be nowhere but in the kitchen," he once told Parks. When she challenged him, asking, "Well what about me?" he lamely replied, "I need a secretary and you are a good one." Nixon would laugh when Parks protested these comments. Other times, when Nixon made such disparaging remarks, Parks "wouldn't do anything but just laugh." Nixon praised Parks for being "faithful as a good hound dog, and I mean that in the best way you can imagine. I never doubted her one minute. She was true as a compass." Though Nixon was one of Parks's greatest champions over the next decades, he did not fully acknowledge Parks's intellectual talents and political acumen, which shaped how he envisioned the roles she should play. Parks was a voracious reader, keeping up with a number of black newspapers and the issues of the day, which gave the branch's work a broader scope.

In 1947, when the Freedom Train was scheduled to come to Montgomery, Parks published a report in the *Memphis World* about the local NAACP's chapter's objections to Montgomery's all-white Freedom Train committee. The especially painted red-white-and-blue train was set to visit all forty-eight states, carrying original copies of the Declaration of Independence, Constitution, and Bill of Rights. The national requirement that the exhibit be integrated—black and white viewers mingling freely—was highly controversial. Southern cities like Birmingham and Memphis refused to agree to these stipulations, and the

Train bypassed these cities. That the Freedom Train included a stop in Montgomery was due in part to the work of Parks and her colleagues, who pressured city officials to appoint blacks to the Freedom Train committee and federal officials to ensure all children would actually enter on a first-come, first-served basis.

Parks took a group of black young people to visit the integrated exhibition in December 1947—which resulted in numerous hate calls to Parks's home. Septima Clark recalled Parks's fear of even discussing the Freedom Train visit during her visit to Highlander years later. "I asked Rosa, 'Would she would tell the people in the workshop about the coming of the Freedom Train to Montgomery,' which she hated very much, because she was afraid that some of the Southern whites would go back and say what she had said [to other white people in their communities] and then she would be in for harassment. Nevertheless, she ventured to tell it." Eight years later, in the backwoods of Tennessee, the difficulty and attendant fear of the Freedom Train organizing still haunted her.

Parks also engaged in her own personal forms of protest, avoiding segregated drinking fountains and elevators. "I tried to use them as little as possible. There were white and colored fountains, so you just didn't drink." Besides her role as secretary of the chapter where she did much of the behind-the-scenes work of the organization, in 1949 she and Johnnie Carr founded and led the NAACP Youth Council, which was initially active but then died out because of lack of membership.

The revival of the Klan and increased white resistance to black voter registration made this a difficult time for Montgomery's NAACP. Membership in the organization fell in 1949 from 1,600 to 148. It was also a difficult time for the Parks family. When her mother got sick, Parks scaled back her NAACP involvement, resigning her secretary position in both the Montgomery branch and Alabama conference in 1949. Unfortunately, perhaps because of the loss of Parks's able and systematic stewardship, Nixon's leadership was increasingly questioned by the national office, and they quietly sought to bring in a more traditional middle-class leader. Nixon lost the state conference presidency in November 1949 to Birmingham insurance agent W. C. Patton and the next year was defeated for Montgomery branch president by Robert Matthews.

Parks continued to help Nixon with his work with the Brotherhood of Sleeping Car Porters. When her mother's health improved, Parks returned to the position of branch secretary in 1952. This caused a slight rift with Nixon, according to Brinkley, because Nixon wanted

Parks working for him and distrusted the current branch president Robert Matthews. Most Alabama blacks in the early 1950s, according to NAACP historian Dorothy Autrey, saw the NAACP as "a futile undertaking. . . . Only a few individuals possessed the vision and the patience required for active participation."

Still Parks kept on. Indeed, in interviews in the years and decades after the boycott, Parks would stress how long they had been working on these issues and how they "didn't seem to have too many successes." Part of what sustained her during these years was an abiding faith in God's vision of justice on earth. A devoted member of St. Paul's African Methodist Episcopal Church, Parks knew a God who sided with the oppressed and drew sustenance from prayer and worship for her continued community work. She loved the Book of Psalms, and the hymns buoyed her, particularly "Woke Up This Morning with My Mind on Freedom."

Activists like Parks and Nixon labored in relative loneliness. The national NAACP, exceedingly careful about the cases it would support, kept a distance from many of their cases—and legal cases that involved sex (real, imagined, or coerced) were often kept at arm's length. Local people who sought to engage the branch in more activism received little direct support from the national office, even as they dutifully sought to expand the organization's membership. At the same time, despite the number of issues that angered Montgomery's black community, "there wasn't really a movement," Parks noted, and most eschewed any form of public opposition.

One of Parks's former classmates, Mahalia Dickerson, came back to Montgomery to set up her law practice. Parks and Dickerson went out to Kilby Prison to work on the cases of blacks imprisoned there, but Dickerson "did not receive the support she needed from the African American community" and left town. Parks also took a particular interest in the case of Jeremiah Reeves. Jeremiah Reeves was a popular senior at Booker T. Washington High School. According to Parks, the sixteen-year-old Reeves was having a consensual relationship with a young white woman from the neighborhood. After many months, and increasingly fearful of being found out, she cried rape. Reeves was arrested for rape, beaten by police, and subsequently confessed after officers taunted him and forced him to sit in an electric chair. Reeves later retracted his admission of guilt and denied ever having had sexual relations under any circumstances with the woman. He was tried and sentenced to death.

"The things that young black men suffered because of white women!" Parks observed in her autobiography. Appeals and organizing led the

Supreme Court in 1954 to throw out his conviction based on biased jury composition. At his new trial in May 1955, his defense argued that the trial was unfair and the case should be dismissed in part because of the "systematic exclusion of Negroes from jury duty in Montgomery County." After two days of testimony, the new all-white jury took only thirty-four minutes to restore Reeves's death sentence. The case had an impact on many of Reeves's fellow students. According to Claudette Colvin, a classmate of Reeves,

Jeremiah Reeves's arrest was the turning point of my life. That was when I and a lot of other students really started thinking about prejudice and racism. . . . When a white man raped a black girl—something that happened all the time—it was just his word against hers, and no one would ever believe her. The white man always got off. But now they were going to hold Jeremiah for years as a minor just so they could legally execute him when he came of age. That changed me. . . . I stayed angry for a long time.

The Montgomery NAACP worked for years to free Reeves. Parks personally corresponded with him and helped get Reeves's poetry published in the *Birmingham World* and the *Montgomery Advertiser*. Buried in the papers that Parks donated to Wayne State University are clippings from the *Montgomery Advertiser* of March 27, 1958 (the day before Reeves was executed), which ran two of Reeves's poems, "Don't Forget About Me" and "God Calls a Little Boy." The poems had stayed with her.

Parks strove to find evidence to prove the white woman was lying and even thought about going out to talk to the woman herself. Her friend Bertha warned, " 'Girl you know your mother and husband aren't going to let you go out there.' But I was ready to risk it if I could have found someone else to go along with me." On March 28, 1958, Reeves was executed. "Sometimes it was very difficult to keep going," Parks admitted, "when all our work seemed to be in vain."

Under Parks's leadership, the Youth Council was rejuvenated in 1954. Many parents were reluctant to have their children involved. "At that time," according to Parks, "the NAACP was considered far too militant or too radical, or too dangerous." Zynobia Butler Tatum, an eighth grader and the daughter of Parks's friend Bertha Butler, who was also active in the NAACP, became the secretary of the Youth Council.

Butler and Parks both lived in the Cleveland Courts projects, the Parkses in apartment 634. Opened in 1937 for blacks (while Jefferson

Courts opened across town for whites), the Cleveland Courts projects represented decent, if cramped, segregated housing for poor and working-class African Americans, with modern cooking facilities and indoor plumbing. The sense of community was palpable, made richer for the Parkses by Rosa's Aunt Fannie's family also residing there. After spending some time in Detroit, Rosa's mother had also come back to live with them. Rosa and Raymond did not have children. In a 1981 interview, Parks noted, "That was one thing missed."

The property was maintained by the government, which in these early years proved to be more reliable than many white landlords. Montgomery's housing segregation was fierce. Decent homes or rentals for black people were exceedingly scarce, even at premium price. For working-class blacks, the problem was even worse. Most properties lacked proper sanitary facilities: 82 percent of blacks lacked hot water in their homes, and nearly 70 percent used chamber pots and outhouses (compared to 6 percent of whites). Indeed, by the mid-1950s the inadequate quality and shortage of housing for blacks had reached crisis proportions, according to Reverend Robert Hughes, a white minister who was executive director of the Alabama Council for Human Rights. Reverend Palmer, a black pastor, noted the city's failure to repair and maintain the sewers and streets in black neighborhoods only to declare certain black areas "slums" in order to take over the land, a tactic Northern munici-palities like Detroit were also using. There were almost no park facilities available for black people, as most of the city's parks were white-only (black people weren't even allowed to cut through them).

The Youth Council met most Sundays at the Parkses' apartment, except for special occasions when they had speakers and would meet across the street at Trinity Lutheran Church. It was a small group, Doris Crenshaw recalled, and many parents wouldn't allow their children to join. "Our meetings were to be serious," recalled Zynobia Butler. Parks stressed "listening skills, taking notes, and neatness. . . . I didn't appreciate having to redo things so often." Indeed Mrs. Parks highlighted comportment and respecta-bility to the Youth Council and taught her young charges the importance of being active. She taught them what had been instilled in her: respectability meant maintaining your own self-worth, comporting yourself properly, and expecting respect from those around you. When Parks took Youth Council members to downtown Montgomery they "always drank from the white water fountain without incident." According to member Claudette Colvin, most of the young people in the group, unlike her, were the children of professionals. Some went to private schools. "Whenever they said they planned to go North for an education after they graduated, Rosa would scold them, 'Why should your families have to send you North? Our colleges right here could offer a good education, too—but they're segregated.'"

Odaliah Vaughn Garnier joined the Youth Council and appreciated how political Mrs. Parks was compared to her own mother. She registered to vote as soon as she turned eighteen, following Parks's instructions at their NAACP meetings. Mrs. Parks encouraged the young people to take more direct action. Doris Crenshaw was eleven when she joined the Youth Council, along with her sister. She became vice president of the Youth Council at twelve and president as a college freshman, and recalled Parks stressing their rights and the power of the vote. They traveled the state attending meetings, doing citizenship education, and urging adults to register to vote, helping prepare them for the questions on the test, and meeting other active young people. According to Crenshaw, "They had this long, thick voter registration questionnaire that people had to answer to vote. We would go over the ques-tionnaire with them and encourage them to go down and vote . . . people were very fearful of registering to vote. So we encouraged them to go down, to not be afraid." In these trips, the young people met various NAACP activists across the state. Parks also made connections and tried to find funds to enable these young people to attend college.

Parks also helped organize the Youth Council to challenge segregation directly, including protests at the main library, which did not allow blacks to check out books, requesting to be served. "They did this again and again" but were unsuccessful in changing the practice. Parks drew solace from the action-oriented nature of the young people she worked with: "One of things I did like about the youth . . . [is] they started right in to write letters to Washington [about anti-lynching legislation] . . . they didn't spend a lot of time arguing over motions and there was a difference in their way of conducting their meetings . . . from the senior branch." Many young people were warned by their parents and teachers not to get involved in civil rights. "There was this very popular phrase saying in order to stay out of trouble you have to stay in your place," Parks recalled. But then, she added, "when you stayed in your place, you were still insulted and mistreated if they saw fit to do so."

THE NETWORK GROWS

In the years before the boycott, the network of personal and political ties that would form the initial infrastructure of the boycott took shape in

Montgomery. Parks became friends with Fred Gray, a young black lawyer who had moved back to Montgomery and begun attending NAACP meetings. Gray had attended Alabama State for college but went to Western Reserve University Law School in Ohio to attain his law degree, taking advantage of Alabama's willingness to pay out-of-state tuition for black students so the state didn't have to desegregate the law school. Gray became the twelfth black lawyer in Alabama and the second in Montgomery.

Parks saw his potential as a civil rights advocate and for nearly a year regularly walked to Gray's office from her department-store job to have lunch and discuss Montgomery's problems. "We became very good friends," Gray explained. In these regular conversations, Parks helped Gray "get on his feet" and encouraged his law practice to pursue issues of racial justice. "She gave me the feeling that I was the Moses that God had sent Pharaoh and commanded him to 'Let My People Go.'"

Like many in Montgomery's black community and across the country, Parks, Gray, and Nixon were heartened by the Supreme Court's 1954 decision in *Brown v. Board of Education*. Excited about the prospect for real change, Parks saw "more possibility of not having to continue as we had." Nixon and several others escorted twenty-three black school children to the newly built all-white William Harrison School. "They wouldn't let them stay there," Nixon recalled. "They run them out, and they run me out too." At an NAACP meeting, the group decided to approach the school board directly to press for a desegregation plan. The branch also began to solicit signatures from parents to push for the implementation of *Brown* in Montgomery. A few parents signed, and the NAACP chapter presented the plan to the Board of Education at the opening of school in 1954. In response, Parks noted, the Board of Education published names and addresses of those signatories, opening them to "any type of harassment that might be inflicted . . . and to intimidate us as a people." Faced with this hostility, black parents were unwilling to pursue the case further and take the city to court. While in the minority, Nixon felt the branch hadn't done enough and continued to press the chapter—along with the national organization—to do more about implementing the decision. The Board of Education continued to stonewall; Parks thought the situation was "hopeless." She grew discouraged in the wake of *Brown* by the "apathy on the part of our people." Expanding the vote continued to be a pressing issue for both Nixon and Parks. In the summer of 1954, Nixon was named chair of a voter-registration effort for the Second Congressional District in Alabama and Parks the corresponding secretary.

Working for the NAACP was unpopular and dangerous in the mid-1950s. At a meeting in September 1955, the branch leadership discussed fears that their mail was being tampered with. Hostility to the organization grew precipitously in the wake of the *Brown* decision. "Today the NAACP sounds like an easy kind of phrase," Studs Terkel observed in 1973 in an interview with Parks, "a fashionable kind of word to say, safe, but in Montgomery, back in '55 . . ." Parks, in an interview in 1967, was hard-pressed to account for "what we actually accomplished" in Montgomery. There were "almost no ways" to see any discernible progress around segregation, despite the various activities of the organization. Nixon too lamented to a reporter that "these crackers have did a good job of keeping the Negro afraid and also keeping him unlearned."

HIGHLANDER

At the urging of both E. D. Nixon and Virginia Durr, in the summer of 1955, Parks decided to attend a two-week workshop at the Highlander Folk School entitled "Racial Desegregation: Implementing the Supreme Court Decision." The Durrs had worked with Nixon on various civil rights cases, and on Nixon's recommendation, Parks had started sewing for the Durr family, one of Montgomery's most liberal white families. Due to their politics, the Durrs had been ostracized by many white friends and colleagues, Clifford giving up a position at the Federal Communications Commission in Washington because he refused to sign a loyalty oath. Virginia was even more of a firebrand, chairing Henry Wallace's 1948 Virginia campaign (Wallace was the Progressive Party's candidate for president), running for Senate herself on the Progressive ticket, and going head-to-head with Senator James Eastland when he called her in front of the Senate Internal Security Subcommittee on charges of having Communist ties. The Durrs moved back to Montgomery in 1951 (both Virginia and Clifford had grown up in Alabama). Most white Montgomerians wanted nothing to do with them, making Clifford's law practice in these years somewhat precarious and Virginia quite isolated. The Durrs had three daughters and not a lot of money, in part stemming from this red-baiting, and their relatives would send them old clothes to help out. Needing more income for her family, Parks began sewing for them in 1954, altering the clothes to fit the three girls and fashioning some of the garments for the Durrs' daughter Lucy's wedding trousseau. Durr and Parks spent a lot of time sitting and talking. Despite and alongside the gulf between white and black women in 1950s Alabama, the two grew friendly, though Parks maintained a certain formality with her employer.

A member of Highlander's board of directors, Durr had seen the work Parks was doing with the NAACP Youth Council and knew how discouraged Parks had grown. As Parks recalled, "After that, I began getting obscene phone calls from people because I was president of the youth group. That's why Mrs. Durr wanted me to come up here and see what I could do with this same youth group when I went back home."

Myles Horton had cofounded the Highlander Folk School in Monteagle, Tennessee, in 1932 as a grassroots, interracial leadership training school for adults. The school held workshops to help local people develop strategies for pursuing social change and cultivate their own leadership skills. In the mid-1950s, Highlander, which had been integrated from its beginnings in the 1930s, had started to turn its attention to civil rights, having previously concentrated on labor and anti-poverty organizing, largely with white Appalachians.

The Supreme Court had issued its historic ruling in *Brown* in 1954 but put off the implementation order of the decision for another year, often referred to as *Brown II*. While *Brown* declared school segregation unconstitutional, *Brown II* in 1955 called for a "prompt and reasonable start to full compliance" and returned oversight for the implementation of desegregation to the states, which needed to proceed "with all deliberate speed." Without a specific timetable and with white resistance to desegregation mounting, this second decision allowed for delay and malfeasance. Civil rights activists and community leaders realized that they would have to press to ensure the decision was actually enforced. Myles Horton saw the need for a workshop focused explicitly on these questions of school desegregation implementation. Though blacks had previously numbered about 10 to 15 percent of Highlander's participants and had not spoken much at the meetings, the workshop Parks attended signaled a change. About half the participants at that workshop were black, and people participated avidly.

Horton had called Durr to tell her he had a scholarship for someone from Montgomery to attend the desegregation workshop. Durr immediately thought of Parks and how Highlander might help renew her embattled spirit. Nixon also urged Parks to go. Durr also called her friend Aubrey Williams, another liberal white Southerner and the publisher of the *Southern Farmer*, for further financial support because Mrs. Parks could not afford the round-trip bus ticket to Tennessee.

Parks described her state of mind as she embarked for Highlander as "rather tense and maybe somewhat bitter over the struggle that we were in." She was "willing to face whatever came, not because I felt that I was going to be benefited or helped personally, because I felt that I had been destroyed too long ago." Parks's language reveals the toll that more than a decade of civil rights work had taken on her. Seeing little possibility for racial justice in her life and frustrated with attempts to pursue any form of school desegregation in Montgomery, she placed her hope in the younger generation and in trying to ensure that the Supreme Court's decision was carried out "as it should have been." Increasingly, she focused her efforts on the youth chapter, from which she hoped more determined action might come.

Upon receiving the Highlander scholarship, Parks wrote a thank-you letter conveying her eagerness to attend the workshop and mentioning that she knew two of the speakers, Dr. Charles Gomillion of Tuskegee Institute and Ruby Hurley, NAACP regional field secretary. Parks took two weeks off from her job as an assistant tailor at Montgomery Fair to attend, a significant request and economic sacrifice.

Parks tried to get her husband to go to Highlander with her, but he refused. According to Brinkley, Raymond was "irate" about Rosa going because he considered the school suspect. This may have stemmed from his work with Communists and former Communists in the Scottsboro case. Rosa's mother was not well, but this did not stop her from going: "Parks and my mother could get along without me. He would cook." As a young person, Raymond had taken care of his own mother and grandmother and, as Rosa's activities took her away from home more often, he assumed some of the caretaker role for her mother.

Because Parks was fearful of being discovered going to Highlander, Durr accompanied her part of the way. "Just getting on the bus," Parks recalled in language that even decades later reveals how nervous she had been, "I found myself going farther and farther away from surroundings that I was used to and seeing less and less of black people. Finally I didn't see any black people and was met by this white person. I said to myself that I didn't know where I was going, but they seemed to be nice enough . . . I was somewhat withdrawn and didn't have very much to say. Finally I relaxed and enjoyed the stay there very much throughout the entire workshop." The county where Highlander was located was all white—and though the school was integrated, Parks was initially nervous at being surrounded by white people.

From July 24 through August 6, forty-eight people—teachers, union activists, civic leaders, and college students, about half of them black and half white—participated in a workshop designed, according to Highlander's report, "for men and women in positions to provide community leadership for an orderly transition from a segregated to a non-segregated school system in the South." The first few days, Rosa Parks barely talked at all, nervous about whether the whites in the group would actually accept her perspectives and fearful about describing the difficult situation activists faced in Montgomery. But she admired Highlander's founder Myles Horton's spirit and sense of humor. "I found myself laughing when I hadn't been able to laugh in a long time." And she started to grow more comfortable.

White and black people at Highlander lived, ate, discussed, and debated together—which was, by Southern standards, unimaginable. Parks particularly liked Horton's tongue-in-cheek response to reporters who repeatedly asked how he managed to get blacks and whites at Highlander to eat together. "And he says, 'First, the food is prepared. Second, it's put on the table. Third, we ring the bell.' " Parks found herself "cracking up many times" at Horton's way of pointing out the absurdity of segregation. Her spirits lifted. The variety of ways that Highlander subverted racial custom delighted Mrs. Parks. One of her favorite aspects of the two-week workshop was waking up to "the smell of bacon frying and coffee brewing and know[ing] that white folks were doing the preparing instead of me."

For many workshop participants, white and black, this experience of living with, eating, and having political discussion with people of another race was transformative. Alice Cobb, a white woman, recalled the first uncomfortable night she went to bed in the same room with a black woman. "The Highlander idea of equality and dignity of persons seemed to begin stirring around then for me in a bourgeois sort of effort to put that poor girl at ease and the odd realization that she was doing the same thing for me."

Septima Clark, a former South Carolina teacher, ran a number of the workshops. Two years earlier, she had attended her first Highlander workshop. Like Parks, Clark was friendly with a handful of white civil rights supporters, yet the interracial living impacted her as well. "I was surprised to know that white women would sleep in the same room that I slept in," Clark observed, "and it was really strange, very much so, to be eating at the same table with them, because we didn't do that." Cobb echoed Clark's feelings. "The eating together . . . I've always felt that eating together is a social sacrament." For Parks and others, the naturalness of the Highlander's integration— evident but not belabored—was key. Parks had participated in integrated groups and meetings, in particular Montgomery's integrated Council of Human Relations. But she had disliked those meetings, telling Virginia Durr, "Every time I went to one of those meetings, I came away blacker than I was before, because everything was discussed in terms of race."

Septima Clark had lost her teaching job of forty years when she refused to give up her membership in the NAACP. After the Supreme Court's decision in *Brown v. Board*, many states redbaited the NAACP as a foreign and potentially subversive organization; the state of South Carolina required all employees to renounce their membership or lose their jobs. Clark had chosen to retain her membership and forfeit her position—and in 1955 had come to work at Highlander full-time. Parks was "very much in awe" of Clark. Despite her own political history, Parks believed Clark's activities made "the effort that I have made very minute" and hoped for a "chance that some of her great courage and dignity and wisdom has rubbed off on me." Parks noted how Clark "had to face so much opposition in her home state and lost her job and all of that. She seemed to be just a beautiful person, and it didn't seem to shake her. While on the other hand, I was just the opposite. I was tense, and I was nervous and I was upset most of the time." Parks found Clark's calm determination remarkable.

The respite she found at Highlander was evident in her descriptions from a 1956 interview in which she described its "relaxing atmosphere" that was "more than a vacation but an education in itself." She found "for the first time in my adult life that this could be a unified society, that there was such a thing as people of all races and backgrounds meeting and having workshops and living together in peace and harmony." The atmosphere proved a salve for some of the psychic exhaustion she had been feeling and began to transform what Parks imagined was possible, a society not riven with racism. "I had heard there was such a place, but I hadn't been there."

The school had a strong Christian sensibility. As with Parks, Horton's revolutionary inspiration was Jesus who, Horton observed, "simply did what he believed in and paid the price." This Christian view of social justice—that Christianity required activism and also buttressed it—squared with Parks's worldview. Christian social thinker Reinhold Niebuhr, one of Martin Luther King's theological inspirations, would be one of the school's strongest supporters.

Johns Island organizer Esau Jenkins explained the purpose behind Highlander's workshops. "Well, we was talking about civil rights, constitutional rights, the Bill of Rights, and anything that is your right—if you don't fight for it, nobody going to fight for it. You going to have to let people know, I'm not going to let you do this to me or do this to my people without . . . my opinion against it." Even though she didn't speak much during the workshops, Parks took copious notes during the sessions, detailing what each speaker said. On one page, she framed the question of gradualism versus immediacy, a key issue in school desegregation implementation. "Gradualism would ease shock of white minds. Psychological effect. Disadvantage—give opposition more time to build greater resistance. Prolong the change." She then outlined how to formulate a social action program:

1. Policy not to use persons with record of trouble with law. Give them something to do where they will not be in forefront of action.
2. So people should be, as far as possible, economically independent. Not owe too many debts or borrow money from certain places.

In another section, she described how teachers lost their jobs if they worked for school desegregation. Parks was thus more than aware of the economic ramifications of being publicly identified as an advocate for desegregation. And then with a prescience she could not have imagined, she wrote, "Desegregation proves itself by being put in action. Not changing attitudes, attitudes will change." The point was to act and through that action, societal transformation would occur. Tellingly, Parks uses the term *desegregation* rather than *integration*—as many of her civil rights peers would—to signify that it was not a matter of having a bus seat or a school desk next to a white person but dismantling the apparatus of inequality.

Participants in the workshop were encouraged to contextualize the problems facing their communities within a global movement for human rights and to come up with concrete steps to create change locally. According to Horton, Parks was "the quietest participant" in the workshop. "If you judge by the conventional standards," Horton observed, "she would have been the least promising probably. We don't use conventional standards, so we had high hopes for her." Despite her reticence, the visit to Highlander was a transformative one for Parks, who had grown increasingly weary of pressing for change with little result.

> I was 42 years old, and it was one of the few times in my life up to that point when I did not feel any hostility from white people. . . . I felt that I could express myself honestly without any repercussions or antagonistic attitudes from other people . . . it was hard to leave.

Highlander workshops always ended with a closing discussion called "Finding Your Way

Back Home." Clark asked participants what they planned to do once they returned home. "Rosa answered that question by saying that Montgomery was the cradle of the Confederacy," Clark recalled, "that nothing would happen there because blacks wouldn't stick together. But she promised to work with those kids, and to tell them that they had the right to belong to the NAACP . . . to do things like going through the Freedom Train." Esau Jenkins recalled Parks referring to many in Montgomery as "complacent" and not likely to do anything bold. Many of the workshop participants agreed with her on the futility of trying to mount a mass movement in Montgomery. Parks worried about how blacks in Montgomery "wouldn't stand together." Horton could see how worn down Parks was. "We didn't know what she would do, but we had hopes that this tired spirit of hers would get tired of being tired, that she would do something and she did."

Parks found it difficult to return to Montgomery, "where you had to be smiling and polite no matter how rudely you were treated." Because Mrs. Parks feared white retaliation for her participation in the workshop, Clark accompanied her to Atlanta and saw her onto the bus to Montgomery. Parks also insisted on being reimbursed for her travel in cash, fearing that a check from Highlander would draw harassment.

A black teacher from Montgomery who also attended the workshop had not even told people at home where she was going, saying she was going somewhere else in Tennessee, for fear that she would lose her job if anyone found out.

Still, a typed press release dated August 8, 1955, and addressed to the *Montgomery Advertiser* and *Alabama Journal* called attention to the Highlander workshop that had taken place from July 24 to August 8 on school desegregation. Probably written by Parks, the fifth paragraph mentions that "Mrs. Rosa L. Parks attended the workshop from Montgomery as a representative of the NAACP Youth Council" and describes how the workshop ended "with specific plans by people from each of the 20 cities and communities represented" to bring about a "prompt and orderly" plan for school desegregation. Upon her return, Parks also reported to the NAACP branch membership about her trip to Highlander.

"Rosa Parks was afraid for white people to know that she was as militant as she was," Septima Clark recalled. Clark's observation in many ways summed up one of the paradoxes of Parks's character. Parks often covered up the radicalism of her beliefs *and* her actions. Her reticence was evident even at a place like Highlander, where she was still reluctant to talk about the Freedom Train visit to Montgomery. Nonetheless, while she was scared of it being discovered she went to Highlander, she still was willing to be listed in a press release that highlighted her attendance at the school desegregation workshop.

Parks looked to Clark and Ella Baker as role models as she sought to figure out how to be a woman activist when much of the visible leadership was made up of men and how to continue the struggle despite the vitriol of white resistance and the glacial pace of change. In spite of many years of political organizing, Parks still felt nervous, shy, and at times pessimistic about the potential for change. This process she went through is often missed in the romanticization of her bus stand as a spontaneous action without careful calibration. When Clark heard that Rosa Parks had refused to give up her seat on the bus five months after returning from the workshop, she thought to herself, " 'Rosa? Rosa?' She was so shy when she came to Highlander, but she got enough courage to do that." Indeed, the popular view of Parks as either an accidental or angelic heroine misses the years of gathering courage, fortitude, and community, which then enabled her to refuse to give up her seat. To be able to understand how Parks could have said aloud in front of other political organizers that nothing would happen in Montgomery, return to her political work in the community, and then five months later refuse to get up, demonstrates the political will at her core. She might not believe that anything would happen in Montgomery, but that didn't mean she would not try to demonstrate her opposition to the status quo.

Returning to her job at Montgomery Fair attending to the garments of white customers, no matter how rudely she was treated, was difficult. With few industrial jobs available in the city, most African Americans in Montgomery found themselves sequestered in service-related labor. In 1950, more than 60 percent of black women in Montgomery worked as domestics and 75 percent of black men were trapped in menial jobs. Only one in ten in Montgomery's black community worked in a professional field.

Having worked a series of sewing jobs, Parks had gotten the position at Montgomery Fair around Labor Day 1954. As the only black woman employed in the tailor shop (the tailor, John Ball, was black), she knew she was "setting a precedent." The situation for black employees and customers at the store was a segregated one—which bothered Parks a great deal. Montgomery Fair was the most prominent downtown department store. Blacks were employed in certain positions but not as clerks. The lounge at the store was reserved for white employees, while the black women workers were confined to a small room by the toilets. Those black people who worked as cooks and dishwashers at the department store lunch counter had to buy their sandwiches and eat them elsewhere. Black people could shop at the store but couldn't try items on. The store's black workers felt this instability. "We had to just face each day not knowing what to expect; if we made any protest or even sometimes if we didn't . . ."

The tailor shop was in the basement of the department store. Parks worked in a small, stuffy back room, made even hotter by the large pressing irons. Because she was a woman, she was not required to fit the male customers. The tailor did that, and she completed the alterations.

"We wear the mask that grins and lies," black poet Paul Laurence Dunbar wrote in 1896. "With torn and bleeding hearts we smile." The mask had never been easy for Rosa Parks. After Highlander it was becoming unbearable. Virginia Durr recalled in a letter to the Hortons in January 1956 that Mrs. Parks "felt so liberated [at Highlander] and then as time went on she said the discrimination got worse and worse to bear." Upon returning to Montgomery, Parks informed Nixon that the Highlander workshop had strengthened her resolve around her Youth Council work. She hoped to impress upon them their worth as equal to other young people.

Just a few weeks after Parks returned from Highlander came the devastating news of the murder of fourteen-year-old Emmett Till in

Money, Mississippi. Till had grown up in Chicago but had gone to visit his uncle in Mississippi for a summer holiday. After making a comment to a white woman who ran a local grocery store, the young Till was kidnapped from his uncle's house by her husband and brother-in-law, tortured, and then murdered. His body was dumped in the river. His mother fought to get his body sent back to Chicago and then had an open-casket funeral. Fifty thousand people saw his casket. Till's mother also allowed *Jet* magazine's photographers to take pictures so the nation would witness what had been done to her son. Parks wept at the photo of Till's body published in *Jet*. The lynching outraged her.

Poet Nikki Giovanni connected Till's murder and the killers' subsequent acquittal to Parks's decision to remain firm on the bus. Giovanni wrote, "This is about the moment Rosa Parks shouldered her cross, put her worldly goods aside, was willing to sacrifice her life, so that the young man in Money, Mississippi . . . would not have died in vain. . . . Mrs. Rosa Parks . . . could not stand that death. And in not being able to stand it. She sat back down."

Around that time, Montgomery had an incident similar to the Till murder. A young black minister Raymond Parks knew was killed for appearing to make an advance toward a white woman. "But the difference in this case from Till's," Parks explained, was that "Emmett Till came from the North and the media picked it up. In this case, of course, it was kept very much hidden so that is why in, around Montgomery it was supposed to have been a good race relations, quote unquote." The young man's mother was "not supposed to complain. There were several cases of people that I knew personally who met the end of their lives in this manner and other manners of brutality without even a ripple being made publicly by it."

With Parks as secretary, the Montgomery NAACP in 1955 continued its voter registration campaign, supported Jeremiah Reeves's legal defense, and protested Governor Folsom's segregated inaugural ball. NAACP field secretary Mildred Roxborough, who stayed with the Parkses when she visited the branch, described her as "stalwart." Parks "would go to meetings when other people were home lounging. . . . She wouldn't miss meetings unless she couldn't avoid it." Parks didn't talk a lot at meetings, but when she did, she "commanded by her demeanor a lot of respect." Roxborough recalled that Parks felt the NAACP chapter "should be doing more than it was doing at that particular time."

While E. D. Nixon was no longer head of the Montgomery NAACP, and class tensions continued to plague black organizing in the city, Nixon's own civil rights activism had not slowed down. A profile of Nixon in the *Chicago*

Defender shortly after the boycott started referred to Nixon and Parks as "the two most active members in the local branch." Nixon had complained to the Durrs when they first moved to town in 1951 that "the Negroes were all split up and jealous of each other and divided into cliques and you couldn't get them together on anything." In 1952, he was chosen president of the Montgomery Progressive Democratic Association. In 1954, Parks was elected secretary and Nixon chairman of the NAACP's Alabama Coordinating Committee for Registration and Voting.

In early November 1955, Nixon invited New York congressman Adam Clayton Powell to speak to the Progressive Democratic Association. Along with black women in Harlem, Powell had organized "Don't Buy Where You Can't Work" campaigns in the 1930s to target businesses that refused to hire black employees and helped lead a successful bus boycott in New York in 1941 that led to the Transit Authority hiring two hundred black workers. In his speech in Montgomery, Powell noted that the economic tactics of the White Citizens' Council (WCC) "can be counter met with our own [black] economic pressure." Powell met with Nixon, Parks, and others that night. His visit likely impacted Parks, Nixon, and many of Montgomery's politically active black citizens, as these Southern activists drew inspiration and strategy from Northern protests.

On November 27, 1955, four days before she would make her historic bus stand, Parks attended a packed mass meeting at Dexter Avenue Baptist Church. The meeting called attention to a series of recent lynchings in Mississippi—the young Emmett Till's murder as well as those of George W. Lee and Lamar Smith. Lee, a Mississippi grocer and Baptist minister, and Smith, a farmer, had both been murdered when they registered to vote and refused to back down to white pressure. Two days earlier, Lee's friend and fellow activist Gus Courts had also been shot. Dr. T. M. Howard, who was spearheading the organizing around the Till case, gave the keynote speech that evening. After Till's murderers were acquitted, Howard had embarked on a speaking tour across the country which included this stop in Montgomery. The meeting left a strong impression on Parks. Sickened by the detailed description of Till's murder, she continued to think about this gruesome killing in the days after the meeting.

Indeed, in the years preceding the boycott, Parks repeatedly struggled with the ways racial injustices were simply covered up to make it seem like all was well in Montgomery. "Everything possible that was done by way of brutality and oppression was kept well under the cover and not brought out in the open or any publicity presented." Demonstrating dissent was crucial, even if it did nothing, so it would not be "taken for granted that you were satisfied."

Mrs. Parks steadfastly continued her work with the Youth Council "and the few young people that I could get to pay attention to what I was trying to get them to see about desegregation of the schools and other public facilities." She was planning a big youth workshop for December 3 at Alabama State College.

Having been politically active now for two decades, Parks and Nixon, along with other Montgomery activists like Mary Fair Burks, Reverend Vernon Johns, Fred Gray, Jo Ann Robinson, and Alabama State professor J. E. Pierce, had tilled the ground for a movement. Yet local leaders continued to struggle with the fear and reluctance of many Montgomery blacks to unite across class lines to face the vitriol of white resistance. The small numbers of black people willing to take action weighed on Parks. Her heavy spirit, however, was about to lead her to an act of conscience and a season of courage bearing fruit few could have imagined.

CHAPTER THREE

"I Had Been Pushed As Far As I Could Stand to Be Pushed"
Rosa Parks's Bus Stand

"WHITES WOULD ACCUSE YOU OF causing trouble when all you were doing was acting like a normal human being instead of cringing," Rosa Parks explained. Such was the assumption of black deference that pervaded mid-twentieth-century Montgomery. The bus with its visible arbitrariness and expected servility stood as one of the most visceral experiences of segregation. "You died a little each time you found yourself face to face with this kind of discrimination," she noted.

Blacks constituted the majority of bus riders, paid the same fare, yet received inferior and disrespectful service—often right in front of and in direct contrast to white riders. "I had so much trouble with so many bus drivers," Parks recalled. That black people comprised the majority of riders made for even more galling situations on the bus. Some routes had very few white passengers, yet the first ten seats on every bus were always reserved for whites. Thus, on many bus routes, black riders would literally stand next to empty seats. Those blacks able to avoid the bus did so, and those who had the means drove cars. Black maids and nurses, however, were allowed to sit in the white section with their young or sick white charges, further underscoring the ways that bus segregation marked status and the primacy of white needs.

Because Montgomery saw itself as a more cosmopolitan city than some of its Southern neighbors, signs or screens separating the black and white sections were no longer used. It was a "matter of understanding [of] what seats we may use and may not use," Parks explained, with the power and discretion, particularly over the middle seats, "left up to the driver." "The bus driver could move colored people anywhere he wanted on the bus," Nixon reiterated, "because he was within his rights under a city ordinance." The arbitrariness of segregation, the power and place it granted white people, was perhaps nowhere more evident than on the bus.

Some bus drivers were kinder, remembered Rosalyn Oliver King and Doris Crenshaw, letting black passengers sit in the white seats while they drove through the black parts of town. But the minute they crossed into a white neighborhood, most drivers would tell the black passengers to get up. Some drivers didn't make black people get up when the white seats filled. "There were times when I'd be on the bus" Parks recalled, "and if what they called 'White section,' or

'White Reserved seats' were occupied and any white people were standing, they would just stand." But kindness did not undermine the force and legal basis of segregation. The majority of drivers made black passengers stand over open seats and forced them to pay and reboard through the back door so they would not even walk next to white passengers. Jo Ann Robinson recalled the demeaning terms often used in addressing African American women—"black nigger," "black bitches," "heifers," and "whores." Dr. King elaborated: " 'Go on round the back door, N—r.' 'Give up that seat, boy.' 'Get back, you ugly black apes.' . . . 'I'm gonna show you niggers that we got laws in Alabama.' 'N—r, next time you stand up over those white people I'm gonna throw you over to the law.' 'I hate N—rs. . . . Y'all black cows and apes, git back.' " For Rosa Parks, the education young children received in the mores of segregation hurt the most, as she hated to see children take an empty seat only to have their parents snatch them up and hurry them to the back before they got in trouble.

A HISTORY OF BUS RESISTANCE

"I was not the only person who had been mis-treated and humiliated," Rosa Parks said in an interview on Pacifica radio station KPFA in April 1956. Most people had been mistreated, some "even worse than [me]," Parks noted. Before

Parks, a number of black Montgomerians had also refused to submit to the terms of bus segregation, often paying dearly for that resistance. That history of brave acts in the decade before Parks's bus stand accumulated and came together in Parks's courageous refusal and in the bus protest sparked by her arrest.

In 1900, when the city first instituted segregation on the buses, Montgomery's black community boycotted and won a change to the city ordinance to specify that no rider had to surrender a seat unless another was available. In practice, drivers routinely violated this ordinance. Protests particularly heated up during World War II—as the contradiction between black military service abroad and unequal treatment at home heightened black resistance. With two Air Force bases (and thus a significant dependence on federal defense money to sustain the local economy) and a large population of both black and white service people, Montgomery, according to historian Glenda Gilmore, "stood at the epicenter of the guerrilla war on buses." The city's buses were rife with altercations between black service people and white bus drivers during the war years. Following a problem with the bus driver, a police officer shot a black airman; in another instance, the bus driver shot a local black GI in the leg when he took a front seat. In a third instance, when a black army lieutenant refused to give up her seat to white passengers, police beat her up and took her to jail. As Gilmore observed, "Rosa Parks would have known each of these hometown stories—and more—by heart."

In 1945, two Women's Army Corps members in uniform were asked to move for a white man. When they refused, saying that there were other available seats, the bus driver hit and verbally abused them. Referring to it as "one of the worst cases" he had seen, Thurgood Marshall warned that it looked "like dynamite to me." Bus resistance by army personnel was often met with violence; as Parks observed, "white people didn't want black veterans to wear their uniforms" because it served as a visible reminder of the fundamental equality imbued in that national service.

These disputes extended to civilians. In 1944, Viola White, who worked at Maxwell Air Force Base (like Rosa Parks during this time), was beaten and arrested for refusing to give up her seat. Found guilty, White then appealed her case to the circuit court. "The city of Montgomery knew they couldn't win," E. D. Nixon explained, "and we couldn't get on the court calendar." The case was held up indefinitely. Shortly afterward, the police retaliated, and a white police officer seized White's sixteen-year-old daughter and raped her. The daughter had the presence of mind to memorize the cop's license plate and boldly reported the crime. After many attempts by Nixon, a warrant for the officer's arrest was issued, but the police chief tipped off the officer, who left town. And then Viola White died, derailing any further legal action.

In 1946, Geneva Johnson was arrested for "talking back" to a driver and not having the correct change. She did not appeal but paid her fine. A few years later, Mary Wingfield was arrested for sitting in seats reserved for whites. In 1949, two New Jersey teenagers—Edwina and Marshall Johnson—refused to give up their seats and were arrested. Sixteen-year-old Edwina Johnson told the driver, "Where we come from we can sit anywhere we wish. I paid my fare— and I'm not going to move."

And in 1950, Hilliard Brooks, a veteran who had just returned from service, paid his fare but refused to exit and enter through the back door. Brooks asked the driver for his money back, but the driver refused. Brooks, who allegedly had been drinking, refused to back down. The police were called. Mattie Johnson, a passenger, witnessed the altercation. "And when you're waitin' on something awful to happen, you feel it more than any other time. It feels like it's pressing down on you, gettin' tighter and tighter around you, cuttin' you off from everything else." A police officer, M. E. Mills, boarded the bus and hit Brooks with his club. Johnson recalled, "My whole body jerked, like I'd been stuck by a pin." Brooks managed to get free and tried to exit the bus. The officer then shot Brooks, who subsequently died from the wounds. Mattie Johnson never rode the bus again. The killing was ruled a justifiable homicide because the officer said that Brooks had "resisted arrest."

The Brooks family, who had two young children and were expecting a third, lived across the walkway from the Parks at the Cleveland Courts apartments. When the incident occurred, Rosa was in Florida, taking care of a three-year-old white girl whose family was vacationing there. Brooks's murder "passed unnoticed except by his family and maybe a few others who were concerned at the time," according to Parks. His wife stopped riding the bus altogether.

The next year, Epsie Worthy exited the bus after the driver insulted her. When he followed her off and began hitting her, she fought back, "defend[ing] herself . . . with all her might." Worthy "gave as much as she took," according to passengers. The police broke up the fight, but Worthy was charged with disorderly conduct and fined fifty-two dollars. The driver was not sanctioned.

Parks was Nixon's right-hand woman during many of these cases and personally knew a number of the individuals who had resisted. For her, riding the bus required a persistent struggle;

in 1968 she told an interviewer that it was a "constant offense" and that she "was always in conflict with it." Many times, when she could, she avoided the bus. Witnessing the mixture of outrage and courage that led people to make such a stand, she intimately understood the punishment—the cost—they had to endure for that refusal. The notion that she was the first—or even third—to resist or that she made her bus stand impulsively misses her familiarity with the many instances and dangers of bus resistance, and the considerable thought she had given the matter.

Along with Parks, other Montgomerians had reached their "stopping point" around bus segregation, including some who emerged as key organizers of the boycott. The bus was a closer, more confrontational experience of segregation than many other public spaces. Part of the driver's power was that he could mistreat black passengers in front of the entire audience of the bus. Indeed, the power of segregation was produced and reproduced each day in the interactions between white bus drivers, black riders, and white riders. Dr. King had been seared by his experience with bus segregation at the age of fourteen. In order to participate in a speech contest, he and a teacher traveled from Atlanta to a small town in Georgia. On the way home, the driver ordered them to give up their seats for white passengers, and though King initially refused, his teacher convinced him to stand. They stood for several hours—and King was "the angriest I have ever been in my life."

So too was Reverend Vernon Johns, who refused to reenter through the back door after paying his fare. After asking for his money back, Johns called on the rest of the passengers to exit the bus with him. No one followed. A few days later, one of his congregants who'd been on the bus communicated the thoughts of some of their fellow passengers: "You ought to knowed better."

Jo Ann Robinson, a professor at Alabama State College who headed the Women's Political Council (WPC), had a painful experience on the bus in 1949. Ejected from an almost-empty bus for sitting too close to the front, Robinson fled, afraid the driver would hit her. "Tears blinded my vision," Robinson remembered, and "waves of humiliation inundated me; and I thanked God that none of my students was on that bus to witness the tragic experience. I could have died from embarrassment." The experience was so traumatic that Robinson couldn't talk about it, even with close friends. But the "hurt of that experience" strengthened her resolve that the WPC needed to demand change on Montgomery's buses.

Along with outright resistance, black passengers developed a series of daily tactics, according to historian Robin Kelley, to contest disrespect on the bus. "In Birmingham, there were dozens of episodes of black women sitting in the white section arguing with drivers or conductors, and fighting with white passengers." Indeed black passengers were arrested—or more commonly thrown off the bus—for "making noise," whether they talked back to the conductor, challenged another passenger, or gave an impromptu speech on racism.

One further insult in Montgomery came from the disconnect between the treatment blacks encountered on the integrated trolley on Maxwell Air Force Base and the city's segregated buses and other public spaces. Indeed, blacks and whites worked together at the Maxwell base, which had an integrated cafeteria, bachelor hall, and swimming pool. Rosa had worked at Maxwell for a time, and Raymond's barber chair was on the base. "You might just say Maxwell opened my eyes up," Parks noted. "It was an alternative reality to the ugly policies of Jim Crow." Parks sometimes rode the bus with a white woman and her child, sitting across from them and chatting. When they reached the edge of the base and boarded the city bus, she had to go to the back. Thus, Rosa Parks had direct personal contact with desegregated transportation in her own hometown. This visceral experience highlighted the sheer arbitrariness of segregated public transportation and made riding the city bus even more galling.

Parks would talk later about how "protest must be in my blood." Many years before her own stand, a driver told her mother, who had sat down near the back next to a young white serviceman, to move or he'd throw her off the bus. Her mother "stood up, very politely smiled in his face, and said, 'You won't do that.'" He returned to the front of the bus. Recalling the scene, Rosa said that she could hardly contain herself. "But before I could say anything, here came a very deep bass voice of a brother in the back of the bus. I don't know who he was or what he looked like, but he said very clearly, very distinctly, 'If he touches her, I'm hanging my knife in his throat.' So he didn't touch her, and I was happy he didn't, because he would have been pretty badly hurt by me with what I had, only my fingers." This image of young Rosa ready to defend her mother with her hands presents an important context for the origins of her own bus stand.

But there were also a number of times when Parks's mother had not been able to resist mistreatment on the bus. These also made a great impression on her daughter. In a 1966 interview, Leona McCauley stated, "Too many times I've had to get up and stand up so a white man could sit." Once a white man started cursing at her at a streetcar stop. "I heard her mention how upset she was but the only thing she could do was move over further from where he was standing," Rosa noted. Black women, thus, experienced particular vulnerabilities on public transportation.

Raymond Parks had largely stopped riding the bus before the boycott began, deciding he'd rather walk than be pushed around, as did Professor J. E. Pierce, who was active with Rosa in the NAACP. Rosa herself walked when she could and tried to use alternate means of transportation, particularly after Colvin's arrest. Along with other acts of resistance, these informal refusals show that bus protest had been percolating before the organized boycott emerged and locate Parks in the midst of those radical currents.

By 1955, the Montgomery NAACP was looking for a court case to test the legality of bus segregation. Some in the Women's Political Council (WPC) had even suggested a boycott. The WPC had been formed in 1946 by Mary Fair Burks, an English professor at Alabama State College. A sermon about black middle-class complacency by her pastor, Reverend Vernon Johns, inspired Burks to gather women from her church and social circle at Alabama State. Though their appearance suggested indifference, she suspected this was "a mask to protect their psyche and their sanity." Out of this initial meeting the WPC was formed as a predominantly middle-class black women's organization committed to address injustice. Burks was the first president, followed by Jo Ann Robinson. "We were 'woman power,'" Robinson explained, "organized to cope with any injustice, no matter what, against the darker sect." Rosa Parks knew the group and saw it as a women's affiliate of Dexter Avenue Baptist Church, a largely middle-class congregation where many of these women worshipped. Though she was acquainted with some WPC women, Parks was not a member of the council, likely because of the class and education divides that cut through Montgomery's black community.

Historian Mills Thornton has called the WPC the "most militant and uncompromising voice" for black Montgomerians in this period. By the early 1950s, people knew to bring their complaints about bus segregation to the WPC. The women of the organization, three hundred strong by 1954, collected petitions, met with city officials, went door to door, packed public hearings, and generally made their outrage around bus segregation publicly known.

Frustration with bus segregation mounted after the Supreme Court's ruling in *Brown*. Black Montgomerians were "worn out with being humiliated," Parks explained; bus segregation "was taking our manhood and womanhood away." What people sought "was not a matter of close physical contact with whites, but equal opportunity." Following the *Brown* decision in

1954, WPC president Jo Ann Robinson sent a letter to the mayor, Tacky Gayle, demanding action on the buses or people would organize a citywide boycott. Pointing out that bus ridership was three-fourths black, Robinson reminded city leaders that the buses "could not possibly operate" if black people stayed away.

Nixon's entreaties to the city had also been met with stonewalling, blame shifting, and claims that black people voluntarily chose these practices. Indeed the defense of segregation in a Southern citadel like Montgomery was not univocal. At times its white citizens invoked the political and moral necessity of segregation, while at other times, like their counterparts in the North, they denied that there was a problem or that the city was responsible for it. And like their Northern brothers, Southerners claimed that segregation was not institutional but a matter of personal predilection, that black people preferred it this way too. According to Parks, when Nixon complained to the bus company about black people being told to go around to the back door after paying their money, "they told him your folks started it—they go because they want to do it."

By 1955, frustration was hitting new levels. Early that year, the daughter of a minister was arrested, but, according to Nixon, "her father didn't want her to be part of a movement like that." So nothing further was pursued.

CLAUDETTE COLVIN'S ARREST

Then on March 2, 1955, Claudette Colvin boarded a bus home from school and refused to budge when the driver ordered her to move. Fifteen years old, the tiny Colvin—who Virginia Durr described as a "little gosling"—attended Booker T. Washington High School. Politicized by the legal mistreatment of her classmate Jeremiah Reeves, Colvin had just written a paper on the problems of downtown segregation. "We had been studying the Constitution in Miss Nesbitt's class. I knew I had rights." On the bus home that day, the white section filled up. A white woman was left standing. The driver called out, and the three students sitting in Colvin's row got up. She did not. The standing white woman refused to sit across the aisle from her. "If she sat down in the same row as me, it meant I was as good as her," Colvin noted. The driver yelled out again, "Why are you still sittin' there?" Colvin recalled. "A white rider yelled from the front, 'You got to get up!'" A girl named Margaret Johnson answered from the back, "She ain't got to do nothin' but stay black and die." There were thirteen students on the bus that day, most of them her classmates.

The driver, Robert Cleere, then called the transit police. In the midst of this, a pregnant neighbor of Colvin's, Mrs. Ruth Hamilton, got on the bus and, unaware of what was taking place, sat down next to her. When the policeman arrived on the bus, there were now two black people in the row. Initially, Hamilton also refused to get up. But upon the scolding of the police, a man in the back got up and gave Hamilton his seat. Colvin held fast, saying that she was tired of standing for white people every day. "If it had been for an old lady, I would have got up, but it wasn't." Colvin refused to surrender her seat because "I didn't feel like I was breaking the law." And indeed, in Montgomery, city code asserted that black people should not have to get up if there wasn't an open seat. Because the transit policeman could not make an arrest, at the next stop the bus was met by a squad car.

The two cops boarded the bus. The driver, according to Colvin, told the cops, "'I've had trouble with that 'thing' before.' He called me a thing." She was roughly handcuffed by the two officers. One WPC member, A. W. West, described the scene when the police boarded the bus: "Bless her heart, she fought like a little tigress. The policeman had scars all over his face and hands." But Colvin maintained that she went limp. "They started dragging me backwards off the bus. One of them kicked me. I might have scratched one of them but I sure didn't fight back." In the patrol car, the officers mocked her and made comments about parts of her body. Colvin worried that they might try to rape her and tried to cover her crotch. She tried to put her mind on other things. "I recited Edgar Allan Poe, Annabel Lee, the characters in Midsummer Night's Dream, the Lord's Prayer and the 23rd Psalm."

Colvin's arrest had a profound impact on Montgomery's black community. "I don't mean to take anything away from Mrs. Parks," lawyer Fred Gray later observed, "but Claudette gave all of us the moral courage to do what we did." Durr also underscored the impact Colvin's arrest had in Montgomery. "I mean this is just like genius, it just strikes; just like God strikes in a way because this child just wouldn't move." Many black people were awed by Colvin's actions. "That little teenage girl must have had a steel testicle," Andrew Young pointedly observed. The arrest angered Rosa Parks—all the committees, meetings, petitions to address bus segregation without "any results . . . just a brush-off."

Bailed out by her minister and mother, Colvin returned home proud but extremely fearful. "I had challenged the bus law. There had been lynchings and cross burnings for that kind of thing. . . . Dad sat up all night long with his shotgun. We all stayed up. The neighbors facing the highway kept watch." Montgomery's black leaders were outraged by Colvin's arrest and some in the Women's Political Council called for a boycott of the buses. Faced with Colvin's arrest, according to WPC president Jo Ann Robinson, some "could not take anymore. They were ready to boycott. . . . But some members were doubtful; some wanted to wait. The women wanted to be certain the entire city was behind them, and opinions differed where Claudette was concerned. Some felt she was too young to be the trigger that precipitated the movement . . . Not everybody was ready." Robinson, Rufus Lewis, and a new minister in town, Reverend Martin Luther King Jr., met with the city to discuss a plan where blacks would not be forced to move once they had taken a seat—and they were given assurances that city policy would be investigated and that Colvin's case would receive a fair trial.

Martin Luther King Jr. had moved to Montgomery in 1954 to succeed the militant Vernon Johns as pastor of the downtown Dexter Avenue Baptist Church. The church had sought a minister more erudite, middle-class, and less confrontational than Reverend Johns, who had long chastised his congregation for their complacency. After Montgomery authorities had beaten a black man to death for a speeding violation following another act of police brutality, Johns posted the title of his forth-coming sermon, "It's Safe to Murder Negroes in Montgomery," outside the church. As Dexter Avenue's billboard faced the Alabama state capitol building, this landed him before a grand jury, who sought to prevent him from preaching the sermon. He preached it that Sunday, anyway:

> Last week, a white man was fined for shooting a rabbit out of season. But of course, it's safe to murder Negroes. A rabbit is better off than a Negro because in Alabama niggers are always in season. . . . A Negro man was stopped by a trooper for speeding and brutally beaten with a tire iron while other Negroes stood by and did nothing. What would God have said when he looked down and saw an enraged police officer take up a young colored boy and use his head as a battering ram when the boy's father said nothing, did nothing? I'll tell you why it's safe to murder Negroes. Because Negroes stand by and let it happen.

Unlike many in the congregation who considered spirituals low-class, Johns occasionally added them to the church service. Committed to independent black economic development, he established an African American food cooperative and often sold vegetables, fruits, and hams in the basement after church on Sundays. The final straw for his parishioners came when he took to selling watermelons on the campus of Alabama State. While many did not appreciate Johns's political sermons, they shook up the congregation, instigating conversations about Christian social action, which laid the groundwork for Dr. King's leadership.

The first time Rosa Parks met the reverend who succeeded Johns was at an NAACP meeting in 1954. "I had arrived early, before the people started to come in. I saw this young person sitting there and nodded hello to him. I had no idea at the time who he was. He looked so young, just like a college student." Parks was thus surprised to find out that this young man was the evening's speaker. Most of the thirty people gathered to hear the twenty-five-year-old Martin Luther King speak on the *Brown* decision were women. When he began speaking, according to Carr, their "jaws dropped." Parks was "amazed that one so young could speak with so much eloquence and to the point." After this meeting, King joined the NAACP's executive committee; he also considered running for president of the organization but decided not to. Parks sent him his letter of appointment to the executive committee. And in January 1955, King addressed the new officers, stating that "we have come a long way but have a long way to go."

THE COLVIN CASE
Rosa Parks and Virginia Durr began fund raising for young Colvin's case, and more than one

hundred letters and a stack of donations streamed in to Parks's apartment. Parks was hopeful that the young woman's arrest would embolden other young people and spark interest in the NAACP youth meetings. She encouraged Colvin to get active in the youth chapter. Colvin recalled her first conversation with Rosa Parks. "She said 'You're Claudette Colvin? Oh my God, I was lookin' for some big old burly overgrown teenager who sassed white people out. . . . But no, they pulled a little girl off the bus.' I said, 'They pulled me off because I refused to walk off.'"

At an NAACP branch meeting on March 27, Rosa Parks highlighted the importance of Colvin's case, noting it could act "as a stimulus in getting members especially in her neighborhood." J. E. Pierce worried about the publicity and the pressure that might "be exerted on the family in some way." They stepped up the fundraising for the case. Leona McCauley baked cookies; Colvin recalled Mrs. Parks scolding her for eating a bunch—"we won't have any to sell." Parks also encouraged Colvin to run in the NAACP popularity contest that the branch sponsored to raise money for the case, which she did, though she didn't win. Parks made the crown for the winner.

At a second meeting with city officials, a group of black community leaders took a petition to the bus company and city officials asking for more courteous treatment and no visible signs of segregation on the bus. Tired of the city's obfuscation, Parks refused to join them: "I had decided I would not go anywhere with a piece of paper in my hand asking white folks for any favors."

Then in April, a young black veteran celebrating his release from the hospital was acting silly on the street and got in the way of a bus. The driver swerved around him but then came back and proceeded to beat the man with his transfer punch, turning his face to a bloody pulp. Mrs. Parks attended the driver's trial and was sickened when he was only fined twenty-five dollars for the assault and allowed to keep his job.

Colvin's case went to court on May 6, 1955. The judge dropped two of the charges (for disturbing the peace and breaking the segregation law) but found her guilty on the third for assaulting the officers who arrested her. The decision revealed the "extreme limits of stupidity and absurdity and horror," Durr wrote a friend, and how authorities were "so scared that the appeal on the constitutionality might be sustained that they dropped all the charges on the segregation issues." Since Colvin had strategically only been convicted of assault, appealing her case could not directly challenge the segregation law. "The thing that is so awful," Durr continued, "is that no one sees how absurd the system makes them appear—how brutal and cowardly—THREE HUGE BIG POLICEMEN against one little scrawny, fifteen year old colored girl."

Following the judge's decision, most black people in Montgomery were outraged. According to Robinson, "Blacks were as near a breaking point as they had ever been. Resentment, rebellion, and unrest were in evidence in all Negro circles. For a few days, large numbers of people refused to use the buses, but as they cooled off somewhat, they gradually drifted back." For the young Colvin, the experience was transformative. After appearing in court, Colvin decided to stop straightening her hair. "By wearing it natural, I was saying, 'I think I'm as pretty as you are.' . . . I told everybody, 'I won't straighten my hair until they straighten out this mess.' And that meant until we got some justice." But many of her classmates didn't react well to her. "Kids were saying she should have known what would happen," one classmate recalled. "Everything was reversed, everyone blamed her rather than the people who did those things to her. . . . We should have been rallying around her and being proud of what she had done, but instead we ridiculed her."

Colvin was seen as "feisty," "uncontrollable," "profane," and "emotional" by some community leaders who worried that she was too young and not of the right social standing to organize a broader campaign around. The Colvin family was poor and lived on the north side of town. After paying the family a visit, Nixon decided Colvin was not the kind of plaintiff they wanted and pulled back from pursuing her case. He also claimed that Colvin's mother didn't want her involved. Jo Ann Robinson vehemently disagreed with Nixon's assessment of Colvin's unsuitability and told him so, though the WPC did fear that the witnesses to the case might get frightened and recant.

Worrying that the press "would have a field day" with Colvin, Parks raised money for Colvin's case. According to black lawyer Fred Gray, who thought the Colvin arrest would make a good test case, Parks "shared my feelings that something had to be done to end segregation on the buses." Ultimately Colvin was deemed an unsuitable plaintiff for a legal case or mass action—which took a toll on the young Colvin.

Parks never said explicitly that she disagreed with Nixon's assessment, although her growing impatience by the end of the summer suggests that this may have been the case. When Parks attended the two-week workshop at Highlander in August, Colvin's arrest—and the community's reaction—was still on her mind. Longing for a stiffening of resolve among Montgomerians to confront the issue of segregation, Mrs. Parks hoped that Highlander would help her find a way to accomplish that. "I wanted our leaders there to organize and be strong enough to back up and support any young person who would be a litigant, if there should be some action in protest to segregation and mistreatment."

According to Colvin, Parks was the only adult leader who kept up with her that summer. Colvin had become a member of Parks's Youth Council before the arrest and continued to attend NAACP Youth Council meetings. Parks made Colvin secretary of the council, trying to nurture the young woman's spirit and budding leadership. Claudette Colvin recalled that she only went to Youth Council meetings "if I could get a ride, because I didn't want to ride the bus anymore. If I couldn't get a ride back, I'd stay overnight at Rosa's—she lived in the projects across the street. Rosa was hard to get to know, but her mom was just the opposite—warm and talkative and funny . . . There was nothing we couldn't talk about." Parks exhibited a certain forcefulness and strictness with the young people. According to Colvin, Mrs. Parks had a different personality inside and outside of the meetings. "She was very kind and thoughtful; she knew exactly how I liked my coffee and fixed me peanut butter and Ritz crackers, but she didn't say much at all. Then when the meeting started, I'd think, Is that the same lady? She would come across very strong about rights. She would pass out leaflets saying things like 'We are going to break down the walls of segregation.' " Parks would make Colvin tell the story of her bus arrest over and over. "After a while they had all heard it a million times. They seemed bored with it."

Late in the summer, Colvin realized she was pregnant by an older man who had befriended the young and vulnerable teenager. According to Durr, Colvin's pregnancy bothered Parks, who regarded it as "a kind of burden that Negro women had to bear for so many generations, you know, of being used . . . and not having their person's [sic] used." Montgomery's civil rights leaders had decided *before* learning of Colvin's pregnancy that they wouldn't actively pursue her case, but now they increased their distance from her, eventually asserting her pregnancy *was* the reason for their decision. Indeed, Nixon would claim that when he went to visit the family in May, Colvin's mother told him of her pregnancy. Other accounts would have Nixon see a pregnant Colvin when he got there. Virginia Durr would claim that Colvin's brother called up to say that Claudette would not be able to come to court because she had taken a tumble. (This would have been impossible, since Colvin's son Raymond wasn't born until March 29, 1956.)

Parks encouraged the young people of her NAACP Youth Council to challenge segregation. In the wake of Colvin's arrest, she instructed her young charges on how to proceed if they were arrested to "make certain that they knew how to conduct themselves in a way that they couldn't be accused of disorderly conduct or resisting arrest." Some of these young people took action, occasionally by taking the front seats. A couple of young men reported back to her that they'd sat in the front "and the driver didn't say anything." Parks figured the reason the driver didn't do anything was "he didn't know what these youngsters would do. I always asked them if they . . . [wanted] to do what we could to break down racial segregation."

On October 21, eighteen-year-old Mary Louise Smith (who was not a member of Parks's Youth Council) was arrested. Smith had attended St. Jude's School, where the nuns taught that all people were equal and deserved respect—which fueled Smith's stand on the bus. That day, she had trekked across town to collect twelve dollars owed to her by the white family she worked for, but they hadn't been home. So she had spent twenty cents on bus fare and was returning home empty-handed. The driver told her twice to move. She refused and was briskly arrested. Her father came down and paid the fine. Smith's family was poor and her father rumored to be an alcoholic. Nixon also paid this family a visit, describing the Smith home as "low type." He claimed that if "the press had gone out there" they would become a "laughingstock to try to build a case around her." Smith later challenged these characterizations, saying her father worked two jobs to support her and her five siblings and did not have time for drinking.

Nixon claimed that both Colvin and Smith were "vulnerable to exploitation by a white lawyer or a white-controlled media," explaining that "white people have used the media to destroy things they dislike." He worried that neither young woman was strong enough to withstand the attacks a case would engender. Some in the WPC disagreed with Nixon, believing that the principles of the case were more important than the plaintiff and that it was time to take a stand. But Nixon was a force to be reckoned with. One of the few activist community leaders, Nixon's backing was necessary for any successful black mobilization in Montgomery. People faced with a legal injustice would telephone him, and he would come to their assistance. He knew many people in the police and sheriff's department, at city hall and at the jail, along with most lawyers, white or black. Thus Nixon's endorsement was seen as crucial. But his leadership, according to Robinson, had its limits. "People respected Mr. Nixon for his bravery. But he wasn't always able to follow up. . . . He was willing, I've never seen anyone more willing, but I think his leadership stopped where he couldn't go anywhere further."

While worrying about finding a plaintiff who could withstand the press, Rosa Parks grew frustrated with the lack of any forward movement. Parks recalled having discussions with Robinson "about how a boycott of the city buses would really hurt the bus company in its pocketbook" but she didn't sense much public support for a boycott.

Civil rights leaders had been engaged in a long-standing negotiation with the city with little result. The city's tactics, nuanced and belabored, dragged Montgomery's black citizens along in a byzantine process of blame shifting where the city and the bus company attempted to foist responsibility for bus segregation onto each other. Moreover, Montgomery's buses were operated by a northern company—National City Lines—so Montgomery's segregation was not simply parochial, and its economic ramifications extended well beyond the Cradle of the Confederacy. Like their counterparts across the South and the North, Montgomery's officials offered meetings and professed concern about race problems yet did nothing. Shortly after the boycott had started, Parks told a journalist of her growing outrage at the "run-around" the city had given Montgomery's activists.

In Montgomery long before our protest began, on some occasions I had been on committees to appear before the city officials and bus company officials with requests that they improve our conditions that existed that were so humiliating and degrading to our spirit as well as sometimes physical discomfort in riding the bus. We would have some vague promises and be given the run-around and nothing was ever done about it.

By the time of Colvin's arrest, she had come to feel that "we had wasted a lot of time and effort" with the petitions and meetings with Montgomery officials. Mrs. Parks was looking for more concrete action.

DECEMBER 1, 1955

"It was a strange feeling because . . . even before the incident of my arrest, I could leave home feeling that anything could happen at any time." On December 1, 1955, Rosa Parks finished work at Montgomery Fair. That Thursday had been a busy day for the forty-two-year-old Parks. During her coffee break, she had talked with Alabama State College president H. Councill Trenholm to finalize plans for her NAACP workshop on campus that weekend. As usual, she had lunch at Fred Gray's office and then spent the afternoon hemming and pressing pants. Her shoulder was bothering her. She was looking forward to a relaxing evening at home and had some NAACP work to do.

She left work. Deciding to wait for a less crowded bus, Parks picked up a few things at Lee's Cut-Rate Drug. She contemplated buying a heating pad but decided they were too expensive. In short, "this day was just like any other day."

The downtown Court Square near Montgomery Fair was decorated with Christmas lights. A banner over one store read "Peace on Earth, Goodwill to Men." This festive atmosphere masked the fearsome race relations that had defined the place for its 150 years of existence. This was the Cradle of the Confederacy. Slaves had been auctioned from that square. Across the street was the Exchange Hotel, which had served as the first headquarters of the Confederacy. Rosa Parks well understood that history of Southern white power and black resistance.

Around 5:30, Mrs. Parks distractedly boarded the yellow-and-olive bus and paid her ten cents. Had she been paying attention, she probably "wouldn't even have gotten on that bus" because the driver, James Fred Blake, had given her trouble before. Back in 1943, Parks had paid her fare, and this very same bus driver insisted that Parks had to exit and reboard through the back door. She felt this practice constituted a humiliation too great to bear. When Parks did not move, Blake grabbed her sleeve, attempting to push her off the bus. She purposely dropped her purse and sat down in a seat in the whites-only section to pick it up. Blake seemed poised to hit her. "I will get off. . . . You better not hit me," she told him and exited the bus and did not reboard. For the next twelve years, she avoided Blake's bus.

As with other segregated situations, like drinking fountains and elevators, Parks avoided the bus and walked when she could. But not owning a car, and given her job and community commitments, sometimes she had no choice. Parks refused to pay her money in front and then go around to the back to board. Some drivers told her not to ride if she "was too important . . . to go to the back and get on." According to Parks, some motormen had even come to recognize her because of this. "It seemed to annoy and sometimes anger the bus drivers." One particular driver, if he saw Parks alone, would shut the bus door very quickly and drive on. Overall, Parks had long attempted to maintain her dignity on the bus, and there were "almost countless times when things happened. . . . But I always indicated that even if I was forced to comply with these rules that it was very distasteful to me." In an interview in 1956 with white liberal Alabamian Aubrey Williams, Parks said that she had never before that evening been directly asked to give up her seat for a white person.

Comfortably setting her parcels down, Rosa took a seat next to a black man in the middle section of the bus. The bus was not crowded, with many seats still open in the front. As she admired the sights and sounds of Christmas, her mind turned to her husband and "how we were going to have a good time this Christmas." Raymond was making dinner, and in fifteen short minutes she would be home. There were two black women sitting across the aisle from her. They were all seated in a row toward the middle of the bus. As she would clarify repeatedly in the years to come, she was *not* sitting in the white section but in the middle section of the bus. The middle was liminal space; it allowed space for paying black customers to sit, but that could be trumped on the discretion of the driver by the wants of a white rider. At the third stop, the white section of the bus filled up. The bus had thirty-six seats. Fourteen whites occupied the front section; twenty-two black people were sitting in the back seats. A white man proceeded to stand behind the driver.

When Blake noticed, he called back, "Let me have those front seats"—meaning the first row of seats in the middle section where Mrs. Parks and three others were sitting. By the terms of Alabama segregation, because there were no seats remaining in the white section, all four passengers would have to get up so one white man could sit down. In Montgomery, technically, black passengers were not supposed to be asked to give up their seat if there was not another one available—but on the "whim" of the driver could be asked to stand for another passenger. When the driver ordered them to give up their seats, no one moved. Getting agitated, the bus driver said, "You all better make it light on yourselves and let me have those seats."

Parks reflected to herself on how giving up her seat "wasn't making it light on ourselves as a people." She thought about her grandfather keeping his gun to protect their family. She thought about Emmett Till. And she decided to stand fast. "People always say that I didn't give up my seat because I was tired but that isn't true. I was not tired physically, or no more tired than I usually was at the end of a working day. . . . No, the only tired I was, was tired of giving in."

Blake told the four black passengers to move. The white passenger never said anything to Parks. When asked by an interviewer in 1967 if the man seemed embarrassed, Parks replied, "I don't remember paying him any attention." What she was about to do was much bigger than him.

Her seatmate and the other two women got up "reluctantly," according to Parks, but she refused. She moved her legs so the man sitting in the window seat could get out and then slid into the seat next to the window. She continued to sit, firm in her decision but unsure what would next ensue.

The tall, blond forty-three-year-old driver got up and walked back to where she was seated. City code gave the "powers of the police officer" to bus drivers. Blake, like all of Montgomery's bus drivers, was white and carried a gun. When the boycott began, there were no black drivers on the city's lines. Born nine months before Rosa Parks in the town of Seman, Alabama, Blake had left school after the ninth grade and been hired by the bus company in 1942. Drafted into the army in 1944–45 and seeing active duty as a truck driver in the European theater, he returned to his job in late 1945 and had been driving the city's buses ever since.

Parks had not planned the protest but "had been pushed as far as I could stand to be pushed." She "couldn't take it anymore. . . . It is such a long and lonely feeling. The line between reason and madness grows thinner [due to the] horrible restrictiveness of Jim Crow laws." And so she decided to withdraw her participation in a system of degradation. Parks felt she was being asked to consent to her own humiliation: "I felt that, if I did stand up, it meant that I approved of the way I was being treated, and I did not approve." "Tired of giving in," Mrs. Parks had reached her stopping point.

"Besides," noted Jo Ann Robinson, "she was a woman, and the person waiting was a man." The fact that she was being asked to stand for a man was significant. In a 1964 *Esquire* article she noted, "It didn't seem logical, particularly for a woman to give way to a man." This carried another cost—that of marking herself as not a lady since etiquette dictated a man would never take a seat from a woman; indeed, he should offer his seat to her.

There were no other seats on the bus so, according to city code, Parks was entitled to keep hers. But as she told an interviewer in February, she had "made up my mind that I was not going to move even if there were seats in back." She also mentioned this to A. W. West, a prominent black woman in the community, who recalled: "When I asked her what happened, she said that she did not move. There were no other seats, however, she stated that if there had been, she had made up her mind never to move again."

Blake wanted the seat. "I had police powers—any driver for the city did." The bus was crowded, and the tension heightened as Blake walked back to her. Refusing to assume a deferential position, Parks looked him straight in the eye.

Blake asked, "Are you going to stand up?"

Parks replied, "No." She then told him she was not going to move "because I got on first and paid the same fare, and I didn't think it was right for me to have to stand so someone else who got on later could sit down."

"Well I'm going to have you arrested."

"You may do that," Parks replied.

Given her NAACP organizing experience, Parks was exceedingly cognizant of the dangers a black woman faced in getting arrested. "I didn't even know if I would get off the bus alive." She knew that Claudette Colvin had been manhandled by police and others had been beaten or shot for their resistance. In her words, "As I sat there, I tried not think about what might happen. I knew that anything was possible." Stories circulated through the black community, according to Doris Crenshaw, of "women being pulled off the bus and raped and not arrested." Parks knew what could happen "but I was resigned to the fact that I had to express my unwillingness to be humiliated in this manner."

Parks thought about the possibility of resisting but decided not to put up any physical fight, even if Blake or the police got rough with her. "I didn't have any way of fighting back. I didn't have any type of weapon. And I would have been too physically weak to try to have done anything to protect myself against any of these policemen, you know, if they had decided to use violence in handling me." Years earlier, in the bus incident with her mother, Parks had imagined using her hands if her mother was manhandled. But here she did not. Parks was a seasoned activist at this point and understood the value in not resisting arrest—the police had charged Colvin not just with a violation of the segregation laws but also with resisting arrest and assault. Still, faced with the possibility that she might be assaulted, she "wasn't frightened at all," she recalled in a 1956 interview. Rather, she was somewhat distracted, thinking about all she had to do for the upcoming Youth Council workshop and the December NAACP elections.

Parks looked to her faith in this moment: "God has always given me the strength to say what is right." She also attributed her courage to the history of the black freedom fighters who had come before her. "I had the strength of God and my ancestors with me." Black women had a long history of bus, train, and streetcar protest, exposing the "irrationality of segregation," according to historian Blair Kelley, and that evening Mrs. Parks extended the tradition. "I could not have faced myself or my people if I had moved," Parks told a reporter in 1957.

Framing her decision as a morally important one, Parks described it in terms similar to Gandhi's ideas about the moral obligation of civil disobedience: "If I did not resist being mistreated, that I would spend the rest of my life being mistreated." She highlighted the "artificial, legal" nature of segregation; to move from her seat legitimated the logic of it. Parks refused.

Parks's frustration came also from how she was

expected to act at work, tailoring clothes in the men's department at Montgomery Fair, and how she was treated in public life. "You spend your whole lifetime in your occupation, actually making life clever, easy and convenient for white people. But when you have to get transportation home, you are denied an equal accommodation. Our existence was for the white man's comfort and well-being; we had to accept being deprived of just being human." Having spent the day altering and pressing white men's suits, Parks again was being asked to lower herself so a white man could be convenienced. She refused. As she had learned from her mother and grandparents, part of being respectable was not consenting to the disrespect of her person.

Blake left the bus to call the supervisor from the pay phone on the corner. "I was under orders to call them first." His supervisor told Blake to put the woman off the bus. " 'Did you warn her Jim?' I said 'I warned her.' And he said . . . 'Well, then, Jim you do it. You got to exercise your power and put her off, hear?' " Blake then called the police. Meanwhile, the tension on the bus grew. Most on the bus, black and white, feared what might happen. They did not want trouble, and many wished she would just stand up. Parks heard grumblings of conversation though she could not make out what they were saying. Some black people exited the bus. "I supposed they didn't want to be inconvenienced while I was being arrested," she surmised.

Police officers Day and Mixon boarded the bus. The police were "the front line of the white segregationist army," according to white Montgomery minister Robert Graetz. While the Klan had for many decades been the central force to keep black people in line, "that kind of illegal [activity] was no longer tolerated, at least officially. Nowadays the task of controlling Negroes was entrusted to the legally constituted constabulary." Montgomery whites saw themselves as sophisticated. They did not have to resort to common vigilantism—at least publicly—and had entrusted the police with maintaining a severely segregated and unequal city. The law was up to the task.

Blake explained to the officers that he had asked for the seats and the "other three stood, but that one wouldn't." This phrasing angered Parks. "He didn't say three what, men or women, didn't refer to anything, just, 'that one,' pointing to me, 'wouldn't stand up.'" Blake addressed nothing further to Parks after he called in the officers.

The first officer addressed Parks and asked her why she did not stand up when instructed to. Parks coolly asked back, "Why do you all push us around?"

He replied, "I don't know but the law is the law and you're under arrest."

Parks thought to herself, "Let us look at Jim Crow for the criminal he is and what he had done to one life multiplied millions of times over these United States."

As she exited the bus, one officer picked up her purse and the other her shopping bag. The police officers talked to the driver "secretly, however I did hear one say, 'NAACP,' and 'Are you sure you want to press charges.'" The driver said that he did, and that he would come down after his next trip. The policemen were reluctant, but they had no choice." Blake wanted to swear out a warrant and after he finished his run would come by to finish the paperwork.

In contrast to other troubles Parks had previously had on the bus, Blake *chose* to have her arrested, rather than simply evicting her from the bus. In an interview on February 5, 1956, Parks put the agency on Blake rather than on the officers, who were willing to just put her off the bus. That decision, according to E. D. Nixon, "was the worst thing ever happened to him." There is no indication from this interview or others that the officers knew Parks, but they seemed to fear the NAACP and what it might do. At 6:06 p.m., the officers signed warrant 14256 charging Rosa Parks with violating chapter 6, section 100, of the Montgomery city code.

In an interview years later, Blake explained, "I wasn't trying to do anything to that Parks woman except do my job. She was in violation of the city codes, so what was I supposed to do? That damn bus was full and she wouldn't move back. I had my orders." But in fact, she wasn't in violation of the city code, and his orders from the supervisor had just been to have Parks removed from the bus—not specifically to have her arrested. That extra step, Blake's vociferous defense of segregation and desire to see Parks punished, proved historic. As Parks observed, the first time she had trouble with Blake he had evicted her from his bus but hadn't called the police. But this evening "he just felt like he wanted to throw his weight around or exercise his power beyond just enforcing segregation law." This was how segregation worked more broadly, endowing a broad cross-section of white people with authority that could be wielded or not wielded at their discretion.

David Levering Lewis, in his 1970 biography of Martin Luther King, claims that Blake recognized Parks's character, which prompted his decision to call the police rather than physically remove her from the bus.

Had Rosa Parks been less primly composed, had her diction betrayed the mangled speech of the ordinary black passenger, the outcome of Thursday, December 1, 1955, could have been different. . . . [Blake] was not generally given to violence, and to use expletives before the amazed and slightly embarrassed white passengers (several of whom were female) struck him as unprofessional. . . . Blake's decision to summon the police appeared to offer the most expedient solution to this extraordinary dilemma.

Parks made the decision to remain in her seat through her own political will and long history of bus resistance. She did not make it because of E. D. Nixon or Myles Horton, though they had certainly been instrumental in her political development. She was not a Freedom Rider boarding the bus to engage in an act of intentional desegregation. If that had been the case, if Parks had been acting on behalf of the NAACP, her former classmate Mary Fair Burks explained, "she would have done so openly and demanded a group action on the part of the organization, since duplicity is not part of her nature."

Still, Rosa Parks was an experienced political organizer. She had been galled by bus segregation for years. So that evening as she waited the minutes for the police to board the bus, she thought about what Mr. Nixon would say and perhaps even how they might use this in their organizing. In the hundreds of interviews she gave around her bus stand, however, Parks rarely acknowledged thinking of Nixon during her arrest and what they might do. Because segregationists were so quick to call her an "NAACP plant," she likely felt that any admission risked giving their slander credence. There is no evidence of any sort of plan, no indication till the moment presented itself that Parks knew she could summon the courage to refuse to move from her seat. It is likely that she, like many black Montgomerians, particularly after Colvin's arrest, had thought and talked about what she would do if she were asked to give up her seat to a white person. But thinking or even talking about it and actually being able to act in the moment are vastly different.

But Parks was well aware of the political situation and the resources she would call on. "I told myself I wouldn't put up no fuss against them arresting me. . . . As soon as they arrested me, I knew, I'd call Mr. Nixon and let him know what had happened. Then we'd see." In another interview, she also mentions thinking about Nixon in that moment. "It was the only way I knew to let him [Nixon] and the, all the world, know that I wanted to be a respectable and respected citizen in the community." And in a 1967 interview, she explained, "I had felt for a long time, that if I was ever told to get up so a white person could sit, that I would refuse to do so."

Parks made an active choice in that instance. As poet Nikki Giovanni framed it, "She saw the opportunity and she took it." In the midst of the fear, humiliation, and inconvenience of being asked to give up your seat on a crowded bus, with the real possibility of violence for refusing, to see an opening is testament to Parks's vision that December evening. In a moment designed to frighten and degrade, she was able to see herself as an agent and claim a space of choice. "It's only a few people that you can find that can get a glimpse of . . . what is going to happen," Reverend Johns observed, "and Rosa Parks was one of those rare people who could catch a vision."

But that agency was also harrowing. There were other people she knew on the bus, but none came to her defense. Calling it "one of the worst days of my life," she said, "I felt very much alone." She fantasized about what it would have been like if the whole bus had emptied or if the other three had stayed where they were "because if they'd had to arrest four of us instead of one, then that would have given me a little support." Parks had not expected that others would follow her or come to her defense on the bus—"I knew the attitude of people. It was pretty rough to go against the system." In another interview, however, she admits to wishing they had and seems frustrated, though unwilling to admit it. "I possibly would have felt better if they had taken the same stand. But since they didn't, I understood it very well. I didn't bear any grudge against them." In a later interview, she put it more starkly, "When I was arrested, no other person stood and said, 'If you put this woman in jail, I am going to . . .'" In numerous interviews over the years, Parks came back repeatedly to how hard her arrest felt in the moment, describing her stand in less than triumphal terms: "At times I felt resigned to give what I could to protest against the way I was being treated."

Parks believed in the responsibility of the individual to stand against injustice. In a speech in Los Angeles a few months after her bus stand, Parks stressed the solitary nature of the protest, which she saw following from the preceding years of relatively lonely activism. "My convictions [against segregation] meant much to me—*if I had to hold on to my convictions alone, I would.* . . . [Emphasis added.] Over the years, I have been rebelling against second-class citizenship. It didn't begin when I was arrested." Parks had taken a number of personal stands against segregation before her bus stand—refusing to use the "colored" bathroom, refusing to pay her money and then reboard the bus from the back door, drinking from the "white" fountain, insisting on taking her youth group to the Freedom Train. Here again, she drew a personal line with no way of knowing that a whole community would soon follow. As she described it in 1978, "There were times when it would have been easy to fall apart or to go in the opposite direction, but somehow I felt that if I took one more step, someone would come along to join me." Getting arrested was considered a mark of shame, but Parks resisted this thinking.

In the years subsequent to her arrest, and particularly in the past few decades, Parks's decision to remain sitting has repeatedly been called a "small act"; even Parks, on occasion, minimized it. But there was nothing small about her action. Renowned black feminist Pauli Murray, in a tribute to Mrs. Parks in 1965, observed: "Here was an individual virtually alone, challenging the very citadel of racial bigotry, the brutality of which has horrified the world over the past few years." Murray had also been arrested for refusing to give up her seat on a bus, in Petersburg, Virginia, in 1940.

"Any one of us who has ever been arrested on a Southern bus for refusing to move back," Murray highlighted, "knows how terrifying this experience can be, particularly if it happened before the days of organized protest. . . . The fear of a lifetime always close to the surface of consciousness in those of us who have lived under the yoke of Southern racism is intensified by the sudden commotion and the charged atmosphere in the cramped space of the bus interior. As one who has known this fear, I suspect Mrs. Parks also felt it, but summoning all of her strength, she disregarded it and held her position."

Parks also contextualized her decision within her role as a political organizer: "an opportunity was being given to me to do what I had asked of others." Seeing herself as part of a fledgling movement, she felt she had a responsibility to act on behalf of this larger community. She had been pushing the young people in her Youth Council to step up and contest segregation and had grown disappointed by the ways adults in the community "had failed our young people." NAACP field secretary Mildred Roxborough recalled Parks's "wonderment . . . thinking I had a role, I became an example of what I preaching." On the bus that December evening, she saw herself at a crossroads and chose to make a stand.

In part, Parks acted because she had grown disheartened by pushing other people to take action who were reluctant to do so. She was frustrated by the Colvin case, by meetings and affidavits that went nowhere, and that December evening her discouragement transformed into confrontation. Indeed, her decision to act arose as much from frustration with the lack of change than a belief that her particular action would alter anything. "I simply did it because I thought nobody else would do anything," she would later explain. But she also chose a more direct form of defiance, refusing to get up rather than just exiting the bus (as she had done previously).

Rosa Parks's protest has often been reduced to the unwitting action of a quiet seamstress with aching feet. That explanation "started . . . after I moved to Detroit. I never heard it before I left the south," Parks observed to a reporter in 1980. Parks critiqued these popular mis-characterizations:

> I didn't tell anyone my feet were hurting. It was just popular, I suppose because they wanted to give some excuse other than the fact that I didn't want to be pushed around. . . . And I had been working for a long time—a number of years in fact—to be treated as a human being with dignity not only for myself, but all those who were being mistreated.

Her quietness has been misread. She may have seemed "schoolmarmish but there was a storm behind it," observed activist-journalist Herb Boyd. That evening, as she waited on that bus, there was thunder in her silence. Years later,

Parks clarified what motivated her stand, reframing the discussion away from its narrow idea of a seat next to a white person to the actual goal of equal treatment and full human dignity. "I have never been what you would call just an integrationist. I know I've been called that. . . . Integrating that bus wouldn't mean more equality. Even when there was segregation, there was plenty of integration in the South, but it was for the benefit and convenience of the white person, not us. So it is not just integration." Her aim was to "discontinue all forms of oppression against all those who are weak and oppressed."

Time and again, Parks explained her protest as an intrinsic part of the political work she already was doing, vehemently denying that her protest stemmed simply from physical fatigue. In an August 1956 speech, she explained, "It is my opinion, it has always been and I'm sure it will always be that we must abolish such evil practices." In 1958, she told a full church in Norfolk, "it wasn't a decision I made that day but the people found out that I had made it long before." And she pointedly made clear that her actions stemmed directly from political commitments she had carried all her life. "As far back as I can remember I knew there was something wrong with our way of life when people could be mistreated because of the color of their skin," she told a thousand people gathered at an NAACP meeting in Baltimore in October 1956. In a later interview with Howell Raines, she explained how her bus resistance "was just a regular thing with me and not just that day." Parks was not unusually tired that day. The source of her decision was a resolve that had long gestated inside her. Simply put, Parks was tired of injustice—"tired of giving in"—and in that tiredness found determination.

In his first mass movement speech, Dr. King echoed this theme of metaphysical tiredness. "There comes a time," King told the thousands gathered at Holt Street Church on the first night of the boycott, "when people get tired." The crowd roared. King spoke of being "tired of going through the long night of captivity. And now we are reaching out for the daybreak of freedom and justice and equality." In many ways, Parks and King tapped into a collective psychic saturation. As one Montgomery domestic explained, "You know, child, you can just take so much and soon you git full. Dat's what happen here."

What Parks found that Thursday evening, what King articulated the following Monday, what black people in Montgomery realized was that the accumulation of tiredness at injustice brought courage and that courage brought a resolve that could withstand whatever lay ahead. In *Stride Toward Freedom*, King wrote, "No one can

171

understand the action of Mrs. Parks unless he realizes that eventually the cup of endurance runs over. . . . Mrs. Parks's refusal to move back was her intrepid affirmation that she had had enough."

Parks's personal act grew out of the lessons she had taken from Highlander. Esau Jenkins stressed how Highlander's philosophy of transformative personal action had operated that December evening. Highlander taught that "if you have to sit for your rights, sit for it. If you've got to crawl for it or wade for it or march for it or demonstrate for it, do that. If that's what necessary to do at that time to bring the focus, the public, on the evil that is being happening to the people, and she said, 'Well, I'm not going to get up this day.'" Parks's experience at Highlander the past summer had given her new vision and raised her expectations. Durr wrote the Hortons crediting Highlander for its role in Parks's action. After Parks got back from Highlander "she was so happy and felt so liberated," Durr wrote, then as time when on "the discrimination got worse and worse to bear after having, for the first time in her life, been free of it at Highlander. I am sure that had a lot to do with her daring to risk arrest as she is naturally a very quiet and retiring person although she has a fierce sense of pride." Septima Clark expressed a similar sentiment in a letter in 1956. "Had you seen Rosa Parks (the Montgomery sparkplug) when she came to

Highlander you would understand just how much *guts* she got while being there." Highlander had furthered Park's sense of outrage and widened her sense of possibility.

"It was inside you the whole time," Studs Terkel observed in an interview with Rosa Parks in 1973. Parks's stand was a deeply political, principled act by a woman who well knew the danger of bus resistance. In her bravery, other people would find theirs as well.

CHAPTER FOUR

"There Lived a Great People"
The Montgomery Bus Boycott

PARKS'S FRIEND BERTHA BUTLER HEARD from a woman who'd been on the bus that Mrs. Parks had been arrested, and ran to Nixon's house to get his help. Nixon's wife phoned him to inform him of Parks's arrest. "You won't believe it. The police got Rosa," Arlet told him "but nobody knows the extent of the charges or whether she's been beaten." Nixon tried calling the jail for information, but they told him it was "none of his damn business" and would not give him any information. He then telephoned Clifford Durr, who called and was able to learn the charge. After finding out that Parks was safe, Nixon was, in a measure, delighted, observing to his wife, "I believe Jim Crow dropped in our lap just what we are looking for." Nixon saw in Parks the kind of test case they had been seeking—middle-aged, religious, of good character, known and respected in the community for her political work, and brave. He explained, "If there ever, ever was a woman who was dedicated to the cause, Rosa Parks was that woman. She had a deep conviction about what she thought was right. . . . No one, nobody could . . . touch her morally, her character or nothin'." He continued, "The press couldn't go out and dig up something she did last year, or last month, or five years ago." Perhaps most important for Nixon, Parks was a "real fighter" and wouldn't be scared off by white backlash. People had to be sure that "the person could stand up under fire and remain courageous through out the pressure of a long court fight," explained Nixon, and he trusted Mrs. Parks's resolve.

Word began to travel. Parks's character and political experience made her a galvanizing figure in many sections of Montgomery's black community. Working class in income (Parks made about twenty-three dollars a week) and middle class in demeanor, she represented a sympathetic class position for a wide spectrum of black Montgomerians to identify with. This—along with her comportment and faith—gave her a wide appeal, likely broader than if she had been poor or squarely middle class. With a barber husband, a live-in mother, and her department-store job doing alterations, she was solidly working class. A devoted churchgoer at St. Paul's AME Church, Parks lived in a tight-knit community in a modest apartment at the Cleveland Court projects—and Montgomery's working-class west side rallied around her. At the same time, Parks's community activism and church work marked her as a steadfast race woman—and thus many in Montgomery's middle class were also outraged by her treatment on the bus. She was middle-aged, trusted, and demure, and while not economically middle class or college educated (characteristics that had tended to be the requisite for Montgomery's black middle-class organizations), she had a character that many middle-class blacks admired—a "lady," according to A. W. West.

Many people of various classes could thus find commonalty with her life and situation. She was "one of the most respected people in the Negro community," according to Dr. King. One Montgomery domestic explained, "Miss Rosie Park, one of our nice 'spectable ladies was put in jail, and the folks got full and jest wouldn't take no more. . . . We shor fixed 'em." Another woman concurred, "They didn't have a bitter need to rest Miss Park. All they had to do was talk to 'er lack she was a lady, but they had to be so big and take her to jail. Dey bit the lump off and us making 'em chew it. . . . Colored folks ain't like they use to be. They ain't scared no more."

Perhaps most important, as Parks herself put it, "the people of the community knew me," and they respected her long-standing community work. The span of Parks's involvement in her church, the Civic League and other voting registration efforts, and the NAACP, according to Alabama State professor James Pierce, was "rather unique." Part of people's resolve came from their identification with her. Reverend French explained, "Not only was Mrs. Rosa Parks arrested but every Negro in Montgomery felt arrested." Because they knew her, they also trusted she would not flinch under pressure or sell them out.

To understand how a boycott was built in Montgomery from Parks's stand requires seeing the power and impact of her action and the host of other people who then turned that action into a movement. In interviews during the boycott, Parks stressed the protracted history leading up to her protest—both her own and that of others who had long been pushing for change—and the actions of many who stepped up after her arrest. Parks herself asserted numerous times that her bus stand was part of a constellation of resistance by a number of people in the city that laid the foundation for a more cohesive movement to emerge. She often prefaced her description of the events of December 1 by describing the boycott's long background and noting that two other women had been arrested that same year for their refusals on the bus. Nixon concurred, "I have told the press time after time that we were doing these things before December 1955, but all they want to do is start at December 1 and forget about what happened . . . over a long period of time to set the stage." Even decades later, Parks was still trying to set the record straight. In an interview in 1988, for instance, she again insisted, "Many people don't know the whole truth. . . . I was just one of many who fought for freedom." She felt a certain embarrassment at how people focused on her to the exclusion of other people's roles.

The infrastructure they had laid, the various movements and meetings Nixon and Parks, Jo Ann Robinson and Mary Fair Burks had organized, the impact of Colvin's arrest—all of this came together in the protest. As Nixon explained, "The success of the bus boycott was due to the fact that we took all the lessons about using the press and public speaking and the courts and politics and white friends and mass pressure and all the rest and used it all at the same time." The years of lonely organizing and the people primed for action provided the brick and mortar to construct a boycott.

GOING TO JAIL

After being escorted into city hall, Parks laughed to herself. "Who would have thought that little Rosa McCauley—whose friends teased her for being such a goody Two-shoes in her dainty white gloves—would ever become a convicted criminal, much less a subversive worthy of police apprehension, in the eyes of the state of Alabama?" Upon getting to the jail, she requested her phone call. Thirsty, she asked for water but was refused; the water was "for whites only."

"Can you imagine how it feels to want a drink of water and be in hand's reach of water and not be permitted to drink?" Parks wrote later. Finally, a policeman brought her some water.

They asked her if she was drunk. She was not. She recalled not being "happy at all" or particularly frightened but found the arrest "very much annoying to me" as she thought of all the NAACP work she had to do. That evening she didn't feel like history was being made but felt profoundly irritated by her arrest, which seemed a detour from the week's more pressing political tasks.

She repeatedly asked for a phone call. Finally, she was allowed to telephone her family. Her mother answered and upon hearing that Rosa had been arrested, worriedly inquired, "Did they beat you?" Both her mother and Raymond were horrified to learn she was in jail, but Rosa assured her mother she had not been beaten. She then asked to talk to Raymond who promised to " 'be there in a few minutes.' He didn't have a car, so I knew it would be longer." Home making dinner, Raymond was angry that no one had informed him of Rosa's arrest. According to Rosa, "There was one man who was on the bus, he lived next door to where we lived, and he could have if he'd wanted to, gotten off the bus to let my husband know that I was arrested. My husband thinks kind of hard of him for not at least telling him."

While in jail, Parks struck up a conversation with her cellmate, who had been in jail for nearly two months. The woman had picked up a hatchet against a boyfriend who had struck her—and, with no money for bail, was unable to let her family know where she was. Parks promised to try to get in touch with the woman's family. Then abruptly the warden came to get her, but she hadn't taken the paper where her cellmate had written down the phone numbers. The woman threw the small paper down the stairs as Parks left, and she surreptitiously picked it up. "The first thing I did the morning after I went to jail was to call the number the woman in the cell with me had written down on that crumpled piece of paper." Parks reached the woman's brother. A few days later, she saw the woman on the street looking much better.

Nixon had gone down to the jail with Clifford and Virginia Durr. The Durrs had no money, and Nixon put up the $100 bail. But he wanted the white couple to go with him to ensure the police actually released Parks after taking the bail money. Around 9:30 p.m., Parks walked out of jail to greet her friends. Virginia was struck by her appearance: "It was terrible to see her coming down through the bars, because . . . she was an exceedingly fine-looking woman and very neatly dressed and such a lady in every way—so genteel and so extremely well-mannered and quiet. It was just awful to see her being led down by a matron." With tears in her eyes, Durr embraced her and was struck by how Mrs. Parks was "calm as she could be, not cheerful, but extremely calm." As they were leaving, Raymond appeared with a bail bondsman, so Rosa rode home with him.

Nixon, the Durrs, and the Parkses convened in the Parkses' Cleveland Courts apartment to talk over the next step. They drank coffee and discussed matters until about eleven that night. Clifford Durr thought he could get the charges dismissed if she wanted him to, because there had not been an open seat for Parks to move to. But Nixon saw this as the bigger opportunity they had been waiting for to launch an attack on bus segregation. "Mr. Durr's right," Nixon explained, "it'll be a long and hard struggle. It'll cost a lot of money. But we'll get the NAACP behind it, I promise you that. It won't cost you and Mr. Parks anything but time and misery. But I think it will be worth all the time and misery." Nixon talked and talked, answering questions and explaining what he saw as the possibilities. Parks knew she never would ride the segregated bus again but had to consider making a public case and step into the line of attack.

Raymond did not initially agree. He "was pretty angry," Rosa recalled. "He thought it would be as difficult to get people to support me as a test case as it had been to develop a test case out of

Claudette Colvin's experience." They discussed and debated the question for a while. After an hour or two, the Durrs left, but Nixon stayed for a while longer. "In the end, Parks, and my mother supported the idea. They were against segregation and were willing to fight it." With decades of political experience, Raymond Parks understood the physical and economic dangers this stand entailed and the difficulties he, his wife, and other activists had faced in building a unified mass movement. The community had not stood together for long in previous cases, particularly in Colvin's, so Raymond worried. The economic and physical violence unleashed on protesting blacks, along with class divisions within the black community, had made a mass movement near impossible in the past. There would certainly be a price to pay for that resistance, and Raymond worried for the safety, physical and emotional, of his wife.

Virginia later highlighted Raymond's reluctance, casting it differently than Rosa did. "He kept saying over and over again, 'Rosa, the white folks will kill you. Rosa, the white folks will kill you.' It was like a background chorus, to hear the poor man, who was white as he could be himself, for a black man, saying 'Rosa, the white folks will kill you.' I don't remember her being reluctant." Historians have latched on to Virginia's version of Raymond's reluctance. But there is a certain racialized and gendered cast to Virginia's explanation—something emasculating in her description of Raymond's fear and the ways she explicitly marked his light skin. It is unlikely that the Durrs had ever visited the Parks apartment socially before, and they did not know Raymond. So the unusualness of the circumstances likely affected how Virginia experienced and remembered the evening. E. D. Nixon provided no such description of Raymond.

Rosa contextualized Raymond's response: "He was concerned about the way I was treated like any husband would be." Fifty-two years old on that December evening, Raymond had a long history of activism. He had known people, as had Rosa, who were killed for their stands against racial injustice—and was even more soul weary than Rosa. He had experienced the ways people grew uncertain and movements crumbled under the immense pressure of white backlash. Virginia did not acknowledge the ways Raymond's own activist experience came to bear that evening, let alone the responsibility he likely felt in trying to protect Rosa from the hardship that pursuing the case publicly would entail. For Rosa, faced with the possibility of retaliation against the entire family, it needed to be a communal decision. Talking to a coworker the next day, Raymond continued to worry that he and Rosa would be killed because of her arrest.

Later that weekend, Rosa asked Virginia to speak at an NAACP meeting. She agreed to do so but "trembled at the thought of it being in the papers the next morning." Even as a middle-class white woman, Durr feared public exposure of her beliefs. In interviews long after the boycott, Durr talked about how terrifying this period was. In 1954, she and Clifford had been red-baited for their civil rights beliefs and their connections to the Southern Conference Educational Fund (SCEF), and she had been called before Senator James Eastland's Internal Security subcommittee and "expos[ed] . . . as a nigger-loving Communist." She refused to answer questions— making national headlines as she stood silent before Eastland, occasionally powdering her nose. Despite their important contributions behind the scenes, the Durrs, in fact, often avoided situations where they would be publicly identified for their civil rights work. When Alabama State professor Lawrence Reddick decided to write a book on the boycott in 1956 and wanted to include description of the Durrs' role, Virginia Durr said no. She explained her decision to a friend, "[Letting ourselves] be written up as having played a part, however it may seem to History, simply means that our tenuous hold here is lost for good. . . . I hated to have to tell him that History cannot feed your children or pay their school bills." And yet,

Virginia was unable to extrapolate her own fears about economic and physical retaliation to Raymond and rendered his fears for Rosa and his family's safety unmanly.

Nixon knew Rosa Parks "wasn't afraid" and that once she committed to things, she did not waver: "If Mrs. Parks says yes, hell could freeze but she wouldn't change." After talking with her mother and Raymond, who both came around to her taking this stand, Parks agreed. Later that evening, she called Fred Gray and asked him to provide her legal representation. Gray recalled that from that moment, "my days of having little to do in my fledgling law practice were over."

BOYCOTT: A COMMUNITY RESPONDS

"God provided me with the strength I needed at the precise time when conditions were ripe for change," Parks observed. This was not some lucky happenstance. Rosa Parks and her colleagues had labored for years to seed the ground for a movement to grow in Montgomery, and those efforts had made the conditions ripe for a movement. In *Stride Toward Freedom*, Dr. King observed that Parks had "been tracked down by the Zeitgeist."

> She wasn't "planted" there by the NAACP, or any other organization; she was planted there by her personal sense of dignity and

self-respect. She was anchored to that seat by the accumulated indignities of days gone and the boundless aspirations of generations yet unborn.

Parks's arrest proved the last straw for many in Montgomery—the "rightness" of the moment created by the people of Montgomery in the years previous to Parks's bus stand and over the next 382 days of the boycott.

As Parks herself would note, "Many people cannot relate to the feelings of frustration that we, as black people, felt in the 1950s. . . . But because we went along with it then did not mean that we would let it go on forever. . . . It was a long time coming, but finally, as a group, we demanded, 'Let my people go.'" Her arrest would provide the impetus. Because she "had been active in the NAACP ever since she was grown," Horton explained, Parks was "a perfect case . . . somebody whom everybody had confidence in, in Montgomery. Some person who people respected to provide the basis on which you could build a movement."

According to WPC founder Mary Fair Burks, Rosa Parks "possessed sterling qualities" that those in the civil rights establishment "were forced to admire in spite of their usual indifference." Initially Burks was surprised to hear that Parks had been arrested. Having attended Miss White's school with Rosa, she remembered her as a "quiet, self-composed girl . . . [who] avoided confrontations and suspension." Yet those same qualities had also enabled Parks to make this stand. After "reflect[ing] on what I knew about her," Burks noted, "I decided it had not been out of character after all. No, Rosa as a rule did not defy authority, but once she had determined on a course of action, she would not retreat. She might ignore you, go around you, but never retreat."

As the community began to react following Parks's arrest, Claudette Colvin experienced a rush of mixed feelings: "I was glad an adult had finally stood up to the system, but I felt left out. I was thinking, Hey I did that months ago and everybody dropped me. . . . They all turned their backs on me, especially after I got pregnant. It really, really hurt. But on the other hand, having been with Rosa at the NAACP meetings, I thought, Well maybe she's the right person— she's strong and adults won't listen to me anyway." Decades later, Colvin reflected on the community reaction. "When I look back now, I think Rosa Parks was the right person to represent that movement at that time. She was a good and strong person, accepted by more people than were ready to accept me. . . . Mine was the first cry for justice and a loud one. I made it so that our own adult leaders couldn't just be nice anymore."

Parks also reflected on why her case incited people to react more than Colvin's had. "Now in the case of this young girl I just mentioned, the dissatisfaction and the resentment was very prevalent. But I never did know why they didn't take the stand in her case as they did mine, unless it was because by my being a mature, middle-aged person, it probably created more sympathy. And I had been working in the community enough for people to know that I didn't initiate this trouble that came on and that it was unjustly put on me." While people proved more willing to stand by Parks than Colvin, part of what spurred that resolve was community anger at the city's empty promises following Colvin's arrest. As black teacher Sarah Coleman explained, "When the high school girl was arrested last spring . . . the bus company promised us they would do something and in six months they never did anything."

A number of people in Montgomery, including Parks, shared Burks's criticisms about the "the usual indifference" of many blacks in Montgomery. King wrote of the "tacit acceptance of things as they were" by the black middle class and the "passivity of the majority of the uneducated." This complacency was rooted largely in fear— fear of being publicly singled out, fear of economic retaliation, fear of imprisonment, fear of violence—the arsenal of weapons whites used well to maintain the racial status quo. A hard life could be made even harder, and the many small comforts of the middle class could quickly disintegrate. "I have known Negroes killed by whites without any arrests or investigation," Parks explained. "This thing called segregation is a complete and solid . . . way of life. We are conditioned to it and make the best of a bad situation." Amidst that fearsome climate, Johnnie Carr noted, "Many Negroes lost faith in themselves."

Indeed, Alabama State professor J. E. Pierce, a longtime NAACP member, initially opposed the one-day boycott because he did not believe the black community would stick together. King had also been struck by the "appalling lack of unity" among Montgomery's many black leaders and feared the division "could be cured only by some miracle." Parks thought her bus incident "would pass without too much notice as many others had."

Before going to bed, Nixon remembered one more person he needed to tell and telephoned Parks's childhood friend and fellow NAACP activist Johnnie Carr, informing her "they put the wrong person in jail." Carr was dumbfounded. "You don't mean they've arrested Rosa Parks," she asked Nixon incredulously. Carr was surprised. "I was noisy and talkative, but she was very quiet and stayed out of trouble. . . . She was so quiet you would never have believed she would get to the point of being arrested." Explaining the plans to pursue the case, Nixon informed Carr he had to leave town on a Pullman run for the weekend, but that there was much work she and Mrs. Parks would need to attend to.

"THE NEXT TIME IT MAY BE YOU": THE CALL GOES OUT

Not everyone went to bed that evening. The boycott was actually called by the Women's Political Council. While the news of Parks's arrest spread like wildfire, "a numbing helplessness seemed to paralyze everyone," according to Jo Ann Robinson. "There was fear, discontent, and uncertainty. Everyone seemed to wait for someone to *do* something, but nobody made a move." The neighborhood was "buzzing," according to Rosalyn Oliver King, Rosa's neighbor at Cleveland Courts.

Gray had called Robinson to talk about Parks's arrest. Robinson called the WPC's leadership. Rather than risk having their efforts thwarted as they had been in Colvin's case, they decided to call for a one-day boycott of Montgomery's buses on Monday—the day Mrs. Parks was scheduled to appear in court.

Despite the dangers of being a black woman out in the dead of night, Robinson left home for Alabama State College. With the help of two students and a colleague who gave her access to the mimeograph machine, Robinson stayed up all night making leaflets announcing the one-day boycott. The leaflets, printed three to a page because they had thousands to make, read,

> Another Negro woman has been arrested . . . If we do not do something to stop these arrests, they will continue . . . We are therefore asking every Negro to stay off the buses Monday in protest of the arrest and trial.

Noting the economic clout the black community had vis-à-vis the buses, the leaflet reminded readers this was the second arrest since Colvin's and "the next time, it may be you, or your daughter, or mother." The leaflet stressed the mistreatment of African American women—perhaps in the hope that this would gird people's resolve to act.

Robinson called Nixon around 3 a.m. to tell him of their plans—but she didn't inform Rosa Parks. In fact, Robinson claims that after talking to Fred Gray on the phone, she jotted down some notes on the back of an envelope which read, "The Women's Political Council will not wait for Mrs. Parks's consent to call for a boycott of city buses." This note, and Robinson's conviction that she didn't need to obtain Parks's consent or to even apprise her of the one-day boycott, likely stems in part from Robinson's determination to act quickly and in part from the class divisions in Montgomery's black community. Though Robinson and Parks had worked together previously, they moved in very different circles. The fact that the reserved Parks had a long history of political activity was not necessarily known to Robinson.

Between 4 and 7 a.m., Robinson and her students mapped out distribution routes for the notices. In the early morning, they were met by nearly twenty women who ensured that "practically every black man, woman and child in Montgomery knew the plan and was passing the word along." Over the next days, the WPC distributed more than thirty-five thousand leaflets to barber shops, stores, bars, factories, and at Dexter Avenue Church, where the ministers would meet Friday night.

When Robinson arrived back on campus to teach her class that morning, there was a message for her to report to the president's office. President Trenholm had found out about the leaflets and was furious, "so angry his cheeks just quivered." Exhausted, and worried that she was going to be fired, Robinson summoned her resolve. "I described the frequent repetition of these outrages, how many children, men, and women, old and middle-aged people, had been humiliated and made to relinquish their seats to white people." Trenholm's mood softened. Robinson promised to keep Alabama State out of their activities and paid the college back for all the leaflets.

Early the next morning, Nixon began calling Montgomery's black ministers. Nixon wanted to get things in place before leaving on his Pullman run. He made his first call to the Reverend Ralph Abernathy of First Baptist Church and then around 6 a.m. called a relatively new minister in town, Reverend Martin Luther King Jr.—to convince them to support the protest. Nixon saw in King the kind of mind, spirit, and oratorical ability to help galvanize the community. King was new to Montgomery and didn't have set alliances, enemies, or much of a public reputation, making him a useful choice in trying to unify the ministers behind this bold action. And perhaps most important, Nixon wanted to use King's church to hold the meeting because Dexter Avenue was centrally located in downtown Montgomery.

Nixon recounted his initial conversation with King. "When he heard me talk about how long it'd take and how hard the struggle would be, he wasn't sure. He was a young man just getting started in the ministry. His family was young. His wife had given birth to their first child, a little girl, less than a month ago." King hesitated that early December morning on what he could realistically commit to, saying to Nixon, "Let me think about it a while and call me back." After making some more calls, Nixon called him back. Having already spoken with Abernathy, King quickly assented. Nixon, Abernathy, and King worked through the morning to get other ministers to turn out that evening. By the end of the boycott, Dr. King had gained a national profile. Nixon, however, always reminded people, "If Mrs. Parks had gotten up and given that cracker her seat, you'd never heard of Reverend King." Parks, on the other hand, always stressed that she wasn't a single actor. "Four decades later I am still uncomfortable with the credit given to me for starting the bus boycott. Many people do not know the whole truth. . . . I was just one of many who fought for freedom."

Before leaving on his run, Nixon had one more person to meet—a young white reporter for the *Montgomery Advertiser* named Joe Azbell. Nixon and Azbell had known each other for several years. Nixon handed Azbell a leaflet, telling him he had an important exclusive and apprising him about the plans for the boycott. Azbell ran a front-page story on Sunday reprinting the entire leaflet—thereby guaranteeing that those blacks and whites who had not heard of the boycott were now well informed. The two local television and four radio stations also picked up the news of a boycott. The protest was now a public event.

Indeed it was "panicky white folks," according to Nixon, who helped make the boycott an initial success and increased police presence, which further dissuaded people from riding the bus. "We couldn't have paid for the free publicity the white folks gave our boycott," Nixon noted.

Parks went to work as usual on Friday but took a cab. The tailor was surprised to see her. "You don't think that going to jail is going to keep me home, do you?" she quipped. Trying to keep a low profile, Parks maintained her composure throughout the days surrounding her arrest, never reaching "the breaking point of shedding tears." The *Montgomery Advertiser* ran its first story on the bottom of page nine, headlined "Negro Jailed Here for 'Overlooking' Segregation." Later that day, the supervisor came by the tailor shop, clearly displeased with the news of Parks's bus arrest.

During her lunch break, Parks took her lunch as usual to Fred Gray's office. To her surprise, she found a swarm of media and learned of the plans for the Monday protest. *Jet* magazine "started taking my picture and asking questions." She was not particularly keen on all the attention and never made a statement to the *Advertiser.* Nixon called to tell her of the meeting at Dexter Avenue Church that evening. She asked what it was about; he replied, "You know—about your being arrested." She agreed to come.

That evening, Parks went to the church, slightly nervous. "At that point I didn't know whether my getting arrested was going to set well or ill with the community—the leaders of the black community." Nearly fifty ministers and other local leaders, including physicians, schoolteachers, lawyers, and union leaders, had gathered to discuss the plans for Monday, but the meeting began poorly. Reverend Roy Bennett, whom Nixon had put in charge, lectured at those gathered for a half hour, without a mention of Parks or the boycott. People started to leave. Even King joked with a friend about wanting to go but being unable to because it was at his church. Finally, others were allowed to speak. Parks addressed the group and, according to historian Douglas Brinkley, "explained to them her weariness with Jim Crow buses, the circumstances of her arrest, and the need for collective action in response to both. Gender was on her side with this crowd: with a touch of chauvinistic chivalry, many of the ministers did not want to be on record as abandoning a good Christian woman in need." And the forty-two-year-old Parks, who had served as a deaconess and Sunday school teacher at St. Paul's, was certainly a good Christian woman. Jo Ann Robinson also took the floor and extolled the need for action. Ultimately, the ministers decided to promote the one-day boycott.

The paradox was this: Parks's refusal to get up from her seat and the community outrage around her arrest were rooted in her long history of political involvement and their trust in her. However, this same political history got pushed to the background to further the public image of the boycott. Parks had a more extensive and progressive political background than many of the boycott leaders; many people probably didn't know she had been to Highlander, and some would have been uncomfortable with her ties to leftist organizers. Rosa Parks proved an ideal person around which a boycott could coalesce, but it demanded publicizing a strategic image of her. Describing Parks as "not a disturbing factor," Dr. King would note her stellar character at the first mass meeting in Montgomery, referring to "the boundless outreach of her integrity, the height of her character."

The foregrounding of Parks's respectability—of her being a good Christian woman and tired seamstress—proved pivotal to the success of the boycott because it helped deflect Cold War suspicions about grassroots militancy. Rumors immediately arose within white Montgomery circles that Parks was an NAACP plant. Indeed, if the myth of Parks put forth by many in the black community was that she was a simple Christian seamstress, the myth most commonly put forth by Montgomery's white community was that the

NAACP (in league with the Communist Party) had orchestrated the whole thing.

Most whites, however, did not seem to know of Parks's actual work with the association. Curiously, the *Montgomery Advertiser* never publicized Parks's connections to the NAACP. Strategically, then, the success of Parks as the symbol of the boycott turned, in part, on obscuring her long-standing political activity. Her history of activism became a secret to keep the movement safe—and she and others would dissemble by calling her a simple seamstress. It was a well-kept secret. It does not appear that state officials, during the boycott, were aware of Parks's NAACP history or other political activities, as these facts were not mentioned when the state outlawed the NAACP in June 1956.

Parks herself would even try to deflect the significance of her action on the bus, particularly when she was interviewed by white journalists during the boycott. She would say she did not know why she kept sitting, but it had been a long day and she did not believe she should have to give up her seat. She gave a more extensive explanation of her decision to black journalists in all-black contexts, or to organizers she trusted; later, with scholars or other interviewers, she would be willing to contextualize her action in her broader history of activism. Given her reserved personality, Parks tended to downplay her own actions and as a seasoned political activist understood the importance of foregrounding the roots of this movement in the broader mistreatment of the black community.

The seeds of the "simple tired seamstress" myth were thus planted in the early days of the boycott to mitigate the repressive atmosphere of the Cold War. Parks's militancy was played down in service of the movement, but the image of her as a tired seamstress would assume a life of its own. Even when black Montgomerians prepared a twenty-year anniversary commemoration of the boycott, there would be a sharp disjuncture between how Parks's action was described in the public program ("a weary seamstress . . . refused to give up her seat to a white man") and how it was referred to privately among the organizers ("this brave and lonely act" where Parks "refused to continue voluntarily submitting to segregated seating on public buses in Montgomery Al."). Similarly, the myth of Parks as a plant and her bus stand as a preplanned, staged event has lived on, but the origins of this myth in efforts by Montgomery's segregationist community to discredit the boycott have long been forgotten.

The myths also assumed a gendered hue—though her job title was "assistant tailor," she would come to be referred to as a "seamstress." This feminized and Americanized her, evoking another famous American seamstress, Betsy

Ross. Reverend French even referred to Parks as a "typical American housewife who shared in the support of her household by working as a seamstress in a downtown department store." Over time, the downplaying of Parks's status as a skilled worker had significant consequences for her and her family. The civil rights community would have difficulty recognizing that the loss of her job and the impossibility of finding another had tremendous consequences for her family's economic security.

Parks's physical attractiveness and composure—her being "above all . . . a lady" as one boycotter put it—were placed front and center in the story. Robinson highlighted Parks's ladylike demeanor: "She was too sweet to even say damn in anger." Referring to her as an "attractive seamstress," King noted Parks's radiant persona, describing her as "soft spoken and calm in all situations. Her character was impeccable and her dedication deep-rooted." Alabama State professor L. D. Reddick described Parks in an article for *Dissent* as "ideally fitted for the role . . . attractive and quiet, a churchgoer who looks like the symbol of Mother's Day." Originally describing her as a "civic leader" on December 11, the *Atlanta Daily World* came to prefer more gendered descriptions of her as "a fine, up-minded, meek-mannered, Christian woman" (the contortions of describing a person who willingly risked an arrest as meek-mannered notwithstanding). The *Chicago Defender* called her "the attractive little spark that ignited the now famous Montgomery, Ala. Boycott." Regularly, descriptions of Parks noted her beauty and adherence to 1950s gender norms. The background material distributed about her by the NAACP described her wearing "smartly tailored suits . . . [who] likes to cook, especially roast and bake drop cookies." As the boycott went on, the NAACP would urge Parks to "obtain 8½ x 11 glossy prints of yourself for publicity purposes."

There was a fixation on how she dressed. Alma John, who interviewed Parks for her New York radio program in May 1956, gushed, "Neighbors, I wish you could all see and meet Mrs. Parks. She is one of the most serene, one of the most beautiful women we've had the honor to meet. . . . She has on a beautiful straw hat, black and white with a little fluted straw around the edge. And she's wearing a very smart dressmaker suit that has a gold and black thread running through it and a white bishop's neck blouse." Youth Council member Rosalyn King remembered that Parks dressed "simply" and "very matronly" and seemed older than she was because of her mannerisms and appearance. Articles in the black press during and even after the boycott stressed that she "did not look like a woman that would start a revolution." The fact that the middle-aged, lighter-skinned Parks did not physically resist arrest—like the young darker-skinned Colvin—furthered the construction of her as the proper kind of symbol. And her beauty became part of what made her the right kind of woman to coalesce around. Horton in 1956 directly addressed why Parks's arrest set off the reaction it did: "Rosa is . . . not only an attractive person to look at but has a beauty of character and was recognized by the people of Montgomery as a person of real dignity and a person that whom [sic] everybody respected. . . . She kind of symbolized some of the finest womanhood in the South. Since she's been active in civic affairs, church work and all, it was just too much to have a quiet, dignified, intelligent person like Mrs. Parks humiliated." Acknowledging Parks's physical beauty, Horton's choice of phrasing—*some of the finest womanhood in the South*—strategically claimed a gendered citizenship and stature for Mrs. Parks that contrasted with the ways she and other black women were treated in Montgomery.

PREACHING THE WORD

On Sunday, King evoked the "awful silence of God," calling on his congregation to join the one-day boycott to challenge "the iron feet of oppression." Other black ministers across the city followed suit. Not only did the ministers' participation in the boycott provide an important mechanism for disseminating news of the protest in a space free of white control, it also provided some protection from charges of red-baiting.

One white minister also joined the call. On Friday, Parks spoke with Reverend Graetz, whose church, Trinity Lutheran, sat next door to the Cleveland Court projects. Robert Graetz had assumed the pastorship of the black Trinity Lutheran Church in 1955, and he and his wife had been viewed as racial oddities since moving to Montgomery from Ohio. The Graetzes sat in the "black" section at the movies. Local whites shunned them in stores. Graetz had heard of the arrest and plans for the boycott but as a white man (even though he ministered to a black congregation) was having trouble getting much information on the events. So he called one of his closest black acquaintances, Rosa Parks, who used his church for her Youth Council meetings. "I just heard that someone was arrested on one of the buses Thursday," he said to her.

"That's right, Pastor Graetz," Parks replied.

"And that we're supposed to boycott the buses on Monday to protest."

"That's right, Pastor Graetz."

"Do you know anything about it?"

"Yes, Pastor Graetz."

"Do you know who was arrested?"

"Yes, Pastor Graetz."

"Well, who was it?"

There was a moment of silence.

Then in a quiet voice she replied, "It was me, Pastor Graetz."

That Sunday, like the Reverends King and Abernathy, Reverend Graetz stood in his pulpit and gave a Christian interpretation of Parks's arrest and the impending one-day boycott. He told his black congregation of his plans to participate in the boycott and to make his own car available to help shuttle people around town, and urged his congregation to do the same.

On Saturday, Parks hosted the already-planned NAACP Youth Council workshop at Alabama State College. Only five young people came. Having devoted a great deal of effort to set up the workshop, she was extremely discouraged by the turnout and increasingly anxious about what Monday would bring.

MONDAY

That Monday, people woke up early. Martin and Coretta King were dressed by 5:30 a.m. Martin believed if 60 percent of the black community stayed off the bus, the protest would be a success. A bus rolled by nearly empty of black passengers; another bus passed empty. They were elated.

Nearly every black person in Montgomery had stayed off the bus. It was a magisterial sight: the sidewalks and streets of Montgomery filled with black men, women, and children walking, waiting, offering rides to people they knew or had never met. "It was really surprising," Georgia Gilmore, a cook and midwife who in the days to come would emerge as a key organizer and fund raiser, recalled. "We thought well maybe some of the people would continue to ride the bus. But after all, they had been mistreated and been mistreated in so many different ways until I guess they were tired and they just decided that they just wouldn't ride."

"Gratifying" and "unbelievable" were the words Parks used to describe the sight that Monday morning—the way people "were willing to make the sacrifice to let it be known that they would be free from this oppression." The reaction far surpassed anything she had ever seen. For Parks, this movement had been long in coming, but that December morning it had arrived. "As I look back on those days, it's just like a dream. The only thing that bothered me was that we waited so long to make this protest."

In a 1966 interview, Parks asserted that her most vivid memory from the entire year of the boycott was waking up December 5, looking out, and seeing the buses "almost completely empty." Robinson explained the "hopeful, even prayerful" feeling that greeted the morning. Most people had not slept well, afraid the one-day action would fail and "the proud black leaders of the boycott would be the laughingstock of the town." But this was not to be. "A quality of hope and joy" marked the day, Durr wrote a friend. *Montgomery Advertiser* reporter Azbell described the mood as "solemn" and noted no black people spoke to white people.

Parks dressed carefully for her court hearing: "a straight, long-sleeved black dress with a white collar and cuffs, a small black velvet hat with pearls across the top, and a charcoal-gray coat." She carried a black purse, and wore white gloves. Mrs. Parks well understood the importance of image to this protest, and she chose her outfit to reflect a dignified and proud citizenship, an in-your-face challenge to the degradation that segregation had long proffered. Rosa and Raymond Parks and E. D. Nixon assembled at Fred Gray's law office at 8 a.m. to figure out the last-minute details and then walked the block and a half over to the courthouse. "I was not especially nervous," Parks recalled. "I knew what I had to do."

Hundreds of people stood outside court and packed the corridors of the courthouse by 8:30 that morning to demonstrate their support. A number of the members of Parks's Youth Council skipped school to attend. Upon hearing the news,

Mary Frances, one of Parks's Youth Council members, observed, "They've messed with the wrong one now," turning it into a small chant. The crowd cheered when she entered the building and called out their willingness to help with whatever she needed. For Nixon, the turnout was astonishing. In the twenty-five years he had been organizing, "I never saw a black man in court unless he was being tried, or some of his close friends or relatives." Up and down the street, "from sidewalk to sidewalk," it was clear that a new spirit had been brought forth in Montgomery. "The morning of December 5, 1955," Nixon proclaimed, "the black man was reborn." Parks felt an enormous sense of relief. The assembled multitude buoyed her spirits: "Whatever my individual desires were to be free. I was not alone. There were many others who felt the same way."

Judge John Scott heard Parks's case in City Recorder's Court. The courtroom itself was segregated, with blacks on one side and whites on the other. Parks, Gray, and the city prosecutor stood. The trial lasted less than thirty minutes. "It was a very emotional experience," Gray recalled, "because, not only was I representing Mrs. Parks as her attorney, but we were friends. In addition, this was my first case with a large audience. . . . Was I nervous? Maybe a little. Was I determined? You bet."

At the hearing, the prosecutor moved to change the warrant, charging Parks with violating state law rather than city ordinance (since Montgomery ordinances did not allow people to be asked to give up their seat if another was not available). Gray objected, but the judge allowed it. Parks did not testify. Blake did, as did two white witnesses, one of whom said there was a seat in the back that Parks refused to take, directly contradicting Blake's testimony that all the seats had been full. Parks was found guilty and fined fourteen dollars. Gray entered her appeal.

Gray and Parks stayed behind to do some paperwork, but Nixon joined the crowd on the street. "If you don't bring her out in a few minutes," people yelled, "we're coming in after her." Delighted by the boldness, Nixon thought to himself, "It was the first time I had seen so much courage among our people!" Still, he worried the police were looking for any excuse to react. After Parks came out of the building, he addressed the crowd, "See this man out here with this sawed-off shotgun? Don't give him a chance to use it. . . . I'm gonna ask you all to quietly move from around this police station now; Mrs. Parks has been convicted and we have appealed it, and I've put her in the car . . . As you move, don't even throw a cigarette butt, or don't spit on the sidewalk or nothing." Given the surge of militancy, seasoned organizers like Nixon wanted to protect and nurture it.

Activists in Montgomery's black community had long worried that it would be impossible to unify the community around a particular action. It was "almost unbelievable," Parks noted, how successful the one-day protest had been. Parks saw one of her Youth Council members and asked why she had not attended the Saturday workshop. The young woman told her that she had been passing out leaflets about Monday's protest. Though Parks did not frame it this way, these young people had learned her lessons well: "They were wise enough to see . . . it was more important to stand on the street corners and pass these papers out to everyone who passed then to sit in a meeting and listen to someone speak."

After her trial, Parks didn't go to work but returned to Fred Gray's law office. She wanted to be helpful. He asked her to answer the phone, something he occasionally had her do, and then left for a meeting with King, Abernathy, and Nixon. "The people were calling to talk to me but I never told them who I was," Parks admitted decades later. "They didn't know my voice so I just took the messages."

This moment reveals one of the paradoxes of Mrs. Parks's own choices about her role in the movement. Parks was a shy person *and* a political organizer who believed in collective action over individual celebrity. These traits combined to produce the mixture of action and reticence that would characterize her public role in the days and years to come. Over the course of the boycott, she would participate in dozens of programs when she saw it as a way to further the protest. (And over the next half century, this would grow to include thousands of appearances.) But time and again, she actively avoided the spotlight and sometimes obscured the role she was actually playing. So Parks did not sit around in Gray's office or go home to rest or go back to work that Monday afternoon. She wanted to be useful, so she answered the phone since many people were calling with questions about the protest. But she did not tell the callers who she was. That erasure would have costs, though; Rosa Parks's own life exemplified many of the currents of African American protest in the twentieth century, but she would come to be known for a "simple act" on a single day. She would stay back, anonymously answering phones, confined to a gender-specific role, while decisions were being made on the leadership of the protest.

The beginning of the Montgomery Improvement Association (MIA) hails from that meeting Gray went to the first afternoon of the boycott, which neither Parks nor Robinson attended. Indeed, while WPC members, churchwomen, and domestic workers would make up the bulk of the boycott's organizational infrastructure, the leadership (most of whom had their own cars and did not ride the bus) was overwhelmingly male. When some of the clergy at the meeting sought to conceal their identities, Nixon responded angrily that they lacked the courage of Mrs. Parks and were acting like "scared boys." "Where are the men?" he challenged. Nixon took up a highly gendered language chastising the ministers and telling them they needed to catch up to the community. "We need to turn history around and stop hiding behind these women who do all the work for us. I say we stand out there in the open and hold our heads high." He then threatened to take the microphone and tell their congregations that these clergy were "too cowardly to stand up on their feet and be counted." King, entering late, agreed, willing to step forward publicly. King was elected to lead the new organization—his name put forward by Rufus Lewis, in part because King was his pastor and in part because he disliked Nixon and feared the militant porter would become the president of the new organization. Others supported the young minister in part because when the protest failed, they would not be blamed. The only woman elected was Erma Dungee as financial secretary. The group drew up three demands: first-come, first-served seating (where blacks would sit starting from the back and whites from the front but no one would be asked to move); respectful, courteous service; and the hiring of black bus drivers.

When asked a decade later whom she would have picked to be the leader, Parks explained that she did not know: "I don't know if I would have had any particular choice. I had met [King] . . . a number of times and heard him speak. And as far as I was concerned, he was well suited for this particular role because he was, as you said, young, eloquent and, as far as I know, well liked in the community. . . . But I don't think I would have wanted to have been the one to have selected any one person at the time." Implicit in Parks's comment ("any one person") and her reluctance to affirm that she too would have picked King, or conversely Nixon, is her experience within an organizing tradition, exemplified by Highlander, that was wary of picking a single leader. Exemplified by her mentors Ella Baker and Septima Clark, the political community Parks came out of encouraged broad-based structures of decision making and leadership as a way to sustain a mass movement.

"THERE LIVED A GREAT PEOPLE": THE BOYCOTT CONTINUES

That evening, fifteen thousand people gathered for a mass meeting at the Holt Street Baptist

Church. Five thousand black Montgomerians packed the church while thousands gathered outside. The streets surrounding the church were clogged with people and traffic. The area was so congested that King had to park many blocks away. Virginia Durr never made it inside, and Reverend Graetz only got to the fellowship hall. Parks fought through the crowds to her designated seat on the platform. With more people outside than inside, the church turned on its outdoor public address system so those standing outside could hear. Relieved by the size of the crowd, Parks described the mood of the meeting as "practically jubilant," though she felt "like it was a bit long in coming because there had been so many incidents when the same action could have taken place. But it seemed that they had not made up their minds until this particular incident."

The spirit was moving in Montgomery that December evening—"something that was just all over you," Gilmore remembered. With only a handful of reporters and few other whites, the audience at Holt Street Church was almost completely filled with black people. The meeting opened with the hymn "Leaning on the Everlasting Arms." "What a fellowship, what a joy divine . . . what have I to fear . . . leaning on the everlasting arms," sang the thousands gathered.

Addressing the crowd, Nixon warned of the

difficult fight ahead. "If anybody here is afraid, he better take his hat and go home. . . . We've worn aprons long enough. It's time to take them off." Nixon's gendered language is worth considering. Nixon seemingly directs his comments to the black men in the crowd, with a call for the men to step up and not be like apron-wearing women. But given that the audience was made up of thousands of women who did domestic labor—as Nixon well knew—the exhortation to take off their aprons also served as a call for black women to recast relations with their white employers and put their own freedom ahead of the employers' demands. The crowd roared as Nixon left the podium. The meeting, according to Nixon, was "the most amazing and the most heartening thing I have seen in my life. The leaders were led. It was a vertical thing." Montgomery's black community was on the move, and those on the podium would have to catch up to them.

Then Dr. King took the pulpit and captivated the crowd. Exceedingly nervous, he had not had time to prepare a speech. But once he started speaking, he found his stride. He spoke of a time "when people get tired. We are here this evening to say to those who have mistreated us so long that we are tired—tired of being segregated and humiliated; tired of being kicked about by the brutal feet of oppression." A tremendous thunder of assent rolled from the crowd. He then called on the dual traditions of Christianity and the Constitution to justify the struggle ahead. "If we are wrong, the Supreme Court of this nation is wrong. If we are wrong, the Constitution of the United States is wrong. If we are wrong, God Almighty is wrong. . . . If we are wrong, justice is a lie." And then Dr. King, with prophetic determination, concluded by extolling the importance of the movement being born in Montgomery for the annals of American history. "Right here in Montgomery, when the history books are written in the future, somebody will have to say, 'There lived a great people—a black people—who injected new meaning and dignity into the veins of civilization.' "

Stunned, people were quiet for a moment and then rose to their feet, cheering and clapping. After he finished speaking, King hugged Mrs. Parks. Outside the crowd erupted in thunderous applause. That evening, the fifteen thousand people gathered there decided to continue the boycott indefinitely and formed a new organization called the Montgomery Improvement Association (MIA). The collection taken that night raised $785.

But Rosa Parks never got to speak. After King spoke, Reverend French presented Parks as "the victim of this gross injustice, almost inhumanity, and absolute undemocratic principle, Mrs. Rosa

Parks." French stressed Parks's reputation as a lady "and any gentleman would allow a lady to have a seat." Introduced as a churchgoer and an industrious, law-abiding citizen, Parks was to play a symbolic role. As Ralph Abernathy explained in his 1958 master's thesis, "Mrs. Rosa Parks was presented to the mass meeting [because] we wanted her to become symbolic of our protest movement." When Parks was introduced, according to Reverend Graetz, it was "almost pandemonium." The crowd rose to its feet, giving her a standing ovation that lasted several minutes. "She was their heroine," Dr. King explained. "They saw in her courageous person the symbol of their hopes and aspiration."

But Mrs. Parks was not invited to address the meeting. The crowd called for her to do so, but their calls were ignored. "I do recall asking someone if I should say anything," Parks later explained, "and someone saying, 'Why you've said enough.'" In her discussions with Jim Haskins for her autobiography in 1988, she elaborated: "Holt Street Baptist Church—you didn't hear me make a speech—I didn't speak—I asked did they want me to say anything—they said you have said enough—you have said enough and you don't have to speak—the other people spoke." In a conversation with Myles Horton and Eliot Wigginton, Parks noted that she just sat up there. "I think everyone spoke but me," she said, though "it didn't bother me at that point." Indeed, while many of the ministers had been reluctant to speak, once they got to Holt Street, many clamored to say a few words.

While Parks imagined that she might speak, she was told that she had "said enough," even though she had said very little between her Thursday arrest and the Monday meeting. Parks never desired public speaking. She may even have felt relieved not to have to address the huge crowd, but she certainly noticed that while they wanted her up on the pulpit, they didn't think she should speak. Reverend Graetz saw the decision not to have Mrs. Parks speak as inextricably tied to gender. "Her personality was diminished," he explained decades later. "It was a male-dominated movement."

As with the treatment of other women in the movement, Parks was lauded by the crowd as their heroine but not consulted for her vision of the struggle and subsequent political strategy. If she had gotten to speak, Parks might have connected the injustice on the bus to the travesties of Scottsboro, the brutal rapes of Recy Taylor and Gertrude Perkins, the murder of Emmett Till, and the impending legal lynching of Jeremiah Reeves. If she had gotten to speak, she might have linked her stand to the courageous work of the Highlander Folk School, to the actions of her own Youth Council at the downtown library, and to the successful one-week bus boycott nearby in Baton Rouge. She might have talked about the loneliness of her stand on Thursday and the power of walking together on Monday. She might have thanked them for turning her individual refusal into a collective protest. She might have said that this movement was a long time in coalescing, but what a joyful and holy day it was now that it had come. All this she knew and might have said—or much more. But she did not get to speak.

Parks's role as a nonthreatening mother figure stemmed from the needs of the movement, which sought to cast her as a nondisturbing symbol, and also from her relationship with many of the young leaders. As Brinkley explained, "At forty-two years old Parks was also a natural maternal figure to the young ministers and lawyers who led the boycott: Gray was twenty-five, King was twenty-six, and Abernathy was twenty-nine." Parks's role as the mother of the movement largely precluded her from having a decision-making or strategic role despite her behind-the-scenes work, the scores of appearances she would make on behalf of the boycott, and her extensive political experience. She would be held up—and paradoxically relegated—to being its symbol.

Black people in Montgomery described their decision to stop riding the bus as "spontaneous" and "undirected" in part to prevent repression of their organization. Amazed by the militant unity of the boycott and fearful of backlash, organizers like Myles Horton echoed this, describing the boycott as "a spontaneous, unplanned, un-thought-out action that no one dreamed of." However, the idea of the boycott as "spontaneous" would also take on a life of its own, distancing the movement from its own roots in the earlier activism of many of its organizers and the bus incidents that preceded Parks's arrest. The seeds of the Parks myth—a "quiet seamstress" refuses to give up her seat and a "spontaneous" protest sets off the modern civil rights movement—emerged in the first days of the boycott initially to protect its organization from a vicious Cold War climate and longstanding Southern fears of outside influence.

THE BOYCOTT

Parks made her first appearance in the *New York Times* in a small wire-service article about the protest on December 6, described as a "Negro seamstress," and was similarly identified by the *Alabama Journal* as a "seamstress at a downtown store." Her address at Cleveland Courts was printed in the *Montgomery Advertiser.* The FBI followed the case "discreetly" from its Mobile office and passed all sorts of information along with newspaper articles to headquarters in Washington, DC.

Parks's role in the protest carried on far beyond

that first day. "I did as many [things for the MIA] as I could." By the next week, an elaborate ride and pickup system had been set up. "The effect has been most startling," Parks wrote a friend from Highlander. People were walking in the most inclement weather, even for miles. And people had banded together to provide a system of rides, formal and informal, for people who needed them. Parks and her compatriots were thrilled and heartened. "Many are still saying they will walk forever," she wrote, "before they will go back to riding the bus under the same conditions." Part of how the "tired feet" explanation gathered so much historical force stems from a conflation of Parks's decision to remain seated with a lovely quote from an elderly boycotter describing her own actions. In the early days of the boycott, Reverend Graetz recounted a woman telling him why she preferred to walk, "Well, my body may be a bit tired, but for many years now my soul has been tired. Now my soul is resting. So I don't mind if my body is tired, because my soul is free." King included this story in his speeches, often quoting her, "My feets is tired, but my soul is rested."

The level of support across the black community was considerable. This was an all-black movement, stressed Ben Simms, a professor at Alabama State, who later became the transportation coordinator. "Of course we had white support but this was a black movement, planned and run by blacks." The boycott was sustained by the development of the car pool. Organizers passed around slips of paper asking: *Can you drive in a car pool? Do you own your car? Insurance? What hours? Who will drive your car? What hours will you serve?* Approximately 300 people volunteered their cars. This goodwill and cross-class solidarity amazed Parks and other organizers. The car was a much-cherished possession and status symbol for the black middle class—and many had kept a studied distance from their poor compatriots. Organizers had originally feared people would be reluctant to have their cars used due to wear and tear and possible damage to their vehicles. Instead, the carpool powerfully drew together black Montgomery's various economic and social classes.

The MIA established forty stations across the city. Drivers charged ten cents, like the bus. People would use the "V for victory" sign to identify themselves to riders and drivers, and the MIA took the "V" as its symbol on its membership cards. This solidarity was buttressed and maintained through the twice-weekly mass meetings that strengthened the collective resolve. Between 1,200 and 1,800 people packed each one, often with no standing room. Abernathy would often warm up the crowd: "Are you tired of walking?"

Voices responded in loud and unanimous tones. "No!"

"Feel like turning around?"

Again, voices rang out. "No!"

"What if no cars are available?"

The people said, "We will walk."

Despite the inadvertent role the *Montgomery Advertiser* played in publicizing the first day of the boycott, their coverage was decidedly negative. The paper was closely tied to Montgomery's City Council, which may also have contributed to its ardent opposition to the protest. In an angry interview Joe Azbell gave to a Fisk researcher in March, Azbell called the boycott "stupid" and the work of a "small proportion" of "big operators" who "have their own cars and they feel important driving a few people around in them." Azbell felt that Montgomery had been one of the "most liberal cities in the South" where "the white people here did everything for the Nigras—they gave them their schools, their hospitals—everything. . . . This is a slap in the face after all they have done for them all that good feeling that was there has been destroyed."

Rumors and misinformation about the boycott ran rampant, more so in the white community than in the black community. Blacks had more access to what whites thought, both through their employers and also the local papers. Despite the biased coverage, *Advertiser* readership remained high among black Montgomerians, according to black schoolteacher Sarah Coleman, because it was "our only channel to what the white community is thinking."

About a month after the boycott began, Fisk University, under the direction of sociologist Preston Valien, sent an interracial team of researchers to Montgomery to document the emerging protest. From January to March 1956, sociologists affiliated with Fisk University's Race Relations Department conducted over three hundred field interviews, using black and white researchers, with black and white citizens of Montgomery. They also did participant observation at MIA mass meetings, dispatch stations, City Commission hearings, and White Citizens' Council meetings.

Rumors snaked through white Montgomery. Most white people were convinced Parks's protest had been cooked up by the NAACP, others claiming a Communist plot, still others believing that the NAACP and the CP were in league together. Some white residents believed Parks had only been in Montgomery for two weeks, a few going so far as to claim that Rosa Parks was not even her real name. Others suggested Parks was actually Mexican and had a car. All made her a pawn of larger agents—

rendering her action someone else's decision. This was the segregationists' version of events—that individual Montgomery blacks would not act in this militant, organized way, and so this action must be coordinated and inspired by an outside organization.

Over time the MIA was spending nearly $3,000 a week on transportation. Reverend Simms, who came to head the Transportation Committee in June, estimated the organization arranged fifteen to twenty thousand rides per day. Ultimately, it employed fifteen dispatchers and twenty full-time drivers. The car pool required tremendous synchronization, flexibility, and fortitude—all coordinated from a building at the edge of Montgomery called the Citizens Club. The police harassment was formidable. Police would often sit at the dispatch points and pull over each car that came through, asking for license and registration, intimidating drivers, giving them tickets for real and imagined infractions.

Parks worked for a month as a dispatcher, taking calls from people needing rides and patching them through to the forty-one different stations across the city. Stations were located in church parking lots, street corners, and stores and changed depending on police intimidation. In meetings and discussions, Parks urged patience and strength to boycotters—"Remember how long we had to wait when the buses pass[ed] us by without stopping." She instructed drivers to pick up as many people as possible and to "be careful," given the harassment the car pools were enduring at the hands of the police. Over time, the donated cars were supplemented with fifteen new station wagons bought with church money for extra protection. Since most white churches already had cars to take their parishioners around, it was difficult to complain about black churches doing the same. Known as "rolling churches," each car had the name of the sponsoring church painted on the front.

The Parks fable depicts the Montgomery bus boycott as the first organized boycott. However, this urban economic action stemmed from a number of antecedents. In the 1930s, blacks in cities like New York, Detroit, and Chicago had boycotted businesses that refused to hire blacks. "Don't buy where you can't work" campaigns sprang up, spearheaded by black women and calling on blacks to boycott businesses that refused to hire any black workers. Then in 1953, Parks had watched with keen interest as a bus boycott broke out in Baton Rouge, Louisiana, which resolved a week later when the city agreed to first-come, first-served seating on the bus. What happened in Montgomery was a grander, longer, and more unified economic movement that ultimately overturned bus segregation completely. But it was not cut from whole cloth in Montgomery in 1955, and it drew on the experiences of activists in other places.

The first days and weeks of the protest were deeply moving for Rosa Parks. Asked later if she ever worried the boycott would fail, she didn't recall "ever feeling that there would be a failure even if it had not lasted the whole year. The very fact that people demonstrated their unity on the first day was very significant and to me that was a success." That unity and collective action had demonstrated to Parks that "whatever people decided they wanted to do could be done" and buoyed her spirits amidst of fear and uncertainty of the boycott year. The boycott, according to Jo Ann Robinson, had a transformative power for it "allowed them to retaliate directly for the pain, humiliation, and embarrassment they had endured over the years at the hands of drivers and policemen . . . there was no need for family fights and weekend brawls."

On December 8, an MIA delegation including King, Robinson, and Gray (but not Parks) met with the mayor and city commissioners. They made three modest demands as a solution to end the protest: first-come, first-served seating on the buses, courteous treatment of passengers, and the hiring of black bus drivers. Even though Nashville, Atlanta, and even Mobile, Alabama, had first-come, first-served seating on their buses, Commissioner Crenshaw rejected this proposal, claiming "it just isn't legal." In the early days of the boycott, Parks called their goals more of a "request than a demand": "we didn't seem to be demanding too much then."

The *Montgomery Advertiser* ran an editorial calling the boycott a "dangerous weapon, like a missile that returns to its launching ground." They reminded black leaders that "the white man's economic artillery is far superior . . . and commanded by more experienced gunners" and that the "white man holds all the offices of government machinery." The paper's editors saw segregation and white power as a fixed truth, pronouncing, "There will be white rule for as far as the eye can see." The *Advertiser* remained fairly steadfast in its anti-boycott coverage throughout the year, often refusing to print positive letters on the boycott because the editors felt it did "more harm than good."

At another meeting with city officials shortly before Christmas, Luther Ingalls, a member of the White Citizens' Council, joined the negotiating sessions. Indeed, from the outset of the boycott and the *Montgomery Advertiser*'s first article, the boycott had been compared with the actions and philosophies of the White Citizens' Council, which publicly advocated economic retaliation to prevent desegregation. Thus, in the paper and in public discussion, the MIA and the White Citizens' Council were often cast as equivalents.

When King protested the presence of people "whose public pronouncements are anti-Negro," he was criticized for introducing mistrust into the meeting. White members of the committee accused Reverend King of dominating the discussion and having "preconceived ideas" himself. What is interesting in this exchange is not that King sparred with many of Montgomery's white leaders but that the terms of the exchange sound so modern. The white committee members did not defend segregation as necessary to maintain white superiority. They saw the conflict as a disagreement of interest groups. King represented one interest group; the White Citizens' Council represented another. King found, as biographer Taylor Branch explained, "that the whites sincerely believed that morality was neutral to the issue [of segregation] . . . depriv[ing] King of the moral ground he had occupied all his life." The immorality of segregation would have to be demonstrated over and over in the months and years to come. Many, even in the Deep South, would cast segregation as a matter of personal preference and predilection, not power or social necessity.

Moreover, many city and business leaders reacted with surprise at the bus protest and downplayed its impact. "It hasn't made any difference except to the bus company. I don't know why there has been so much hullabaloo about it. . . . Most people are not paying any attention to it." Some white leaders blamed the problem on a handful of "rough" bus drivers—and wished blacks had brought grievances to their attention, since they could have been remedied. Some even claimed that Parks's arrest was the first they had ever heard of black problems with bus segregation. Nevertheless, underneath the resistance of many whites lay a grudging surprise and admiration. Researcher Anna Holden over-heard a couple of women sitting at the Kress lunch counter talking about the "niggers": "Well you can't help but admire them. They've kept it up all through all this bad weather—walking in all this cold and rain." Many whites who saw themselves as moderates nonetheless chose to sit by while other white people resorted to violence and economic retaliation against the boycott.

Faced with the city's intransigence, the resolve of the MIA grew. Part of what spurred the determination of the boycotters in the early months was the city's absolute unwillingness to grant the MIA's initial modest demands. Robinson recalled, "They feared that anything they gave would be viewed by us as just a start. And you know, they were probably right."

Nonviolent direct action was not the way most white or black Montgomerians dealt with social problems. Like most Alabama whites (even liberal middle-class families like the Durrs), most black people owned guns. When Reverend Graetz was questioned in an interview during the boycott as to whether black people were going out to buy guns because of the protest, he said no. "Most negro families have guns, have always had them. . . . [They] didn't rush out to get them. They already had them." Nixon, Raymond Parks, and Jo Ann Robinson all owned guns. Even Dr. King, whose graduate studies had pointed him toward the power of nonviolent civil disobedience, came to organized nonviolence through the Montgomery boycott. Bayard Rustin recalled getting to the King home for the first time and finding armed guards and guns tucked into some of the armchairs. As he noted, "I do not believe that one does honor to Dr. King by assuming that, somehow, he had been prepared for this job. . . . The glorious thing is that he came to a profoundly deep understanding on nonviolence through the struggle itself."

Though never renouncing her long-standing belief in self-defense, Rosa Parks also saw the power and efficacy of organized nonviolence through the boycott. She grew tremendously impressed with the ways King used it to draw people together, maintain unity, demonstrate the collective power of the black community, and keep public attention trained on the protest. Given the ways that boycotters and particularly those people who drove the carpools were continually verbally and physically harassed by the police and white vigilantes, there was a tremendous potential for violence. And whites in Montgomery seemed eager for violence, disbelieving that black people could remain disciplined. Some even hoped for it, because it would have provided the excuse to dramatically crush the protest. According to Rufus Lewis, unified nonviolence disrupted the expectations of most white Montgomerian: "Whites can't help but have high regard for Negroes now, since there has been no violence. There have been a number of good articles written by whites about the unity of Negroes." Though "not altogether" converted, Parks saw that this nonviolent protest "was more successful, I believe, than it would have been if violence had been used."

THE BOYCOTT CONTINUES

"The colored people here are still not riding the bus," Parks wrote to a friend at Highlander right before Christmas. "Private car pools and taxi cabs are co-operating to help under very trying conditions. The police are arresting drivers on the least provocation, in some cases for nothing." In her letter, Parks described working "very hard" at Montgomery Fair but said she would not celebrate the holiday in "the usual way." Her extra money was going to the MIA's transportation fund. To put further pressure on the city, the MIA had called for a boycott of Christmas shopping—asking people to take the money they would have spent on Christmas and donate a third to charity, put a third in savings, and give the remaining third to the MIA to sustain the boycott. It would be a "more traditional, less commercial" Christmas for Parks's family, befitting her religious and political ideals.

Parks corresponded with a number of people during this period, trying to get support for the boycott. One letter from Diane Shapiro, whom Parks had met at Highlander, noted, "We all knew about the bus strike but none of us associated it with you." And help and mail poured in, much of it addressed to Parks. The most common gift was shoes, and Parks thrilled in "passing out the bounty," according to Brinkley. On Christmas day, surprised by the city's unwillingness to meet its modest requests, the MIA published an ad in the *Montgomery Advertiser* and *Alabama Journal* laying out its grievances. "The bus protest is not merely in protest of the arrest of Mrs. Rosa Parks but is the culmination of a series of unpleasant incidents over a period of years. It is an upsurging of a ground swell which has been going on for a long time. Our cup of tolerance has run over."

One of the hardest things for Parks during the first month of the boycott was the disdainful way she was treated at work. "They'd ignore me as though I wasn't there," she recalled. Many of the women in alterations who worked in the next room to her "refused to have any conversation or to speak to me at all. Those I would meet sometime walking through the store . . . acted the same way and didn't even seem to let the crisis we were going through matter to them." Parks worked "5 long tense weeks with people who did not speak to me even once after the bus incident." She tried to ignore this behavior, refusing to respond to her coworkers' rudeness, but it pained her nonetheless.

On January 7, 1956, a month after her bus stand, Montgomery Fair notified Rosa Parks they were letting her go. They had decided to close the tailor shop. When she asked why, they said the tailor was leaving to start his own business and they were not replacing him. She was a trained seamstress and could do the work of the tailor (stitching, sewing sleeves, hemming, and so on) but as a woman worker in a men's shop "was not required to do any fitting of men's clothing." The only other worker at the shop was a young man with no tailoring experience. She received two weeks' severance pay. When news spread through the black community that Montgomery Fair had fired her, an informal boycott emerged against the store. Some black people canceled their credit accounts at the store.

A week later, Raymond was compelled to quit his job after his employer, Maxwell Air Force

Base, prohibited any discussion of the boycott or Rosa Parks in the barbershop. Raymond Parks's barber chair had long been a place of discussion and debate. Raymond had a large white clientele, and some of his white customers had drifted away after the boycott began. Others came in making belittling remarks about "that woman" on the bus, and now Raymond Parks was being muzzled. Moreover, one day Raymond had been eating his lunch in the base's desegregated cafeteria when two white women sat down at the end of the long table where Raymond was seated. He stayed and finished his lunch, which angered a white man working in the concession. Overall, this was an untenable situation for a proud, political man, so Raymond Parks left his job at the base. The Parks family was now without income.

The phone rang constantly with death threats and coarse insults. "There were people who called to say that I should be beaten or be killed," Parks recalled, "because I was causing so much trouble. And then there were some who called to inquire whether I had lost the job and . . . finally when I was dismissed from the job, I remember one person calling and saying she was sorry and then laughing at the end of the conversation before hanging up." Most of the time she didn't talk with these people. "When I discovered that they were this type, divisive or abusive, I would just hang up immediately." Her mother and husband ended up answering most of the calls since they were home more than she was. Parks particularly hated it when her mother answered these calls.

According to Detroit friend Mary Hays Carter, Rosa reached a point of relative peace around her own possible targeting. She quoted Parks as saying, "Well you have to die sometime. I never set out to plan to hurt anyone and if this boycott happened to be attributed to me and my activity, then if they could kill me, I would just be dead," and laughed it off. Partly, Parks was able to get to this place of inner peace because of her faith. In late January, praying at St. Paul's, Parks experienced a wash of religious conviction and a sense that all of what was happening—her arrest, the boycott—was God's plan. All she needed to do was to "keep the faith." An intense calm swept over her.

Like Parks, many of the boycott organizers were receiving regular death threats and hate calls. The King household was bombarded. According to *Jet* magazine, when people called in the middle of the night to threaten "that N—— who's running the bus boycott," Coretta Scott King would sometimes calmly reply, "My husband is asleep. . . . He told me to write the name and number of anyone who called to threaten his life so that he could return the call and receive the threat in the morning when he wakes up and is fresh."

Raymond, however, found this a difficult time and began drinking a lot. "He was very shaken and very upset . . . because we had lived under this tension for so long." This period may have been harder on Raymond Parks and Leona McCauley than on Rosa Parks because it was they who were home answering more of the incessant hate calls and death threats. Rosa was away from home making appearances for the MIA around the country, so she escaped some of the daily vitriol that her husband and mother endured. For Rosa, the period of the boycott was also easier than her previous activism because "the public knew about it," as opposed to the previous decades, when she was "without any mass cooperation or any support from either black or whites."

Numerous black women stepped up to ensure the boycott's continuance. In the early days of the boycott, Georgia Gilmore and her friends had decided they would try to raise money for the emerging bus strike. While none of them had much money, they knew how to fund-raise and began to sell sandwiches, dinners, pies, and cakes to raise money each week. They came to be called the Club from Nowhere and presented the money they raised each week in the mass meetings. Another group of women, headed by Inez Ricks and calling themselves the Friendly Club, took up the challenge and began their own bake sales. A bit of a competition developed. Every Monday both clubs would present their fund-raising efforts at the mass meeting to a standing ovation.

"I learned much myself," Parks later reflected. For her it was a lesson in organizing, in how people had to move past fear on their own and how much power they possessed once they did.

> I learned that no matter how much you try, how hard you work to give people an incentive it is something you yourself cannot give to another person. It has to be in the person to make the step, to have the belief and faith that they should be a free people. The complacency, the fear and oppression that people had suffered so long after the Emancipation of Chattel Slavery. The replacement of Chattel Slavery with mental slavery so people believed, actually believed that they were inferior to others because of the positions that they had to hold. When the oppression they had to endure was thrown off and they began to stand up, to be vocal, be heard, to make known their dissatisfaction against being treated as inferior beings, it is my belief now . . . that we will never go back to that time again.

Parks had spent more than a decade before the boycott wrestling her own fear and drawing on her own faith to make stand after stand against racial injustice. She had grown disillusioned by the ways many others seemed unwilling to do the same. The unity the community maintained for the 382-day boycott was deeply inspiring.

Women provided the backbone of the boycott as walkers, drivers, organizers, and fund-raisers. But they didn't necessarily say they were boycotting. As Virginia Durr explained, "Often I'd stop and pick them up. Never did one of them say that they were walking on account of the boycott. 'No, ma'am, I don't have nothing to do with that boycott. The lady I work for, she was sick this afternoon, and couldn't drive me home.'" For protection, many black women feigned indifference and let the white women they worked for assume what they wanted about the protest—and then went on to the mass meetings at night. In interviews with Fisk researchers in the first months of the boycott, numerous white women claimed their black maids were too afraid to ride the bus and just wanted the boycott to be over. But the black women interviewed by black researchers were steadfast. "I'll crawl on my knees," one woman told a Fisk University researcher, "'fo' I get back on dem buses."

Some women were forthright with their employers about their role and opinions in the protest. Forty-five-year-old Beatrice Charles described a confrontation with her employer, who threatened to fire her because of her support of the boycott. "Well Mrs. I just won't come at all and I sure won't starve. You see my husband is a railroad man, my son and daughter have good jobs and my daddy keep plenty of food on his farm. So I'm not worried at all, 'cause I was eating before I started working for you." Another domestic, Dealy Cooksey, told of arguing with her white employer, who claimed King was just swindling Montgomery blacks. "I said back to her, 'Don't you sey nothing bout Rev[erend] King. You kin say anything else you want to but don't you sey nothing 'bout Reverend King. Dat's us man and I declare he's a fin un. He went to school and made somethin' out of hisself and now he's tryin' to help us. Y'all white folks done kep' us blind long enough. We got our eyes open and now us sho ain't gon let you close 'em back." Both Charles's and Cooksey's employers backed down.

The level of fear that black people felt about the boycott being brought down by the city was enormous, and the discipline people kept in terms of protecting the organization of the boycott and its leaders was considerable. That fear certainly heightened the belief that Parks's long-standing political commitments were nobody's business and needed to be kept out of public view. Dissembling provided protection.

The mass meetings continued to be packed.

People got to the meetings hours ahead of time to get a seat. Many women who did domestic work would get off work, bring their lunch, and settle into the pews to wait, often singing to pass the time. A number of the older women soon had their own customary seats. Some took charge of prayers or song. Professor Lawrence Reddick observed, "The really stirring songs are the lined, camp-meeting tunes, of low pitch and long meter. They seem to recapture the long history of the Negro's suffering and struggle."

Parks would come to the meetings, but after the first one she didn't sit on the dais. She was never asked to speak, which, according to an interview she gave in early February, she "appreciate[d] . . . for other people have suffered indignities, and it is really our fight rather than mine." According to Reverend Graetz, Parks attended mass meetings but "was treated like she didn't have anything to say." By the spring she was making speeches and doing fund raising across the country on behalf of the boycott, but those appearances were rarely announced in the mass meetings back in Montgomery, unlike those of the ministers, whose work on behalf of the boycott was often proclaimed from the pulpit. Parks's symbolic status was crucial to MIA, but the work she was doing on behalf of the protest was less visible. This may have contributed to the jealousy some felt toward her.

Reverend King, who had just turned twenty-seven on January 15, was a sensation at the mass meetings, particularly among many of the older women. Exceedingly proud, they thrilled that this extraordinary gifted young man, attractive and well-spoken, had arisen in their midst. Some dressed in their Sunday best, hoping the reverend would be pleased with them and acknowledge their service. Most treasured him and defended him to the hilt, even when it meant challenging their white employers. The impact that King's emerging leadership had on Montgomery's black community in those first months is hard to capture. Nearly everyone—Parks especially—thrilled to the amazing good fortune at having this bold young minister who was making the community proud. For Parks, the way that this had become everyone's fight and produced new leadership was especially cherished. It made it easy to background her role and that of other longtime activists like Nixon.

The boycott crippled the bus company, and a month after Parks's arrest, they raised fares, laid off dozens of drivers, and curtailed service by cutting off many bus routes. Adult fares jumped from ten to fifteen cents and student fares from five to eight cents. Rumors circulated that the city might even lose the bus franchise.

Attempts to break the boycott were legion. Walkers—and those driving the carpools—were often pelted with food, stones, urine, and other things. Police continually pulled over car poolers on real and often imaginary violations, and drivers received dozens of tickets. Within the space of a few months, Jo Ann Robinson had racked up seventeen tickets. A police officer in a squad car threw a rock through the front window of her home, and two men in police uniforms threw acid all over her car. Many drivers found their vehicles vandalized. People had their gas tanks filled with sugar and their brakes tampered with. According to Robinson, police officers (or men dressed as police officers) were responsible for a great deal of the violence—paint and manure thrown on homes, bricks thrown through their windows, yards and automobiles destroyed, nails scattered on streets to puncture tires. Crosses were burned on the campus of Alabama State. Martin Luther King was arrested for "speeding," though city officials claimed that the officers did not know it was King when they pulled him over.

Still people were determined to keep going. As one elderly boycotter explained, "We have fooled the (White) people and ourselves too. Neither one of us recognized our (Negroes) power—now that we see what we can do—we are going to do it until we get what we want." Parks herself saw the ways that the increasing pressure and resistance to the boycott bespoke the power of it. "If you are mistreated when you ride and intimidated when you walk," she pointedly observed in February, "why not do what hurt them most—walk and let them find $3000 per day to pay for it . . . until they better learn to treat us."

In the fall of 1955, a local group of the White Citizens' Council was established in Montgomery to provide organized economic, political, and, at times, physical resistance to impending desegregation. Under the leadership of a group of white lawyers, the Council initially did not attract very many members—"less than 100 low-status members," according to the *Southern Patriot*. With the start of the boycott, the membership of the White Citizens' Council skyrocketed to fourteen thousand members within three months. Even Mayor Gayle joined the organization and, according to Parks, "was proud to announce it in public." Then came the news that Police Commissioner Clyde Sellers had joined the WCC, which increased black people's fear that the police would simply become an arm of the Council. Still, some white businessmen kept their distance from the Council, particularly as black Montgomerians boycotted businesses associated with the WCC.

Many whites, including many political leaders, professed surprise at black grievances, claiming black people hadn't brought these problems forward previously. Some claimed that a handful of mean bus drivers who were too "rough" with black passengers had been dealt with. As one leading businessman involved in some of the initial negotiations explained, "We admitted there had been injustices. We investigated charges against the drivers and found that the company had some rough necks who were rough with everybody. We were in touch with the bus company and they discharged five of the troublemakers during the session." Framing it as a discrete issue caused by a handful of bad apples employed by the bus company who were subsequently disciplined, they avoided the question of a systemic practice—or even the idea that bus segregation was systematically inequitable and disrespectful.

The bus company conversely sought to shift the blame to the city. As bus company president J. H. Bagley explained:

> We don't have anything to do with making the laws—you see we operate under the city commission and they regulate the seating and what they asked for is against the law. We do what the law says and if they change the law, we will change—this is between them and the city commission and the laws of Ala, the bus company has nothing to do with it.

However, the bus company was never willing to side with the black community in any of its legal challenges, sticking with the status quo.

Right before Christmas, the Central White Citizens' Committee ran ads in the *Advertiser* and *Observer* calling on "citizens of Montgomery" to ride the bus. Flyers also circulated through Montgomery's white community urging people to ride the bus. On February 10, more than ten thousand white people from Alabama and Mississippi converged on the Montgomery Agricultural Coliseum to hold a White Citizens Convocation with featured speaker Mississippi senator James Eastland. Waving Confederate flags and singing "Dixie," they spoke of "states' rights" and the "mulatto decision" of the Supreme Court and giving "the niggers a whipping"—with a particularly "harsh lesson" for Rosa Parks. With their "way of life" believed to be under siege, the White Citizens Council came to play a decisive role in the public life in Montgomery. Virginia Durr wrote a friend in February about the expanding power of the WCC, which "grow[s] apace day by day and there is real black mail going on. They work the blocks and the buildings and ask each one to join and if they don't—Well there is no doubt you get on a blacklist."

It became increasingly dangerous for white Montgomerians to criticize the Council or to have any association with blacks. Those whites who did associate with the protest came under attack; verbally harassed and ostracized, they often lost their jobs and sometimes were physically targeted. The few whites who supported the boycott were endlessly red-baited, threatened, and physically targeted. White Northern liberals grew increasingly self-righteous in their attacks on white Southerners yet many lent little tangible support to visible white and black civil rights activists.

On January 30, white vigilantes threw a bomb into the King home with Coretta and baby Yolanda inside. King, who was at a meeting, was quickly summoned home. No one was hurt, but hundreds of black people gathered in anger. Frightened, angry, but able to draw on a reserve of courage and conviction, King came out and quieted the crowd. "Brothers and sisters, we believe in law and order. Don't get panicky. . . . Don't get your weapons. . . . I want it to be known the length and breadth of this land that if I am stopped, this movement will not stop." According to observers, Commissioner Sellers and Mayor Gayle (who curiously were some of the first people on the scene) seemed disappointed by King's reaction. The next day, Nixon's house was also bombed. Nixon was away on a Pullman run but Parks rushed over to help clean up.

The violence had heightened the climate of fear. "We do not know what else is to follow these previous events," Parks wrote a friend, but we are "praying for courage and determination to withstand all attempts of intimidation." She asked the MIA for night watchmen at her apartment. "Some strange men have been coming into my neighborhood inquiring about this woman who caused all this trouble. I'm not worried about myself but it does upset my mother quite a bit." The MIA took responsibility for providing Parks with protection. Likely, Parks's neighbors at Cleveland Courts also played a significant role in saving the Parks's apartment from attack—the sense of community and the presence of people around at all times of the day and night provided an important buffer that King, Abernathy, Nixon, and Graetz, who all lived in houses, did not enjoy.

Still, the Parks family was not deterred. Parks wrote a friend that they were "more determined than ever to stand up till the end." When Nixon's house was bombed, Rosa and Raymond together helped to clean up the debris and rubble and get things back in order. According to a friend, the couple was "part of a clean up crew of people that would essentially help people whose homes had been bombed." Mr. and Mrs. Parks "when they would hear the bombs go off, would run toward them and Mr. Parks in doing this once, stepped on 11 sticks of dynamite with everyone screaming for him not to go in the direction that he had gone." The FBI took notice of the violence but saw no need to investigate and expressed no problem with the Montgomery police department's inability or unwillingness to identify suspects. BOYCOTT STILL CONTINUING, they cabled national headquarters.

According to Martin Luther King, "so persistent and persuasive" was the argument among Montgomery whites that Parks was an NAACP plant that "it convinced many reporters from all across the country." Still, the dozens and dozens of stories run in both the *Montgomery Advertiser* and the *Alabama Journal* never mentioned Parks's actual work with the NAACP over the preceding decade—despite on occasion mentioning E. D. Nixon's ties to the organization. (In 1955, Nixon no longer served as branch president, but Parks was the organization's secretary, a position she gave up shortly after the boycott began.) According to WCC leader Luther Ingalls, "The Parks woman tried five or six times to create an incident before they finally arrested her—I got that from the drivers. You know she used the white toilet at Montgomery Fair. . . . You can see what she is after." Though these charges were off base, segregationists were often quite accurate, perhaps inadvertently, in terms of Parks's larger goals.

BROWDER V. GAYLE

Meanwhile, lawyer Fred Gray and other activists had taken up a "second front." Montgomery's civil rights leaders had learned from the case of Viola White how city officials would try to hold Parks's case up in circuit court. Moreover, given Parks's connections to the NAACP and the red-baiting of the organization in Alabama in 1956, they believed a federal case with different plaintiffs might be better. So they decided to file suit directly in federal court, bypassing the state court. As E. D. Nixon explained, "They . . . wanted to wear us out, wear us out and never move that case up the Circuit Court, and they was dumbfounded when they found out that we done decided to go into federal court." Clifford Durr feared that because Parks had refused to give up her seat when there were no other seats available, her case could be decided in her favor (vis-à-vis Montgomery city law) without resolving the larger issue of the constitutionality of bus segregation.

The first draft of this federal case included Parks as the first plaintiff; however, the final one filed in federal court did not. Gray worried that having Parks on the suit would muddy the complaint because her criminal case was on appeal in state court. He did not want to give any grounds for the federal case to be dismissed because the issue was already being heard in Alabama state court. Moreover, given the red-baiting of the NAACP, Parks's long-standing ties to the organization made her less than ideal for the suit. Indeed, Parks had resigned her position as secretary of the branch after the boycott got under way in order to "not have it said that the bus protest was organized by 'outside agitators,' and organizations from the North."

Fred Gray began looking for plaintiffs to bring this federal challenge to bus segregation. They wanted a diverse group—hoping to have at least one minister as part of the suit. Aurelia Browder, Susie McDonald, Claudette Colvin, and Mary Louise Smith had encountered discrimination on Montgomery buses and agreed to become plaintiffs in a civil action lawsuit. No men stepped forward to join them. Rather than make another defensive move following from an arrest, on February 1, they took a proactive step in challenging bus segregation by filing a class-action suit in federal court. Jeanetta Reese was named as the fifth plaintiff on the original suit but pulled out a day later, claiming she had not agreed to the suit. Both Reese and her husband had been threatened. When activist Bayard Rustin visited Reese in her home, she explained to him her decision to pull out, "I had to do what I did or I wouldn't be alive today." A week after the suit was filed, Fred Gray's draft status was reclassified as 1-A. Then, in an attempt to disbar him, he was indicted for improperly representing Jeanetta Reese.

THE STUBBORN WOMAN
WHO STARTED IT ALL:
THE PRESS AND THE INDICTMENTS

In late December, dismayed by the coverage of the Montgomery protest, Reverend Graetz wrote *Time* magazine a letter, criticizing as "one-sided" local coverage that "omitted pertinent facts that would have put a much more favorable light on what the Negroes are asking for." Identifying himself as a white minister of a black congregation, Graetz asked the magazine to dispatch a reporter to the city to "get a good look at the way a one-way press and a one-race police force band together to discredit fifty thousand people who are tired of being treated like animals on the city buses, and who are registering their feelings by refraining from riding those buses." Up to this point, the boycott had received scant attention in the national media, and the local white media, as Graetz pointed out, had sought to discredit it. The *New York Times* and the *Washington Post* initially had relied on the wire services to cover the protests. Black newspapers had been much quicker to recognize the historic significance of the boycott, sending reporters and covering it more extensively.

White resistance gained traction in February. On February 5, a riot erupted at the University of Alabama following the admission of Autherine Lucy, the first black student. The university subsequently expelled Lucy "for her own safety." Angered by the federal suit, the city stepped up its harassment and began to look for new tactics, since the tickets and police intimidation had not worked to dissuade the boycotters. Dredging up a 1903 law that outlawed boycotts (in response to black streetcar protests), in February, the city called more than two hundred blacks to testify before a grand jury about who was behind the boycott. One hundred and fifteen boycott leaders (later reduced to eighty-nine)—including more than a half dozen women, including Parks and Robinson—were indicted on February 21, 1956.

To preclude King from being isolated and demonstrate that they had nothing to hide, the group decided to turn themselves in. "Efforts were being made to have [Martin Luther King] bear the blame for the boycott," Reverend Solomon Seay explained. "Those poised for this important event in history did not allow him to bear the blame alone. We all decided to go to jail rather than wait for the arrests." Parks, along with Nixon, were among the first to present them-selves to the sheriff: "Are you looking for me? Well I am here." As person after person was booked, the largest indictment in Alabama history, the atmosphere outside the county courthouse was proud, determined, and almost jubilant.

This mood was very different from that of her first arrest, two and a half months earlier. "We were surrounded by crowds of people," Parks recalled, "and reporters, and photographers all across the country were on hand and when I went in to be fingerprinted and arrested there was a photographer to take our pictures and we had such a spirit of unity that there were people who felt somewhat left out when they were not among those arrested." The interviewer then asked if it was "more popular to be arrested the second time than the first?" "Yes," Parks replied. "The first time I was very much alone because none on the bus who witnessed my arrest volunteered to accompany me or show sympathy in any way." The mug shot of Parks taken that February day—along with a photo of her being fingerprinted by police officer Drue Lackey (who would later become Montgomery's chief of police)—would become iconic, often misidentified as the photo from her arrest on December 1.

While Parks and the others were inside, the crowd, many carrying shotguns, started getting restless. The police were increasingly worried. Reverend Simms described the scene: "Black women with bandannas on, wearing men's hats with their dresses rolled up. From the alleys they came. This is what frightened white people. Not the collar and tie group."

One of the police hollered, "All right, you women get back."

These great big old women with their dresses rolled up told him, and I never will forget their language, "Us ain't going nowhere. You done arrested us preachers and we ain't moving."

He put his hands on his gun and his club. They said, "I don't care what you got. If you hit one of us, you'll not leave here alive." That was the thing we had to work hard against, keeping these blacks from killing these whites.

The arrests served to strengthen the feeling of resolve at the evening's packed mass meeting at Abernathy's church. Many ministers spoke—though Parks did not. Casting it as a conflict "between justice and injustice," King called on the gathered crowd to "let nobody pull you so low as to hate them." The crowd roared its approval. King went on, "I have done three things that are 'wrong.' First of all, being born a Negro. That is my first sin. Second being tired of segregation law I've committed the sin of being tired of segregation. I have committed the sin of being tired of the injustices and discrimination heaped upon Negroes. Third having the moral courage to sit up and express our tiredness. That is my third sin." After King finished the speech people called out from the audience "Gone too far" and "Can't quit now."

The day of the arraignment, the *Montgomery Advertiser* ran an ominous story on its front page.

> Federal Bureau of Investigation agents are known to have secured a complete list of Negroes indicted and arrested on charges of boycotting the Montgomery City Lines. FBI agents had no comment on the securing of the list. It was understood, however, that the list was to be sent to the Washington FBI office for informational use.

The indictments and increasing pressure served to galvanize the community and deepen its commitment. Indeed, according to Parks, the more resistance the protest sparked, the more determined they got: "The white segregationists tried to put pressure to stop us. Instead of stopping us, they would encourage us to go on." The MIA's demands stiffened to full desegregation of the buses.

On February 22, circuit judge Eugene Carter turned down Parks's appeal of her December conviction and sentenced her to fourteen days in jail. Parks then appealed the decision to the state supreme court. Meanwhile, after their petition to dismiss charges against the remaining eighty-nine defendants was rejected, Gray and the other eight defense attorneys (all black, including Robert

Carter of the national NAACP) asked for separate trials for each of the defendants. Determined to put the system on trial, they waived the right to a jury trial, which meant Circuit Judge Eugene Carter would decide all the cases.

The mass indictments and subsequent trial drew the national news media. The *Washington Post*'s editorial page called the indictments "a monumental display of folly" while terming the boycott "impeccably lawful, orderly, dignified— and effective." The *New York Times* weighed in a bit tongue-in-cheek on the "crime wave" in Alabama that had led to the arrest of more than one hundred citizens for their actions related to the boycott, fearing that "the Communists, who hate democracy, will have this tragically true story to add to their existing assortment of lies." Still, the *Times* added, "The wisdom of this boycott in a city where race relations are said to have long been good cannot be argued at this distance. . . . This newspaper has faith that the people, of Alabama, of whatever race, do in the majority believe in democracy. We have faith also that they have intelligence enough to realize that equal rights do not dictate to anybody of any race his choice of friends." And in an article ten days later, a *Times* reporter described Gray and Graetz's "drift away" from moderation as they now were calling for full desegregation of the buses. Moderation to the *New York Times* meant advocating for respectful, first-come, first-served segregation.

Reporters swarmed into Montgomery from all over the country. The *New York Times* and *Washington Post* sent their first reporters. Journalists from India, England, and France journeyed to Alabama to cover the trial. This coverage furthered the determination of black Montgomerians—the world was now watching their actions. Black congressman Charles Diggs of Michigan came as an "interested spectator," bringing with him $5,000 from Detroiters to aid the boycott. The New Orleans Ministerial Alliance sent $3,000.

Many in Montgomery's white community found this national exposure hypocritical, feeling like they (and the South more broadly) were being singled out by Northerners, even though the North had similar problems. As the boycott dragged on, newspapers like the *Advertiser* began publishing stories of Northern segregation. Some in Montgomery's white community thought they should go for the "paper integration" favored by the North. John Hardt, who taught at Maxwell Air Force Base, lamented the attitudes of some white Alabamians, "Why can't they go ahead and say 'yes' we'll accept the Supreme Court decision and then do like they do in the North—manage the school districts so that there is actually little or no integration. You already have residential segregation and accepting the decision would mainly be a matter of accepting it on paper, with very little actual integration." In March, when 19 senators and 892 congressmen issued the "Southern Manifesto" as a response to the *Brown* decision, Parks and white Fellowship of Reconciliation field secretary Glenn Smiley authored an unsigned statement from the MIA calling the manifesto "inflammatory."

Hoping to discredit the minister and break the back of the protest, the city decided to try Martin Luther King first and separately. The gallery was packed with scores of people jammed in the hallways, trying to get a peek at the proceedings. Numerous people testified about their decision to stop riding the buses, not on the direction of King or the movement but based on the mistreatment they had long endured on the bus. Those called to the stand were evasive on the movement and strategic in locating the protest in their own decisions and beliefs. As Gladys Moore testified on March 22, "Wasn't no one started it. We all started it over night." Raymond Parks and Sadie Brooks (the wife of Hilliard Brooks, who had been killed for his bus protest a few years earlier) testified to their own long-standing grievances.

Raymond Parks spoke of two incidents on the bus that had given rise to his own decision to stop riding. One time a bus driver had refused to stop at the designated stop—and took the passengers ten to twelve blocks past the original destination. Another time a bus driver refused to pick up two women because they were black, and Raymond recalled hearing the term "nigger" being used multiple times. But Raymond refused to state directly why and when he had stopped riding the bus, frustrating the state prosecutor:

Q: You say you are riding buses now?
RP: No, sir, I didn't say that.
Q: I thought you said you were riding buses every day?
RP: I said I wasn't riding to Maxwell Field over here through town. And I haven't rode this bus out this way because—
Q: Have you been riding the City Line buses in the last two months?
RP: No, sir.

Raymond then testified that the morning of Rosa's arraignment he rode the bus out to Maxwell and then came back for the trial and had not ridden the buses since. It is hard to assess the validity of that statement since nowhere else has it ever been suggested that Raymond did not boycott that first morning.

Much of the national press was "overwhelmingly favorable, sometimes fawning" toward the boycott, according to Gene Roberts and Hank Klibanoff in their study of the media and the civil rights movement. "For the first time in their lives . . . [they were] covering a story that had no grays." Alistair Cooke of the *Manchester Guardian*, however, took pity on the economic costs being born by the city's bus company and described Parks as "the stubborn woman who started it all . . . to become the Paul Revere of the boycott." Wayne Phillips of the *New York Times* had a different take on the boycott. He credited Parks's reputation as one of the keys to the protest movement "which was certainly strengthened by the fact that Mrs. Parks was an intelligent, hard-working woman with a strongly developed conviction that segregation was evil, a leader in her church and one of the leaders in the local chapter of the National Association for the Advancement of Colored People."

In May, *Browder v. Gayle* went before Judges Rives, Lynne, and Johnson. Reese testified for the prosecution, and, unlike the black people in the courtroom dressed in their Sunday best, appeared in her domestic uniform and was let in the back door by her employer, the sheriff. Claudette Colvin, according to historian Frank Sikora, was the "star witness." Trying to provoke Colvin to admit to a conspiracy to boycott, the prosecutor asked who their leader was. Colvin testified, "Our leaders is just we, ourselves. . . . We all spoke for ourselves." Mary Louise Smith also testified. At lunch after the testimony, Colvin met Smith for the first time. "I liked Mary Louise," Colvin recalled, "and I was proud that two teenaged girls had stood up."

Because of the *Brown* decision and the mounting racial tension surrounding the boycott and Autherine Lucy, Alabama authorities began to take steps against the NAACP. On June 1, 1956, state attorney general John Patterson secured a court injunction barring the NAACP from further activity in Alabama on the grounds that it was a "foreign" corporation. The injunction specifically mentioned the boycott and Autherine Lucy's desegregation of the University of Alabama. Patterson's attack on the organization, according to Parks, came "because the people had become so unified in this protest, and it was our only civil rights organization in the city, and people were paying memberships faster than we could actually take them in. So, in order to retard the progress that this organization was making in the state of Alabama, it was outlawed a few years. But it did not separate the people because the organization was outlawed. The MIA just became stronger."

Rosa Parks outside the Highlander Folk School Library, circa 1955.

COURTESY HIGHLANDER CENTER

Parks, Septima Clark, and Parks's mother pose during Parks's visit to Highlander in December 1956 to meet with students desegregating schools in Clinton, Tennessee. COURTESY HIGHLANDER CENTER

From left: Martin Luther King, Jr., Pete Seeger, Myles
Horton's daughter Charis, Parks, and Ralph Abernathy
gather for Highlander's twenty-fifth anniversary
celebration, 1957. COURTESY HIGHLANDER CENTER

Septima Clark and Parks share a relaxing moment at Highlander, circa 1955.   COURTESY HIGHLANDER CENTER

Parks and her husband, Raymond, go to court for her arraignment on December 5, 1955, the first day of the Montgomery bus boycott. COURTESY AP IMAGES

Parks with Martin Luther King, Jr. circa 1955. WIKIMEDIA COMMONS

Parks and Stokely Carmichael outside Rev. Albert Cleage's Central Congregational Church in Detroit, late 1960s. PHOTOGRAPH BY WILLIAM CARTER, COURTESY DOROTHY ALDRIDGE

Rosa Parks speaking at the conclusion of the Selma to Montgomery civil rights march, 1965. Ralph Abernathy is on the left. © STEPHEN SOMERSTEIN

Parks gets a kiss from her mother, Leona McCauley, after returning home from the civil rights march in Selma, Alabama, in 1965. COURTESY DETROIT NEWS ARCHIVES

Parks, Eleanor Roosevelt, and Autherine Lucy prior to a civil rights rally at Madison Square Garden, 1956.

LIBRARY OF CONGRESS

Parks and E. D. Nixon reunite in Detroit in 1976.
COURTESY DETROIT NEWS ARCHIVES

Parks surveys the book tables at the National Black Political Convention in Gary, Indiana. LeRoy W. Henderson

Parks leads a march down Woodward Avenue in Detroit, August 1976.   Courtesy Detroit News Archives

Two Montgomery comrades, Parks and Virginia Durr, come together in South Hadley, Massachusetts, 1981.

Parks applauds a speech by Congressman John Conyers at a labor rally in Detroit, late 1980s.

Parks protests apartheid in front of the South African Embassy, Washington, D.C., 1985.   COURTESY JIM HUBBARD

CHAPTER FIVE

"It Is Fine to Be a Heroine but the Price Is High"
The Suffering of Rosa Parks

WITH THE CITY STANDING FIRM for segregation, the economic and physical harassment of boycotters intensified. Parks's action had come at a significant sacrifice to her family's economic stability. When Montgomery Fair discharged her a month after her bus stand, this jeopardized the family's stability, as they relied greatly on her steady income. A week later, forbidden from discussing the protest at work, Raymond resigned his job at Maxwell Air Force Base. Shortly after, their landlord raised their rent ten dollars a month. The Parks family was now in severe economic trouble.

While the physical violence the boycotters and leaders endured is an integral part of civil rights history, this economic catastrophe—the sacrifice Rosa's bus stand entailed for her family and, more broadly, the economic retaliation against civil rights activists—is not as widely recognized. Indeed Parks's sacrifice—the toll her bus stand took on her and her family—barely gathers a mention in the triumphal story of her journey from Montgomery to the Capitol rotunda.

Learning to live with such economic insecurity was excruciating, particularly the paradox for Parks of being "famous" and yet having no money. Additionally, the phone rang constantly with hateful messages: "Die, nigger. Die" or "You should be killed." Sometimes she was verbally accosted on the street. The fear of white violence was ever present.

The faith and fortitude it took to stay active proved immense. To live with death threats and witness friends' homes bombed, to lose her job and wonder how her family would survive, to spend a decade being famous yet still without steady employment, and to have that stress significantly compromise her health and that of her husband—that was Rosa Parks's experience during and after the boycott.

Historian Chana Kai Lee notes the importance of examining the difficulties women activists like Parks and Fannie Lou Hamer experienced: "It seems only fair and profitable to try to talk about her pain too, but not in a way in which we emphasize only her survival of that pain and those challenges." Understanding the fullness of Parks's political life requires looking at the economic insecurity, health issues, fear, and harassment she endured the year of the boycott and for the ensuing decade. Being a heroine was difficult.

The erasure of Parks's hardships stems partly

from the ways she was publicly cast as a tired seamstress, rather than a longtime political activist. Montgomery activists, including Parks herself, had realized the importance of a symbol to coalesce around; to do so, they separated and celebrated the courageous stand she made on the bus from her larger political and employment history. But the danger of symbols is that they get fixed in time. They require honor but not necessarily assistance, so the fact that the figure was a real woman with a real family who was suffering became difficult to see. Add Parks's gender—and the ways that economic instability is often not understood to have the same impact on a woman as on a man of that era—and Parks's sacrifice recedes further into the background. Moreover, symbols become the property of the whole movement. So who would claim responsibility for the quiet suffering of the "mother of the movement"?

In a larger sense, the boycott fable is the founding story—the golden goose—of the civil rights movement, with its untarnished happy ending and its ability to reflect the best possibilities of the United States. A classic American tale, it is the story of an ordinary citizen who with a simple act inspired the nation to make good on its ideals. To see the Parks family suffering for a decade after the boycott's successful end—to confront the cost and complexity of that success and the economic retaliation that many civil rights activists endured—mars the legend. In many ways, that fable's utility requires the now-classic photo finish, the ubiquitous image of Rosa Parks seated in profile on a desegregated bus.

Looking at Rosa Parks head on requires going beyond that picture and ultimately provides a more sobering view of the prolonged resistance to civil rights throughout the country. Parks's politics and a deeply segregated and discriminatory job market left her without stable work in the Confederate South and the liberal North for nearly a decade. That decade of suffering occurred as the modern civil rights movement reached its apex, a decade now tinged in the rosy glow of nostalgia and redemptive suffering. But there was nothing foreordained about where the Rosa Parks story would end, no easy solace that Parks could claim to alleviate the fear or the poverty. Not all suffering led to change, as civil rights stalwarts like Parks knew well. In 1966, Parks sidestepped a question in an interview with New York state senator George Metcalf, who was writing a book profiling important black figures. Metcalf asked whether "all the tortures and everything you suffered were worth it?" Parks did *not* say an unequivocal yes, responding instead, "I didn't think of it in just that way. I think I would have preferred if we would return to normal without segregation. It would have been better. I didn't regret the fact that we had made at least this gain of ending segregation on the buses." Having endeavored to conquer her fear in the decades of activism before the boycott, Parks had delighted in the community uprising. She worked to keep the terror of harassment and instability at bay as she played an active role in maintaining the boycott, and continued her political activities once it finished. She did not sugarcoat the costs of that work but often kept the difficulties to herself.

FIRED

Parks was very reluctant to attribute her firing from the Montgomery Fair Department Store unequivocally to her bus stand: "I cannot say this is true. I do not like to form in my mind something I do not have any proof of." As judicious as she was in her assessment, there can be little doubt that her bus stand cost her a position at the department store. After she was laid off, Parks redoubled her work for the boycott. She gave speeches, traveled on behalf of the NAACP and MIA, attended meetings, helped distribute clothes, food, and other necessities to people affected by the boycott, and served briefly as a dispatcher—all the while worrying about her own family's economic well-being and doing whatever sewing work she could find on the side.

During the first weeks of the boycott, the MIA relied on local fund-raising but soon recognized the need to solicit outside support. In February, longtime New York–based organizers Ella Baker, Bayard Rustin, and Stanley Levinson formed In Friendship. Heartened by this budding Southern militancy, the group sought to provide material support for the boycott and civil rights workers across the South facing reprisals for their activism.

Given the Cold War context—not to mention that civil rights activities had long been discredited as the work of "outsiders"—taking outside money put the movement at risk of charges of subversion and carpetbagging (with its Reconstruction-era overtones). However, the costs of sustaining the car pools were considerable, not to mention the numbers of people facing reprisals for their participation. The MIA needed outside financial support, beyond what Montgomerians could provide.

By the winter, friction had developed between King and NAACP executive secretary Roy Wilkins over how the NAACP was still keeping the boycott at arm's length, even as its own fund-raising was benefiting from the protest's inspiring example. The NAACP had maintained its distance from the boycott in its early days, in part because the boycott, with its initial limited demands, was not, at first, a full-on assault on segregation. Seeing it as too "mild," Wilkins wrote Alabama field secretary W. C. Patton that the boycott sought to "improv[e] segregation by making it more polite." Though this went unmentioned, the grassroots militancy of the boycott differed from the organization's usual program of legalist strategies. James Peck (who later joined CORE's Freedom Ride) wrote a letter criticizing the NAACP for its unwillingness to back the boycott. Indeed the national office of the NAACP blocked talk by some members urging a national boycott of the bus company.

To Montgomery officials there was nothing mild about the boycott. As the protest continued, King continued to press the NAACP for help while expressing his concern that NAACP fund-raising was eclipsing the MIA's. Wilkins pledged to cover the legal costs associated with Parks's appeal and the indicted boycott organizers. Still, even when the boycott's goals turned to full desegregation, the NAACP kept its distance from the boycott itself. While providing legal assistance, they waited to see the outcome of the mass trial that followed the February indictments before assessing the efficacy of passive resistance and economic suasion. At its June national convention, the NAACP continued this equivocation, passing a resolution saying that "we are not yet ready to take a position on [passive nonviolent resistance]." This friction and the rivalries between groups would have severe consequences for Parks. No civil rights group— not the NAACP she had worked for over the past decade nor the MIA she helped create—felt primarily responsible for Parks's imperiled situation, even though she fund-raised for both during the year of the boycott.

Parks wrote on a slip of paper during the boycott, "I have no quarrel with MIA about being given or not given a job." While certainly not feeling entitled to a job, this note demonstrates that she recognized the possibility of a job for her within the organization. The MIA hired four women to be its office staff: Erma Dungee as financial secretary, Maude Ballou as King's personal secretary, Martha Johnson as the MIA's secretary-clerk, and Hazel Gregory as the MIA's general overseer. Jo Ann Robinson described the four as sophisticated, socially prominent, well-trained "young ladies" who were members of the WPC with professional husbands, which suggests that these women occupied a different social position than Parks. Meanwhile, no one would hire either Rosa or Raymond Parks.

One day, Virginia Durr had stopped by the Parks's apartment. Leona McCauley had a hankering for sweet potatoes, but the family had no money for such luxuries. Recognizing the depth of the trouble the Parks family was facing, Durr set about to find some money or a job for

Mrs. Parks. For Durr, who was an outcast in Montgomery because of her civil rights beliefs, this project provided a respite from her own isolation and a way to be useful. There is no record from Parks about how she felt or if she knew the extent of Durr's outreach.

Durr threw herself into this cause, writing to friends across the country for assistance. To Myles Horton of Highlander, she explained, "It is fine to be a heroine but the price is high." To another friend, she noted that Parks "has the heaviest burden to bear." Horton wrote back hoping to "figure out a way to get some money somewhere to help her out" and asking whether Durr and Parks might come to a March meeting at Highlander. "It would be an inspiration to have her [Parks] here," Horton explained. Horton subsequently wrote to Parks telling her how "proud we were of your courageous role in the boycott," and offering his sympathies regarding her economic situation. Horton's response would become the standard treatment for Parks over the next years and decades. Fame—even that imbued with the deepest admiration and respect—did not necessarily translate into security. People would honor her work and solicit her political participation, often without attending to her pressing economic needs.

Durr wrote Horton again two weeks later about Parks's difficulties: "You would be amazed at the number of pictures, interviews etc that she had taken and all of that takes up time and then too all the meetings and then having to walk nearly everywhere she goes takes time too. . . . Most people want to contribute to the Boycott itself rather than to an individual, but that particular individual is to my mind very important."

Parks herself wrote to Horton a week later telling him of the termination of her job. "Mrs. Durr is very concerned about our welfare. I appreciate her friendship, especially at this trying time." Parks cited Durr's concern to invoke the urgency of her situation; as a respectable black woman, she sought to maintain her dignity. While Horton would grow into a friend, she had only met him once at this point and likely found it easier to mention the difficulties of her situation through the words of a white woman who was his friend.

Historian Darlene Clark Hine has written about the culture of dissemblance, a politics of silence that developed among black women in response to the pressures of living with sexual and economic violence. "Only with secrecy, thus achieving a self-imposed invisibility could ordinary black women acquire the psychic space and gather the resources necessary to hold their own in their often one-sided and mismatched struggle against oppression." As Hine argues, black women of this era purposely shielded their innermost feelings from public view. One imagines this was particularly acute for someone like Parks, who was reserved to begin with and then spent the second half of her life under constant public scrutiny. Committed to maintaining her dignified appearance to advance the movement, she kept many of her feelings and troubles to herself. Parks had long chafed at the ways black people had to subsume their needs to whites, but she, like many black women, was skilled at this survival strategy. She put this ability to different use in her public role as a boycott symbol, which required backgrounding her own needs and pain, at times, for the good of the movement. Even as she noticed and attended to the suffering of others, she often seemed determined to keep quiet about her own difficulties. Her own personal sense of dignity became linked to her ability to withstand the pressure.

Horton wrote back to Parks and committed to paying her expenses so she could come to the March Highlander meeting. He subsequently wrote Durr celebrating Parks as "a symbol of the thing we all believe in." Recognizing the importance of white support in the midst of this struggle, he telegrammed Parks the night after the mass indictments came down: "The passive resistance movement your calm and courageous action set in motion there in Montgomery deserves the backing of all who seek justice. Highlander is proud of you."

In late February, King prepared a memorandum to Abernathy concerned about Parks's desperate financial situation "because of her tremendous self respect she has not already revealed this to the organization." King recommended that "$250 be given to her from the Relief Fund. Ordinarily, I would not recommend this much to any one individual, but I think her situation demands it, and the Montgomery Improvement Association owes this to Mrs. Parks above any other. Actually you may make it three hundred dollars ($300.00) if you feel so disposed. Please check with the committee and get this to Mrs. Parks immediately." Three hundred dollars was subsequently disbursed from the MIA treasury to Parks.

The economic toll of the boycott was certainly not limited to the Parks family; it reached across the black community. Working with the MIA Welfare Committee, Parks sought to find employment for laid-off workers because a "lot of people lost their jobs." Faced with the host of reprisals, the MIA became a broad-based social service agency. According to financial secretary Erma Dungee Allen, they bought food and paid people's rent, gas, water, and doctor bills; sometimes they even bought washing machines and other household goods. In many ways, Dungee Allen felt that some of these were "free rides as far as I was concerned. But they [the MIA leadership] seemed to think this is what we had to do." Dungee Allen explained that King was "real sympathetic" to people's needs and "usually the poorest ones" came to the MIA. The MIA understood that meeting people's basic needs would allow for a more engaged movement.

Parks was doing a great deal of speaking and numerous appearances for the MIA—a "tremendous hit," according to Clifford Durr, as one of the MIA's most able speakers and fund-raisers. While she regularly turned over the money to the MIA, not all the ministers did the same. Some kept a portion as an honorarium for their time and energy. Reverend Graetz, who, like Parks, fastidiously turned over his speaking money to the organization, recalled someone in the MIA asking, "Did you keep enough out for yourself?" Shocked, Graetz learned others kept a portion for themselves as compensation for their effort. More than the ministers, Parks did need a portion of the money raised from her public appearances but, like Graetz, never engaged in this practice. Parks also did numerous speaking engagements for the NAACP, some of which garnered her a modest stipend. (On one ten-day tour, the NAACP split the money fund-raised from her events between the local branch and the national office, while giving her twenty-five dollars a talk.)

Financial issues in the MIA grew controversial. Some of the ministers—and occasionally Nixon himself—took part of the funds for their own needs, when hosting organizations thought all of the money was going to the boycott itself. "We had a whole lot of money at that time," Nixon admitted, "and some of it we handled unwisely." In June of 1956, Reverend Uriah Fields, the former secretary of the organization, accused the MIA's leaders of "misappropriation of funds." Days later, after meeting with King, Fields recanted, though he never fully took back his criticisms. In June, Reverend Simms assumed the leadership of the transportation committee, which had grown to require "full time supervision" and established a precise system of record-keeping.

Along with suffering economic hardship, the Parks home received regular hate mail and constant death threats. This harassment took a significant toll on Parks's mother and husband in particular; since she traveled a lot during the boycott year, they often answered the phone. The suffering of her husband took its toll on Rosa, too; as he grew more depressed, she worried. Yet, while scholars have begun to foreground the crucial support that wives of civil rights leaders made, in a troubling gender omission, there has been almost no discussion of the role of husbands. Raymond's support in helping Rosa achieve what she did that year and beyond and the impact their fearsome situation had on him rarely figure into the story. Too often, when Raymond does make a brief cameo in the popular narrative, he is viewed as not sufficiently admirable because he stayed behind the scenes. Rosa considered Raymond a partner and felt he facilitated her activism during the boycott and in the following decades when she continued her public role. The respect he had for her and her work sustained her. While worrying about her safety, he was willing to prioritize her political work—a shift from the early years of their marriage when he was the more prominent activist.

As poet and friend Nikki Giovanni observed, "Nobody would say that Coretta wasn't courageous because she worried about Martin. So why say it about Raymond?" Indeed, Giovanni saw Rosa and Raymond Parks as "of one mind," committed in partnership to the same political struggle. *Jet* magazine would later describe them as a "modern day power couple" in reference to their shared political commitments. According to friends, Rosa was good at finding ways to do what she believed necessary and skirt around Raymond's fears for her safety. According to Reverend Graetz, "She was more firm than her husband wanted her to be. He . . . worried she would be attacked. He didn't want her to be so active." His wife, Jean Graetz, elaborated: "She knew how to get around what he was keeping her from doing. She knew how to get things by going around the opposition. Mrs. Parks wasn't in your face. . . . She had other ways of convincing people."

In describing Rosa and Raymond's partnership, Giovanni recalled the first time she met Rosa Parks, which was in the early 1980s. "Black love is Black wealth," Parks said when Giovanni introduced herself—quoting a line from Giovanni's poem "Nikki-Rosa." Surprised, Giovanni was touched that Parks knew her poetry. That poem criticized the ways the outside white world often did not understand the value of the black family, concluding with the stanza:

> and I really hope no white person ever has cause
> to write about me
> because they never understand
> that Black love is Black wealth and they'll
> probably talk about my hard childhood
> and never understand that
> all the while I was quite happy.

Far beyond the difficulties, to Rosa Parks this love and a shared vision of justice were crucial. And Raymond's love and support was foundational. In many ways, what Raymond did behind the scenes for her over the next decades—backing her up, helping her make travel arrangements, keeping their household functioning, sharing her political outrage—kept her going and enabled her political activities.

The inauguration of the bus protest meant war to segregationists. This put visible black activists like the Parkses, the Kings, the Nixons, Jo Ann Robinson and Fred Gray, in the line of fire. Leona McCauley talked on the phone for hours with friends to keep Raymond from having to answer those hate calls. Rosa increasingly found herself able to keep the terror at bay, later explaining, "I have learned over the years that when one's mind is made up, this diminishes fear; knowing what must be done does away with fear." Part of this stemmed from her faith and reliance on prayer. "There were times when people asked, How did I do it. . . . I prayed hard not to give in and not to fall by the wayside. I believe prayer changes things." But Raymond did not find any such peace.

The impact of living with this racial terror, relentless harassment, and economic insecurity overwhelmed his spirit. Besieged by death threats, unable to find steady work, and worried about their security, Raymond began drinking heavily and chain-smoking. Unnerved, he suffered a nervous breakdown during the boycott. Virginia Durr prodded Rosa to take Raymond to a psychiatrist at Maxwell Air Force Base. Durr claims that the psychiatrist felt Raymond "had no identity" and felt that "if Mrs. Parks had been a more yielding, soft and a kind of helpless woman, he might have found his identity in being a husband but since she was such a strong, brave, intelligent woman that she further made him feel the loss of identity. Anyway, he thought Mrs. Parks ought to give up all her civil rights work and go back to being a little sweet housewife," a suggestion Durr found "absurd."

There is no record from Rosa Parks of this doctor's visit or her reaction to it. But she did not give up her civil rights work. She was always quick to note Raymond's support of her, which may suggest he didn't buy into this thinking either. Rosa contextualized Raymond's difficulties as akin to the psychological impact of living in a war zone, analogous to the trauma of battle. Troubled that he was regarded as peculiar or weak, she stressed how bad their situation was, how most people were torn up by such acute stress.

While Raymond may have manifested his pain more visibly, the stress also took an increasing toll on her health. She developed painful stomach ulcers and a heart condition that would plague her for many years. She had chronic insomnia, a problem she had developed even as a young child when the Klan would ride through Pine Level. Her mother was also sick a great deal the boycott year. And E. D. Nixon would develop high blood pressure in the wake of all the stress. The battle exacted its price. But Mrs. Parks didn't talk about that cost. As a longtime Detroit friend later observed, she "never got into it much. You really have to pull things out of her." In Parks's interviews with Jim Haskins in the late 1980s, however, they talked about the burden this work and the accompanying fear had on many other civil rights activists they knew throughout the South and how many of those activists drank a lot "to be able to sleep at night."

The harassment—and the personal toll it took—was not restricted to black activists. Nor was the sense of living in a war zone. Across town, city librarian Juliette Morgan was one of the few whites supporting the boycott. Her public solidarity with the protest led to unceasing harassment at the hands of segregationists. Long committed to civil rights, Morgan had written a letter to the *Montgomery Advertiser* in the first days of the boycott, describing how "history was being made" by Montgomery's black community. She linked the bus protest to the moral imperatives Gandhi and Thoreau had laid out. "It is hard to imagine a soul so dead, a heart so hard, a vision so blinded and provincial," Morgan wrote, "as not to be moved with admiration, at the quiet dignity, discipline and dedication with which the Negroes have conducted their boycott." Morgan also wrote about her embarrassment at witnessing black passengers being mistreated on the bus.

While dozens of white Montgomerians privately wrote to affirm Morgan's message, publicly she came under attack. Many writers called for her dismissal. Morgan lamented the "silent liberals" who "want to say something but are afraid to speak out." The library initially backed her but insisted she not write anything further or engage in any civil rights work. After the riot following Autherine Lucy's admission to the University of Alabama, Morgan wrote another letter, this time praising the editor of the *Tuscaloosa News* for his stand against the White Citizens' Council; she criticized "cowardly Southern white men" for their harassment of the boycott and of Lucy. A shower of mental and physical harassment followed, as Morgan became a target of white vigilantism. The harassment, according to Jo Ann Robinson, was "unending"—phone calls, prowlers, rocks thrown at her windows for a year. The White Citizens' Council distributed leaflets about her and succeeded in getting the library to compel her to resign, pressuring the mayor to withhold its funding. Morgan lived with her mother, who harangued her for taking such a stand and felt Juliette was ruining her life. Subsequently, Morgan had a "nervous break-down," according to Parks. A year and a half after the boycott began, Morgan took her own life. No black Montgomerians were allowed to attend her funeral.

As the boycott moved the ground beneath the city's feet, violence, harassment, and economic intimidation were time-tested and effective tactics to put civil rights workers back in "their place." Systems of racial distinction require constant reassertion. Those who stepped over those boundaries, like Rosa Parks or Juliette Morgan, were in effect calling the whole system into question. Virginia Durr captured the importance and the cost of such stances, writing to a friend, "Thank God for the exceptions—but they do have a hard time." The Montgomery bus boycott profoundly asserted a social order where black and white people were civic, political, and social equals, threatening the assumptions of the existing socioeconomic structure, which was inextricably wedded to white supremacy. A community of black people and a smattering of white allies looked the old order, that terror, in the eye day after day.

What makes this difficult to fully appreciate is that certain core precepts of the boycott have subsequently been adopted as common sense: that segregation was a systematic apparatus of social and economic power and that resistance to it was possible. Most Americans now look back in the glow of that new truth, assuming they too would have remained seated, written letters to the local paper, risked their jobs to print thirty-five thousand leaflets, or spoken out in favor of boycotting the buses. But as Nikki Giovanni captured in her poem "Harvest":

> . . . Something needs to be said . . . about Rosa Parks . . . other than her feet . . . were tired . . . Lots of people . . . on that bus . . . and many before . . . and since . . . had tired feet . . . lots of people . . . still do . . . they just don't know . . . where to plant them . . .

The bus protest left many casualties and required constant vigilance. Raymond Parks slept with his gun during this period. So did Jo Ann Robinson. "I was afraid to shoot the pistol, but it was a comfort to have it there. . . . If anybody had attempted to break in, I am sure I would have used the gun." Living with the very real possibility of white violence, many in the black community worried tremendously and had their guns nearby for self-protection during the yearlong struggle.

TRAVELING
Throughout 1956, Mrs. Parks traveled throughout the country making appearances on behalf of the bus protest and the NAACP. Crucial to sustaining the protest, these appearances raised money and

brought national attention to their efforts and to the repression black Montgomerians faced, turning a local movement into a national struggle.

In March, Parks returned to Highlander to speak at a workshop. She described the dramatic change the boycott had brought to the city. "Montgomery . . . [is] just a different place altogether since we demonstrated." Being asked to give up her seat was "too much. . . . it meant that I didn't have a right to do anything but get on the bus, give them my fare and then be pushed wherever they wanted me." She also highlighted how others in Montgomery "had experienced something of the same" humiliating treatment that had spurred the protest. The public role of the ministers, Parks felt, was as an important new development in Montgomery. Laced throughout Parks's remarks was her surprise and delight at the movement that had emerged in Montgomery. Horton echoed Parks's incredulity, curiously referring to Parks's stand as a "very little thing."

In a letter to Horton in April, Parks described the uncertainty many felt "never know[ing] what to expect, however, we are keeping on no matter what may happen." She spent most of the spring traveling, crisscrossing the country from Detroit to Seattle, Los Angeles to New York to San Francisco on behalf of the movement. Raymond was "concerned for my safety," but it was a "wonderful trip" with "no unpleasant experiences."

In speeches she gave that year, Parks talked about the boycott as just the beginning of a broader struggle and asked that people pray for her as she returned to Montgomery. Parks's desire to have people praying for her reveals the fear she was living with that year and the sustenance she derived through collective support. Having organized in relative loneliness for a decade previous to the bus protest, she drew tremendous strength from the outpouring of support for their movement.

In March, Parks flew to Detroit—her first airplane flight. She saw her brother, raised money for the MIA in a number of churches, and spoke to Local 600, a militant Detroit UAW local. Demonstrating her willingness to separate herself from the agenda of the NAACP, who frowned on this association with radical trade unionists, Parks maintained alliances with the black left. She did not distance herself from those "reds" who, by the mid-1950s, had been blacklisted and whom those in some civil rights circles had excommunicated for fear of being red-baited themselves. In June, she sent union activist Ernie Thompson of the radical National Negro Labor Council a letter of thanks, evoking the need for struggle over empty sentiments: "It awakens within our mind the fact that there are people of good will in America who are deeply concerned about justice and freedom for all people, and who are willing to make the noble precepts of Democracy living facts lifted out of the dusty files of unimplemented and forgotten court decisions." The decision to maintain these alliances with the Left, particularly during the boycott and the vicious anti-Communism infecting Alabama, evidenced her political independence.

While frowning on such alliances, the NAACP found Parks to be a popular speaker and membership recruiter. She spoke to the Seattle and Los Angeles branches, her talk at the latter entitled "When I Rebelled Against Second Class Citizenship." While visiting Oakland, she met Durr's good friend the writer and Communist Party member Jessica Mitford. Durr later wrote Mitford that Parks's travels were "like a fairy tale, orchids, flowers, presents, banquets, and speaking to audiences of 3000 people" though Parks had not appreciated that there were also "snoopers" who were trying to cause trouble for Mitford.

In early May, Parks journeyed to Anderson College in Indiana, then spoke at an NAACP event in Pittsburgh, followed by two weeks of events in New York on behalf of the NAACP and the Highlander Folk School (though the NAACP did not endorse this support of Highlander). She stayed with Stewart and Charlotte Meacham, white Methodists and later anti–Vietnam War activists, and then lived in a small room at the Henry Street Settlement on the Lower East Side.

The scope of Parks's visit to New York demonstrates her involvement in a network of seasoned organizers. The trip proved personally thrilling. Parks toured Harlem with Ella Baker, went to meetings with Dr. Kenneth Clark and Reverend James Robinson, and got to meet two of her heroes, labor leader A. Phillip Randolph and NAACP leader Roy Wilkins. She spent an evening with Thurgood Marshall and his wife, Cecilia, staying out with them and the King family until 1:30 in the morning. She also visited the Statue of Liberty. "We went to the top of it, 22 stories," she wrote her mother. Amazed by this whirlwind of events, she made many notable acquaintances and had encounters far beyond what she could have ever imagined six months earlier.

On May 24, In Friendship, along with the Brotherhood of Sleeping Car Porters, held a massive civil rights rally and fund-raiser at Madison Square Garden in New York. Ella Baker and others had worked for six weeks to pull off this "Heroes of the South" event. Sixteen thousand people packed the Garden—much to the surprise of the *Pittsburgh Courier*, which noted that the Garden was rarely used for political events given its difficulty to fill. King was originally supposed to headline the event but had to pull out. Parks and Nixon represented the boycott, though the posters advertising the event never listed Parks. Eleanor Roosevelt, A. Phillip Randolph, Roy Wilkins, Adam Clayton Powell, E. D. Nixon, and Autherine Lucy all spoke.

Mrs. Parks also addressed the crowd, declaring that if she had the choice, she would refuse to give up her seat again. A star-studded array of celebrities—Sammy Davis Jr., Cab Calloway, Pearl Bailey, and Tallulah Bankhead—participated in the festivities. Bankhead kissed Parks and Autherine Lucy onstage, emphatically declaring, "There have been generations of Bankheads in Alabama, but I'm not proud of what's happening there today." The rally raised $6,000. Parks wrote home calling the event a "tremendous affair."

She also rode the bus in New York, prominently taking a seat in the front. The whole event was photographed by the *New York Amsterdam News*, which wrote that Mrs. Parks sat where she chose and was well treated by *black* bus driver Delbert Bradley. While in New York, she also received a plaque from the Committee for Better Human Relations, at the Savoy Ballroom. Accepting the award, she teared up, explaining it was the first one she had ever received. Such accolades for her activism were new for Mrs. Parks, as was all the travel and attention. She vowed to keep going until "all our demands are met." Keeping a full schedule, still she worried that she was "needed in Montgomery."

Parks also attended two meetings for Highlander. After the NAACP's invitation to speak at the New York branch, according to Horton, "they ignored her." Horton arranged for her to meet Ralph Bunche and Eleanor Roosevelt, introducing the "first lady of the land to the first lady of the South." Versed in the perils of taking bold stands in 1950s America, the First Lady asked Mrs. Parks if she had been accused of being a Communist. When Parks said yes, Roosevelt replied that she expected Horton had warned Parks about this. Parks said no. As Horton recalled,

> Mrs. Roosevelt criticized me for not telling her. I said, "If I'd known what she was going to do, I'd have told her. But when she was at Highlander she said she wasn't going to do anything. She said that she came from the cradle of the Confederacy, and the white people wouldn't let the black people do anything, and besides, the black people hadn't been willing to stick together, so she didn't think she'd do anything. I didn't see any reason to tell a person who wasn't going to do anything that she'd be branded as a

Communist because I knew she'd never be called a Communist if she didn't do anything."

Parks told Roosevelt that after the boycott began, Horton traveled to Montgomery to tell her what was in store for her. The former first lady well understood the price that Parks would pay for her stand.

Meeting Parks became the subject of Roosevelt's "My Day" newspaper column. Describing Parks as "a very quiet, gentle persona," Roosevelt wrote it was "difficult to imagine how she could take such a positive and independent stand." Still she challenged the idea that Parks's stand just happened out of the blue. "These things do not happen all of a sudden. They grow out of feelings that have been developing over many years. Human beings reach a point . . . 'This is as far as I can go,' and from then on it may be passive resistance, but it will be resistance." Two days later Parks journeyed on to Washington, DC, to address the National Council of Negro Women with Septima Clark. Parks returned home glowing with excitement over her trip to New York, talking about the "wonderful reception" she had received.

Nonetheless, Parks's health suffered during this period. The stress of the public scrutiny, the economic and personal troubles her family faced, and the constant threat of violence had given her acute insomnia and ulcers. Exhausted and sick, she still continued her travels. In early June, she flew to San Francisco for the forty-seventh annual NAACP national convention. She was met by a reporter who "announced arrogantly that he was going 'to take me apart and see what made me tick.'" He peppered her with a series of aggressive questions accusing her of seeking publicity, impugning her morality, and referring to her as a prostitute. Parks grew upset and began shaking, her teacup rattling. Overwhelmed by the onslaught, she "couldn't stand him any longer" and broke down in "hysterics. . . . I mean I started screaming—I'll kill you—I just cried[.] [T]that's the only time I had done that in a press conference." Pleased he had gotten under her skin, the reporter left. Parks remained crying.

"I don't know what made me go off like that," Parks would write later in her autobiography. This was one of the only times in her history of activism that Parks describes crying in public. Indeed, in all of Parks's public appearances, this is the only time she seems to have lost her composure. Given how much stress Parks faced for decades (before, during, and after the boycott), and the thousands of appearances she made, her public equanimity was remarkable. According to her niece Rhea, both her Aunt Rosa and father had learned "not to display their

304

emotions, to always be in control of their faculties." Parks likely internalized the stress, as her struggles with insomnia and ulcers attested.

Parks compared the difficulties maintaining her composure to those Autherine Lucy faced. Lucy had also struggled not to let the endless harassment get to her when she attempted to integrate the University of Alabama as a graduate student on February 3, 1956. The public scrutiny was endless for both women; explained Parks, "I was not accustomed to so much attention." Parks gave a brief, moving account of her experiences in Montgomery at the NAACP convention, which, according to the *Philadelphia Tribune*, bolstered the fund-raising efforts and led to $10,000 being raised for the Fight for Freedom Fund.

Besides writing Horton at Highlander, Durr had reached out to friends and political associates across the country about the Parks family's economic troubles. Through these efforts over the winter, she raised $500 for the Parks family. Faced with mounting debt, a worsening ulcer, a sick mother, and a husband who was depressed and drinking, Parks reluctantly accepted the money. "So reserved and proud," Durr would write an associate, "if it were not by necessity, she wouldn't take a nickel in contributions." This provided some temporary stability for the family. But by July, Durr wrote a friend, this money had run out. "I wish all those fine people who liked her so much and sent her orchids would get together and send her some dough as she really needs it. She can't get a job anywhere here and can't leave as both her Mother and Husband are sick. . . . For her to have to go back to sewing for little or nothing is sad, sort of like Cinderella." Durr raised another $350 over the summer.

Despite the toll on her personally, Parks publicly urged perseverance. At a talk to the National Council of Negro Women in June in Washington, DC, she promised to "continue in every way I can" and urged people not to "give up faith, and one day we will have the Democracy we are hoping for." Here and in other speeches that year Parks made clear the boycott was aimed at something much bigger than a seat on the bus—the promise of full citizenship. At an NAACP mass meeting in Baltimore in September, Parks told the crowd it might "take plenty of sacrifice" but she felt "sure that we will win in the end." In interviews, Parks often contextualized her own stamina as having grown within the years of difficult organizing before there was a mass movement. For Parks, despite the tremendous hardship the boycott imposed, this was, in some ways, an easier period for her given the solidarity within Montgomery's black community. "Because there were so many people involved . . . it was not discouraging as it had been before the incidents and before others joined in."

In August, Parks accompanied the Graetz family to Highlander to mark the one-year anniversary of her visit, which Graetz described as "a badly needed vacation." Highlander sought to broaden its civil rights workshops that summer beyond school desegregation to voter registration and nonviolent resistance to segregation. At one of the workshops, Parks again recounted the events of December 1 and the larger philosophy behind her action. "It is unfair, unjust and un-Christian and as long as we continued to be pushed around, we were getting treated much worse." She told the group, "There had to be a stopping point so this seemed to have been the place for me to . . . find out what human rights that we had, if any." Like King, Parks called upon Christianity and the Constitution in her speeches as to why segregation was wrong and had to be ended. Her firm tone here—"what human rights we had *if any*"—was echoed in her other public speeches that year. On the panel were fellow Montgomerians Graetz and Alabama State professor J. E. Pierce; during the question-and-answer session, no one asked Parks any questions, furthering the misimpression that her role in the boycott was confined to the first day.

But the vacation was short-lived. Midway

through the week at Highlander, a call came in to the school: Reverend Graetz's house, which was a half block from the Parks residence, had been bombed. The Graetzes had also been subject to an unending stream of threats (hate-filled callers day and night) and various acts of sabotage (including excrement being strewn in their house). With Parks in tow, the Graetzes left Highlander early—a much more somber drive than the trip up to Monteagle. "We were all tense, not knowing what we would find when we arrived home," Graetz recalled. No one had been hurt in the bombing, but the blast was so powerful it shattered the windows of several nearby houses.

The house was not as badly damaged as they had feared. "Unknown to Jeannie and me, Mrs. Parks quietly began sweeping the kitchen and picking up broken dishes." In describing this bombing of Graetz's house, Taylor Branch wrote that "an intrepid neighbor snipped the smoldering end off a fuse leading to eleven sticks of dynamite." This may have been Raymond Parks. Raymond also came over to help clean up the Graetz home.

Mayor Gayle accused the movement of staging the bombing. A week later, Graetz wrote the attorney general to criticize police malingering around the violence taking place in Montgomery and request that the Justice Department intervene.

THE BOYCOTT ENDS:
A HEROINE BETWIXT AND BETWEEN

On June 19, 1956, the U.S. Court for the Middle District of Alabama ruled for the plaintiffs in the *Browder* case, declaring that the "separate but equal" doctrine set forth by the Supreme Court in the 1896 *Plessy v. Ferguson* "can no longer be applied." Mass excitement rippled through Montgomery's black community. But the city appealed the decision to the Supreme Court. Then on November 13, 1956, the Supreme Court unanimously upheld the district court decision, nullifying Alabama's state and local laws requiring segregation on buses. Parks called it a "triumph for justice."

Mrs. Parks was serving on the MIA's publicity committee at this point. During the fall she journeyed to Baltimore, Cleveland, Columbus, and Savannah, helping build membership for the NAACP while bringing the news of the inspiring boycott to black communities across the country. She went to Memphis for a Women's Day program and to Birmingham for the Alabama State Coordinating Association for Registration and Voting. Then, in November, she embarked on another fund-raising tour for the NAACP to raise money for the national office and local branches, with a $25 stipend for her per branch.

A punishing ten-day schedule with ten separate speaking engagements, dinners, and other informal meetings began in Boston on November 10. Then she went to Springfield, Massachusetts; Albany, New York; Main Line, Pennsylvania; Corona-East Elmhurst, New York; Atlantic City and Trenton, New Jersey; and Brooklyn, the concluding stop, on November 20. Much of her travel was done by train—Boston to Springfield, November 12, Springfield to Albany, November 13. On November 14, she went from Albany to New York City, then later that day from New York to Philadelphia, and then late that evening from Philadelphia to Newark, arriving at 12:39 a.m. For the shorter distances, she took the bus. It was an enormously tiring agenda. Her speeches drew sizable crowds: 225 people turned out for the Corona Queens meeting, while in Springfield, nearly 400 people gathered to hear her speak. Durr wrote Horton that she wished he could join Parks in New York, "as she needs direction . . . yet she has the courage of a lion." By this point, Parks had raised thousands of dollars for the boycott and also for the NAACP. The travel had been heady; still, she told a *Jet* reporter in 1960 that it wasn't "as glamorous as it seems" and noted that none of it had netted her more than $100 beyond expenses.

The Supreme Court ruled in *Browder v. Gayle* against Montgomery's bus segregation on November 13, 1956, and its order mandating integration was received by city leadership on

December 20. The 382-day boycott drew to an end. For Rosa "it didn't feel like a victory, actually." Despite the momentousness, Parks knew there was still a great deal to do on the road to freedom. Jo Ann Robinson echoed this feeling:

> It was terrible to watch women and children weep, hearing the news, and even more awful to see grown black men stand and cry until their whole bodies shook with bitter memories of the past. . . . The victory, however, brought no open festivities, no public rejoicing in the streets. . . . Too many people had suffered too much to rejoice. . . . The time was too sacred, the need prayerful, the masses tearful and filled with thanksgiving.

For Parks, Robinson, and many others in the city, the boycott and resistance that ensued had taken a toll. The unity had been even more wondrous—sacred—and thus a certain solemnity greeted the end of the protest.

On December 20, 1956, a community that had walked and carpooled for more than a year stepped aboard the bus and sat where they pleased. Much of the media that day ignored Parks in favor of King and the other ministers. With the country transfixed by King's leadership, reporters and photographers descended on

Montgomery in droves to capture his reaction to bus desegregation, photographing him and other boycott leaders dozens of times early that December morning sitting in the front of the bus. "Some of the books say I was with them but I was not," Parks clarified. She was home looking after her mother, who was not feeling well.

It was *Look* magazine that found her at Cleveland Courts and staged the photo of her that would later become iconic. In it, Parks sits in a front seat looking out the window with a stone-faced white man sitting behind her. That man was not some Montgomery rider, however, but UPI reporter Nicholas Chriss. The photo was staged with Chriss posing as a fellow passenger. "A great scoop for me," Chriss wrote later, "but Mrs. Parks had little to say. She seemed to want to savor the event alone." In the midst of the photo shoot, they boarded a bus being driven by none other than James Blake. The reporter seemed oblivious to the historical irony. "We ignored each other," explained Parks. "Clearly he was not interested in being photographed with me, or any other black person for that matter." Despite being "apprehensive" and not "too happy about being there myself," Parks later described being "glad I let them take [the picture]."

Blake, who worked for the bus company until his retirement in 1974, never claimed his role in the drama and avoided most interviewers.

Reached in his home on the twenty-fifth anniversary of the boycott, Blake responded, "I am tired of being haunted by Rosa Parks." Blake's wife felt he had been unfairly maligned by the events. "None of that mess is true. Everybody loved him." Blake died in 2002, seemingly still bitter and unchanged. At a commemoration honoring the first black bus drivers a couple of years after Blake's death, however, some black drivers spoke about how they had worked closely in the union with Blake. They considered him an ally and spoke of how he had changed and did not want to be remembered only for the events of 1955.

E. D. Nixon later described the power of that December morning when Montgomery's buses were desegregated. "It's hard on me remembering that morning. . . . It was like it wasn't happening. Then it hit me . . . I cried like a baby." Nixon claims that he rode with Parks that day, though no other accounts have Nixon with her during the photo shoot. "And when I saw Rosa climb aboard and look around, her eyes glistening like I knew she, too, had been crying, I thought it was gonna come on me again, but it didn't. Her eyes caught mine, and we knew what we'd done, and we both grinned real big and didn't say nothing. . . . It was the best ride I ever had in my life, just riding through downtown and out to the west and back again, going nowhere but feeling like we was

313

heading to heaven." Whether this ride actually took place that day or another, the successful end of the boycott was not only the culmination of a year of work by Montgomery's black community, but for Nixon and Parks more than a decade of painstaking struggle. Nixon's characterization of a ride that felt like it was "heading to heaven" was testament to the near-religious experience of this victory.

Bus desegregation was met with a flurry of violence in Montgomery. King's door was destroyed by a shotgun blast on December 23. On January 9, 1957, four Baptist churches were bombed. Ralph Abernathy and Robert Graetz's homes were bombed and virtually destroyed. The Graetz family, including their new four-day-old baby, was asleep when the bomb was thrown. Luckily, no one was hurt, though the damage to the house was extensive. Mrs. Parks rushed over to help. A second attempt was also made on the King home. Virginia Durr wrote a friend about how "frightening" this new surge of violence was: "so complete, vicious . . . a real collapse of law and you know that you have no protection against people that hate you." And then a gas station was destroyed after one of the employees offered a description of the bombers.

Seven men were arrested for these bombings; because some of the bombs had not gone off, the grand jury only indicted four. Two were tried but "even with signed confessions," according to Parks, were acquitted. The other two were given amnesty. The boycott might be over but the violence and fear remained.

A NEW VOTER REGISTRATION CAMPAIGN?
Like many activists across the South, Nixon and Parks remained committed to the power of the black vote to break the back of white supremacy, seeing a statewide voter registration campaign as the next logical campaign after the boycott. Despite their earlier efforts, most black Alabamians were not registered to vote. Their idea was to base the project in Montgomery with an office in Fred Gray's law practice—and employ Parks full-time to coordinate it. The whole plan required about $3,000 a year—$25 for rent and $35 a month to pay Parks (considerably less than what she had earned at Montgomery Fair) plus expenses for phone and mailing—and had the added benefit of giving Parks steady work. With considerable organizational skills, Parks was already secretary for the district coordinating council and had long worked alongside Nixon on issues of black voter registration.

Virginia Durr also saw black voting power as imperative for changing the political landscape of Alabama—and believed Nixon and Parks had a political savvy that the MIA's leadership, including King, lacked. Durr regarded King's embrace of nonviolent direct action and desire to avoid partisan politics as somewhat naive. "While I think [King] is terrific as a spiritual leader," she wrote a friend, "he knows absolutely nothing about politics. . . . Mr. Nixon wants to play politics in the American tradition. . . . He thinks the Negroes should make it clear that they are going to depend on the Courts and on political action to back them as well as God."

Durr solicited her white colleagues on the Left at Highlander, SCEF, Emergency Civil Liberties Committee (ECLC), and other organizations to raise money for this voter registration program. She asked for Highlander's help in creating this program with a paid position for Parks. Horton wrote back that the plan was an "excellent" one but he could not commit to funding such a voter project in Montgomery (though Highlander would later help sponsor the citizenship schools). Apologizing for the mistaken belief that Highlander would have to provide all the money, Durr reminded Horton that "the South will not be safe until at least the elementary rights of free citizens are enjoyed here" and extolled Parks's virtues as a seasoned political organizer to push for Highlander's assistance. Durr wrote letter after letter seeking support for this project. Receiving a rejection from another colleague, she was livid, writing a friend, "So Rosa is left with nothing to do and no office and Mr Glen Smiley [of the Fellowship of Reconciliation, who was working closely with King] has the floor with LOVE LOVE LOVE." As 1957 began, Durr remained convinced that the next needed step was a mass voter-registration campaign. "Speeches, prayers, exhortations etc. do not take the place of block by block canvassing and having a central place and a voter's list and someone to keep after people all the time," Durr explained in an appeal to another political associate—and the person with the skills to coordinate it was Rosa Parks. Durr worried that if this voter registration program was taken up by the MIA, "Mrs Parks won't have a job there (the jobs all go to college people)."

Horton did invite Parks back to Highlander in December to meet with a group of black students from Clinton, Tennessee to discuss their recent experience with school desegregation. The students were in need of support—and Horton thought Parks was a good adult to provide such counsel. Nixon drove Rosa and her mother to Tennessee. "It was a rather unpleasant ride," Parks remembered, as Nixon was down on King and the MIA. Once they arrived at Highlander, according to Brinkley, "Everybody at the school, including Septima Clark, turned out to greet Parks like a conquering heroine, teasing her about her world fame and later reading Psalms 27 and 33 in her honor." Later in the week, Horton offered Parks a full-time job at Highlander. But Parks's mother said no. "She didn't want to be 'nowhere I don't see nothing but white folks,'" so that ended that," Parks explained. "Anyway, I was in no position to take off from Montgomery and stay somewhere else at that time." Septima Clark also maintained that Highlander wanted Parks to speak in parts of Alabama and Mississippi and Louisiana "but she didn't feel as if she could do it. She felt . . . that the hostility was so great. She didn't think that she could do that."

Bus desegregation did not improve the Parks family's personal situation. Both Rosa and Raymond still found white establishments unwilling to hire them, and the hate calls had not subsided. She took in sewing (and Raymond did some barbering), but this did not bring in much money because white people would not hire her. Though economic retribution imperiled many civil rights activists in Montgomery and elsewhere, the troubled economic situation the Parkses faced was distinct from that of most boycott leaders. King, Abernathy, Nixon, Robinson, Gray, Graetz, Pierce, and Simms all had jobs that continued through and after the boycott. Parks did not, but she largely shielded her need from public view. As Virginia Durr wrote a friend, "I cannot understand why the Negro community has not taken better care of her but it hasn't. She is a proud and reticent woman and that might be the reason. She does not mind receiving any money I get for her but cannot seem to get it for herself."

The plan of action Nixon and Parks put forward differed from the approach advocated by King and the ministers who in January 1957 formed the Southern Christian Leadership Conference. King and Abernathy thought their next target should be the airport, which Parks, along with Gray and Graetz, thought was foolish given how few blacks actually used the airport. But, the MIA's leadership was also wary of Nixon and Parks's voter registration project, fearing this new project sought to take the MIA's place. By late 1957, the SCLC would focus its energies on a Crusade for Citizenship, a Southern education, action, and mobilization campaign to encourage black voter registration—not completely dissimilar from Nixon and Parks's original plan.

Divisions between King and Nixon that had simmered during the boycott heated up in the MIA. And Parks sided with Nixon. Durr described the schisms as "the old class split" that had previously plagued Montgomery's NAACP, where some of the ministers treated Nixon and Parks with condescension. These class divides also had ideological components—the MIA leadership was wary of Nixon's militancy (connected as he was to A. Phillip Randolph),

319

and perhaps Parks's as well. Moreover, Nixon resented the ways the young King received all the credit and adulation for the movement at the expense of other leaders.

Parks's troubled economic situation became grist for the widening feud within the MIA. In a February 15, 1957, letter, Virginia Durr wrote a friend of the "blazing row" taking place within the organization; Parks has "been a heroine everywhere else, [but] they have not given her a job here although she has needed one desperately . . . She is very, very disgruntled with MLK and really quite bitter which is not like her at all." To another friend, Durr explained that while the MIA had $50,000 in reserve and a payroll of $500 a week, they refused to hire Parks. "They know she cannot get a job, they know she has suffered and is suffering and they blandly do nothing about it at all and this drives me nearly nuts and makes me distrust them very much indeed." In its surveillance of the Durrs, the FBI took notice of Durr's belief that the MIA "was controlled by a small clique" and her concern over Parks's situation.

The MIA did have money in its treasury. According to conservative estimates quoted in the *Pittsburgh Courier*, the MIA had raised $200,000—with Nixon acting as the treasurer. Though the MIA paid a number of people— $62.50 for a private secretary for King, $5,000 a year to its executive secretary as well as salaries to other staff workers—Parks was not offered a position. King historian David Garrow noted that "dissension developed over the organization's continued refusal to put Mrs. Parks, a Nixon ally . . . on the payroll." Birmingham author Diane McWhorter contends that SCLC cofounder Fred Shuttlesworth also criticized the MIA leadership for not taking care of Parks. Still everyone sought to keep the schisms behind closed doors. King later reflected, "Some people never knew the suffering she was facing." King knew about Parks's suffering, but his sympathies are unclear, since he seemingly could have assisted her. Many decades later, Robert and Jean Graetz talked about how "the world blamed all of us in Montgomery for not finding her a living" but said the community did not have the resources to do this for Parks or anyone else suffering from white retribution. Still, the Graetzes had no insight into why certain other people were hired by the MIA but not Mrs. Parks.

Gender had played a role in the organizational and leadership structure of the boycott. While women "really were the ones who carried out the actions," Erma Dungee Allen explained, the visible leadership was male. King, according to Septima Clark, "didn't respect women too much" and "never felt that women should have much of anything." This may have contributed to the

MIA's blindness to Parks's substantial need and to the decision within the organization not to offer Parks a position, despite her political experience and administrative skills. There were women employed by the MIA as office workers. But Parks did not have ties to any of the ministers, nor could she have simply been relegated to the role of acolyte. Mrs. Parks had a husband and no children, so given the gender conventions of the time, the ministers might not have seen her need. Moreover, on top of the more general gender biases, the construction of Parks as a symbol—a simple, tired heroine—made it difficult to see her as either a capable organizer or a martyr who had sacrificed much for the sake of the struggle. Parks's reserve and unwillingness to ask for help only furthered this omission. Finally, Reverend Fields's accusations of cronyism and mismanagement had scared and saddened King. Some of those charges had come indirectly from Nixon (MIA's treasurer), even though Nixon distanced himself from Fields. Relations between King and Nixon became strained after that. In some ways, for King to change course and hire Parks might have admitted to the cronyism in not hiring her a year prior.

The most compelling evidence of Parks's view that she was mistreated is an early outline of her autobiography, prepared with Jim Haskins in the late 1980s, that included an extra chapter entitled

"In the Shadows," which suggests how slighted she felt. The description for the proposed chapter notes,

> Jealousy and dissension within the Montgomery Improvement Association—Rosa Parks has lost her job at Montgomery Fair department store over the incident that sparked the boycott and feels that she should be given a job with the Montgomery Improvement Association—but King refuses, and Rosa feels angry—she goes through extreme financial difficulties—by the time Rosa is offered a job in the voter registration drive that King decides to start, she has accepted a job at Hampton.

Since no such chapter appears in the book, it may be that Parks ultimately felt this was better left in the past.

Little assistance was forthcoming. Parks went back to Highlander in February for another "Public School Integration" workshop. In March, Septima Clark wrote to Myles Horton that she had just answered a letter (from an undisclosed writer) that expressed distress regarding Parks's situation and anger at Highlander's inaction. Clark had apprised the writer that Horton "felt that the only way to do anything for Rosa in

Montgomery was to work through the M.I.A., and in that meeting you held while they were here you told them that a separate fund raising would back fire. . . . I further told them of the conversation I had with Rosa about not feeling like doing anything and that she had an offer to publish a book on the protest if she could take time out to write down the facts. I feel that the whole thing is largely emotional and not to be taken too seriously." The author of the letter was likely the white Southern liberal Aubrey Williams. According to Durr, Williams's dismay resulted in Highlander giving Parks $50 a month, "but it took them a long time to get around to it and only after Aubrey really blew his top. Myles took in over $69,000 last year and I think he can afford it very well." A couple months later, Durr wrote again, saying the Highlander money had only constituted one payment of $50 to Parks and that Aubrey Williams had again gotten angry with Horton for exaggerating the help Highlander was providing her.

Tensions mounted. A few months later, Nixon resigned from the MIA, writing to King, "I do not expect to be treated as a child." Despite his advocacy for her within the MIA, Nixon had also grown increasingly frustrated with Parks's national stature, seeing his own role go largely unacknowledged. When the national NAACP called inviting Parks to speak in DC, Nixon volunteered himself but was told they wanted "Sister Rosa." He exploded in anger at this slight. Later in 1957, Nixon was able to get some money to fund voter efforts through the MIA, but at this point Parks was no longer involved in the project.

The stress took its toll on Parks and her health suffered, though she continued to travel. Raymond's lack of steady work and drinking continued. Durr wrote a friend in April that she found Rosa and her mother ill and worried about her ability to withstand the pressure: "I am afraid she [Rosa Parks] is having some slight heart attacks and had one in Trenton, or nervous attacks or something." Unwell herself, Leona McCauley grew worried about her daughter's safety. According to a friend interviewed years later, Rosa's mother became "very suspicious because of the very underhanded things that have happened to her and her family since Rosa sat on that bus and refused to move." Her family urged Rosa to leave, according to the friend, "because they could see that Mrs. Parks never quit trying to help the NAACP or [stopped] any of her activity." Wanting to spend more time with Sylvester, Rosa's mother began to pressure Rosa and Raymond to move with her to Detroit.

Still Parks continued to make appearances for the movement. In May, billed as the "plucky woman . . . who refused to follow the usual handkerchief head," she embarked on another

NAACP fund-raising tour to Missouri and Kansas as a featured speaker to build local membership and raise money for the national organization. Then she journeyed on to Philadelphia where she spoke at a mass meeting with A. Phillip Randolph and on to Washington, DC, where she made a short speech at the Prayer Pilgrimage for Freedom. Nearly twenty-five thousand people gathered at the Lincoln Memorial on May 17, 1957, to commemorate the third anniversary of the *Brown* decision. The protest, organized by Randolph and Rustin, drew attention to Eisenhower's lack of leadership and to rising white violence. Initially, Rustin had stressed that King focus on "economic and social changes" but after reporters began to claim that the planning had been infiltrated by Communists, they tempered the message. Rustin urged Parks to emphasize the national character of the civil rights struggle and the importance of the vote and ending segregation—points that Parks was all too cognizant of.

By the summer, Rosa was in poor health and financial trouble and worried about Raymond's physical and mental health. White businesses were still unwilling to hire them, and sewing for black families brought in little money. With few economic prospects in the city and still receiving constant death threats, the Parkses decided to move to Detroit at the urging of her brother,

Sylvester. Given the conditions the family now faced in Montgomery, Raymond was much more amenable to leaving Alabama. "I always felt that I wanted to go somewhere else to live. But I probably couldn't have convinced my husband" until after the problems in Montgomery.

The decision also came partly from the unfriendly reception Rosa was receiving from certain members within Montgomery's civil rights community. Many had grown jealous of Parks's national stature and made disparaging remarks about both Rosa and Raymond. Even Nixon had grown resentful of her public profile. One minister referred to her as "an adornment of the movement," while Reverend Abernathy called Rosa a "tool" and referred to Raymond as a "frightened lush." The women plaintiffs of *Browder v. Gayle* resented how much attention Parks had received compared to them, as did Jo Ann Robinson, whose own boycott leadership was not fully recognized. Rosa was bewildered by the animosity and frustrated with the schisms in the MIA and her spirit had plummeted.

According to Brinkley, "Much of the resentment sprang from male chauvinism [from many of the ministers and E. D. Nixon]." That summer, Parks tacitly acknowledged the impact this bitterness had upon her in an interview with the *Pittsburgh Courier*. "I can't exactly say that the reaction from what happened in the boycott made me leave. I really had been thinking about leaving for a long time. But I guess something did have a part in our deciding to go, or rather my husband's deciding for us." In an interview in 1980, Virginia Durr noted, "I know people who have treated her very badly. . . . I could tell you a lot more that I'm not telling, because I wouldn't say anything that would embarrass Mrs. Parks."

Parks was a woman of action, but one who did not favor direct confrontation. Their decision to leave Montgomery in August 1957, eight months after the boycott ended, after having lived there together for twenty-five years, is revealing of her discontent—and it drew the attention of the black press. Calling her a "spunky little woman," Chester Higgins's article in the *Pittsburgh Courier* asked whether Parks was leaving "by choice": "Mrs. Parks was seldom mentioned as the real and true leader of this struggle. Others more learned—not to take a thing from Dr. King—were ushered into the leadership and hogged the show. . . . Perhaps as a proud and sensitive personality, she resented standing in the wings while others received the huzzahs. She wouldn't talk about this." What Parks was willing to say was, "After I was arrested on this charge, the white trade began to fall off. I simply didn't have enough work to keep me busy and I was politely laid off. The Negroes couldn't furnish me with enough work. My husband worked, it is true, but I have been working at my profession for years. I couldn't just sit and idle away."

Parks's comment is telling because she asserts her desire to work as not solely about needing the money but as part of her identity. Like civil rights pioneer Ida B. Wells a half century earlier, Parks had consciously decided not to go into teaching, despite her love of young people, because she found the conditions too degrading. And like Wells, who was run out of Memphis for her bold journalism around lynching, Parks found herself exiled from her hometown of more than thirty years because of her stand against segregation.

The black press began to take notice of the trouble and these divisions. "She got no part of the money being paid out by the MIA—of which she was the direct cause!" Trezzvant Anderson, a reporter for the *Pittsburgh Courier*, wrote incredulously in November. He spent a day with Parks as she prepared to move to Detroit. Explaining how Parks was an "expert seamstress" with some of the "city's very best among her steady customers," Anderson wrote that Parks "paid the price" for her refusal on the bus. Describing her with "dimmed tears in her eyes," "disillusioned," and "sick at heart," Anderson wrote that "not once did Rosa Parks grumble or complain."

The MIA newsletter of November 18 challenged the *Courier*'s account, claiming that "Mrs. Parks was not 'asked' but 'begged' by Dr. King to accept a job from the MIA office. She refused on the grounds that she was away from the city on speaking engagements too often." Parks had been employed for a month in March 1956 as a dispatcher. The MIA's rebuttal, however, was revealing. If true, then Mrs. Parks ultimately turned down a paid position with the MIA because she was doing too much public speaking on behalf of the boycott to be a responsible office assistant. This tendency corresponds to a similar situation that Congressman John Conyers recalled having with Parks decades later when she was working in his office. She had come in to talk to him about a wage reduction—"the only wage reduction conversation I've ever had" with any staff member, Conyers noted—because she felt she was away from the office too often on public appearances. He scoffed, telling her that he was honored to have her working in his office and doing public speaking. But years earlier, the MIA appears to have had a much different reaction to Mrs. Parks's concerns, raising the question of why they didn't create a position incorporating public appearances and office work.

The slightly critical tone Anderson took in the article must have drawn controversy. Both he and the *Courier* published statements to "set the record straight—the MIA gave her one $30 paycheck, a gift of $500 on the eve of her departure for Detroit, plus a donation of $300 during the boycott."

When interviewers touched on these subjects, Parks tended toward long pauses and halting statements. Some interviewers didn't inquire. In Parks's 1985 interview for *Eyes on the Prize*, when asked about how she got to work during the boycott, she noted being "discharged from my job after the first in January." The interviewer didn't pursue the issue. In Nixon's *Eyes on the Prize* interview, when he explained that Parks had to move to Detroit because "nobody would hire her," the interviewer said he thought Parks was working for him. Nixon grew flustered. "She wasn't working directly for me, she was workin' . . . at a clothes store when this thing happened." Then Nixon turned the conversation back to the arrest and there was no further discussion in this interview, or others, about any responsibility Nixon had for her situation.

Yet, in a 1970 interview, Nixon, while sidestepping his own responsibility, explained his frustration with the black community, and the ministers in particular, for not standing up for her.

> Mrs. Parks stood up for the black community. But the community didn't stand up for her, not by a long shot. The whites wouldn't give her a job, and the

Negroes wouldn't support her. One day I said to Reverend King, "With all the money we got here, Mrs. Parks ought to have a job—and we could give her $100 a month whether she got a job or not." He said, "I don't know, brother Nixon, we can't hardly do that." But when they bombed the Reverend King's parsonage, the Montgomery Improvement Association paid a guard $30 a week to be in the door and read the funny papers every night until it was morning. I know, because as the treasurer I signed the checks. When Mrs. Parks finally left Montgomery, the MIA had about $400,000. They could have taken $100,000 and set up a trust fund for Mrs. Parks, and with the $5000 a year interest she could have stayed here. But we done the same thing the white man wanted. After the whites made it hard for her to get a job, all the doors closed on her, and the Negroes kept them closed. . . . But everybody just forgot everything, went wild over King. I respect King, but I'm for Mrs. Parks, too. The point is that she should never have had to leave. But nobody would give a dime.

Nixon's frustration with how the ministers treated Parks dovetailed with his own disenchantment over the ways he'd been treated by King and the MIA and his role in the boycott ignored.

Militant blacks like Parks who publicly defied segregation were taught a lesson through economic intimidation. Particularly because Montgomery prided itself on its sophistication, getting a person fired was a more civilized way to maintain the racial status quo than physical violence. This tactic was widely used against civil rights activists. Historian Charles Payne has documented that every single woman voting rights activist he interviewed in Mississippi lost her job. To Nixon, the ministers' unwillingness to give Parks a stable position had served white interests. Other comrades echoed these sentiments. In a 1976 interview, Septima Clark criticized the boycott leadership's disregard for Parks. "I thought they should have put her down for a certain amount each year until she could find something to do."

Over the years, Mrs. Parks remained evasive on the subject. Resolutely self-sufficient, Parks said in a 1970 interview that she did not want to "place any blame on the community, because I do feel it was my responsibility to do whatever I could for myself and not to look to the community or to Dr. King or anyone else for my support or livelihood. I felt as long as I was well and could move around, I should be on my own, rather than looking to anyone to reimburse me or reward me for what I might have done." For a middle-aged, respectable race woman, asking directly for help or being publicly angry about the lack of help contradicted her sense of dignity. Parks was tender toward the suffering of others and, understanding the structures that produced such suffering and inequality, saw no shame in people needing help. But she was less able to publicly acknowledge her own need. Historian John Bracey has theorized that a race woman of Parks's era and temperament would have felt, "I should not have to ask for things. . . . You know what I did, who I am. If I have to go ask for it, I don't want it. You should keep me from suffering."

In deciding to pursue her bus case, Parks had committed herself to maintaining a certain comportment. The importance of furthering the struggle meant she would keep many of her personal difficulties to herself.

RED-BAITED

The trouble Parks encountered in finding work was not an isolated case but rather the result of a systematic effort to economically incapacitate anyone who pressed for civil rights, in part achieved by terming them subversives. "They always accused of being communists," Parks observed, "any body who stood up for their rights." As Eleanor Roosevelt had warned her,

Parks's political activities and connections led quickly to charges of Communism.

By the 1950s, the United States' Cold War with the Soviet Union had a rabid domestic side. Communists were feared to be infiltrating the fabric of American values and institutions, and Wisconsin senator Joseph McCarthy and a phalanx of politicians vowed to root them out at every turn. Civil rights activists became one of the prime targets. One of the curious features of civil rights red-baiting was how it had everything and nothing to do with Communism. From the 1930s, the Communist Party USA had been one of the few groups pursuing many of these racial cases; thus many current and former CP members, black and white, were part of the backbone of the struggle for racial justice. Nonetheless, vigorously advocating racial equality was one of the easiest ways to get labeled a Communist, regardless if you did it from a church pulpit, purged Communist sympathizers from your organization, were a WWII veteran and patriot, feared Communism yourself, or had no connections to anyone related to or sympathetic with the CP.

Flowering during the first days of the boycott, the red-baiting of Rosa Parks continued long afterward. Amid her attempts to maintain a low profile, Parks had not shied away from people on the Left. That continued even after she was targeted. She and Raymond had worked on the Scottsboro and Recy Taylor cases alongside CP members and affiliates. During the boycott, she had willingly associated with the National Negro Labor Council and Local 600, even as these groups were home to many black Communists. She personally knew a number of current and former black Communists and corresponded with them over the course of her life. In the spring of 1957, she was asked to speak to the Emergency Civil Liberties Committee (run by Durr's friends Corliss Lamont and Clark Foreman which formed in 1951 to defend political activists, including some Communists, from charges by the House Committee on Un-American Activities). NAACP director of branches Gloster Current warned her "of the 'leftist slant' " of the organization, and to "think it over carefully before accepting an engagement." Parks did not directly challenge Current but foregrounded the group's help in the boycott, redirecting how the conversation played out, and remained committed to giving the speech.

Parks understood the ways that challenges to the racial status quo led to claims of Communist subversion. Her longtime work with the NAACP had rendered her suspect, and she had given up her position in the organization to protect the boycott and "not have it said . . . [it] was organized by 'outside agitators.' " Indeed, in the wake of the *Brown* decision, the bus boycott, and Autherine Lucy's attempt to integrate the University of Alabama, the NAACP (despite its own internal red-baiting) was banned in Alabama, and in many other states, as a foreign corporation. Governor Patterson saw the organization "pos[ing] a threat to our citizens who have no recourse at law for injury done by the corporation to them," charging that the NAACP's actions "resulted in violations of our laws and end in many instances of breaches of the peace." Its membership records—which the NAACP refused to turn over—were demanded by the state, and the organization was fined $100,000.

Parks's ties to Highlander made her particularly suspect. On Labor Day weekend of 1957, Parks returned to Highlander for the twenty-fifth-anniversary celebration of the school. Celebrated in Highlander's press release as a featured speaker and leader, she described Montgomery as an "integration beachhead." Reverends King and Abernathy joined her there. During his keynote on the last day of the anniversary celebration, King affirmed the sentiment of those gathered: "You would not have had a Montgomery Story without Rosa Parks."

Abner Berry, a black writer for the Communist paper the *Daily Worker*, also attended the events, as did an undercover agent from the state of

337

Georgia, Edwin Friend, who took a series of photographs, including a picture of King, Parks, and Berry sitting in the audience. That photograph was subsequently displayed throughout the South as proof that King had attended "a Communist training center." When King came under attack for attending this Highlander celebration, photos revealed Parks visible by his side. Indeed, Parks would periodically remind people that she was the one who had actually attended Highlander's workshops and meetings, not King. "I had been there several times," Parks explained to Studs Terkel in 1973. "He only accepted an invitation to be the guest speaker when they had the 25th anniversary. He stayed just long enough to make a speech and to be on his way." Her clarification reflected Parks's core feistiness; if there was going to be red-baiting, she wanted accuracy in terms of who did what.

The school's commitment to interracialism signaled subversion to state authorities. Georgia's governor, Marvin Griffin, claimed Communist infiltration: "The leaders of every major race incident in the South" had all been to Highlander. In 1957, making liberal use of Friend's photographs, the Georgia Commission on Education published a broadside entitled *Highlander Folk School: Communist Training School, Monteagle, Tenn.: Every American Has the Right to Know the Truth.* The commission printed 250,000 copies, and factoring in reprints made by White Citizens' Councils and Klan groups, over one million copies of the brochure were distributed by 1959.

Preserved in the papers that Parks donated to the Wayne State library twenty years later was an original copy of the pamphlet. The broadside began,

> On the preceding pages you have seen pictures of the leaders of every major race incident in the South from May 1954 until the time of this meeting, Labor Day, 1957 Weekend. . . . It has been our purpose, as rapidly as possible, to identify the leaders and participants of the Communist training school and disseminate this information to the general public. This Commission would appreciate you furnishing to us any further identifications you can make . . . Only through information and knowledge can we combat this alien menace to Constitutional government.

It unfolds to feature fifteen pictures with captions. Five have Rosa Parks plainly visible (though captions only mention her in four). Curiously, there is no mention of her in the caption of the photo of King, Berry, Horton, and Parks, though she is clearly visible. By the mid-

1960s, this picture would be plastered on billboards across the South accusing King of attending a "Communist training school." For someone who eschewed the limelight as much as Parks, such attention was agonizing.

Covered up in the national fable, Rosa Parks was actually viewed as a subversive threat for the better part of two decades. The brochure's captions identify her as "one of the original leaders of the Montgomery bus boycott" and "the central figure in the agitation which resulted in the Montgomery Bus Boycott." Another description disparages the ability of Montgomerians to have independently executed the successful boycott, which called for "planning and direction beyond the ability or capacity of local people." Within the racial imagination of the brochure's writers, the effectiveness of the boycott could only be possible with the involvement of the Communist Party.

When *Pittsburgh Courier* reporter Trezzvant Anderson investigated the brochure's allegations of Communist infiltration, commission head T. V. Williams coyly equivocated—"I didn't say Rosa Parks was a Communist"—but maintained these race leaders had convened at Highlander under Communist auspices. When asked for proof of Parks's Communist affiliations, Williams insisted to Anderson there was a file, but that he simply could not find it at the moment.

Regarding Parks as a dangerous leader and

powerful instigator, white officials saw nothing random or accidental about her protest. Aware of some of the "trouble" she had caused long before the boycott, they knew "what she was after"— and it was not just a seat on the bus. White officials and citizens harassed her accordingly. For much of the 1950s and 1960s, Parks's address was often included in the media coverage about her, and much of the hate mail she received excoriated her as a traitor.

However frightening this harassment was, Parks did not shy away from her connection to Highlander even as the school got red-baited by state authorities. In 1959, local police, on the orders of the state attorney general, raided Highlander. Parks wrote Clark in August 1959 "anxious" to know what happened and offering "to do what ever I can." She longed to start a local Highlander support group but did not have the "strength and energy" to make the contacts. Having read that the court was trying to close Highlander, she observed, "It seems so hopeless at times, but with so many taking a stand, something will have to happen."

MOVING ON

Besides her brother Sylvester, Rosa's first cousins Thomas Williamson and Annie Cruse had also moved to Detroit. The hate calls to the Parks's home in Montgomery had continued unabated, and their incessancy bespoke a credible threat. Rosa was deeply shaken—and ready to leave Alabama. So was Raymond. Hearing this and fearing for their lives, Williamson quickly cobbled together $300 to wire the family so they could make the trip. Parks explained the decision as "the best thing I could do at the time."

Chagrined by Rosa's decision to leave, local activists rallied. Ralph Abernathy went to her home to apologize and asked her to stay. As a going-away present, the MIA raised $500 through donations solicited at churches around Montgomery and on an evening in late August hosted a service for the couple, crowded with well-wishers, at St. Paul's AME Church. According to Durr, Parks gave a "wonderful" speech in which she "told them that they could never win unless they fought for the right of everyone to have opportunities, and not just themselves."

A decade later, Nixon recalled his own speech that evening: "Here we forgot about this woman who's responsible for all that's happened in Montgomery and throughout the South and glorified a man who was made because of her. . . . I told the women, 'At least I'd expect you to help fight to see that Mrs. Parks don't leave town.'" Nixon criticized those gathered for "raising a little pitiful seven or eight hundred dollars and . . . then stick your chest out and think you've done something." It is not clear whether Nixon actually made such a critical speech that night, or just wished he had. The money raised that evening, according to her family, accounted for nearly all the resources the Parks family had when they arrived in Detroit.

And so in August 1957, the Parks family bade a bittersweet goodbye to Alabama. The transition to Detroit was not easy, though they welcomed the chance to be near family. Shortly after arriving in Detroit, she wrote King a letter thanking him and the MIA for the "kindness and generosity shown us before our departure from Montgomery." She had "no words of expression of gratitude for what has been done to help us. It will always be among my most cherished memories." She was "sorry to leave at this time" but "perhaps it was best" since her mother was happy to be near Sylvester, and Raymond was working and "improving in every way."

Still, Parks missed "the people I had been seeing. Going to the various meetings. Something to think about." Right around the time the family moved to Detroit in August, she had gone to visit Hampton Institute in Virginia. Alonzo Moron, the head of Hampton, whom Parks knew from Highlander, offered her a job as hostess at the Holy Tree Inn, a guest house on campus. In September, she headed out for another NAACP fund-raising tour and in October moved to Hampton. "After so much turbulence, ill-will, heartache and uprooting," Parks told a reporter, "I am looking forward with great pleasure to my work on this serene beautiful college campus." It is a testament to the dire economic situation that her family was facing—and her own sense of autonomy—that she went by herself to work at Hampton.

Her time there was somewhat difficult. The job was quite "confining and at times boring." She missed Raymond and wrote to her mother about being lonely "because none of the people here are concerned about me except for my service on the job." She knew her family needed the money. The job came with a yearly salary of $3,600, and she was resolved to stay. Parks's ulcer was bothering her; she was having trouble eating solid food and had lost much weight. Most of her clothes no longer fit, but she did not have the time to alter them. She was being looked after by a doctor for free, she wrote her mother, because "I am the Rosa Parks of the Montgomery Bus Protest." Over the year Rosa spent at Hampton, her mother wrote numerous times about the financial difficulties the family was having back in Detroit, asking occasionally for money. In one painful letter, Leona McCauley describes how Sylvester was working but had not gotten paid and how his wife and children were crying because they had no food. Raymond was hospitalized in July 1958 for pneumonia. This worried Parks greatly, particularly because she was so far away and the hospital care that black people received in Detroit was meager, the facilities inferior to those of whites.

Mrs. Parks appreciated the Hampton students and took heart in their energy. In 1958, she returned to Montgomery for a visit and "found the bus situation much improved." Durr urged her to move back. Rosa had gone alone to Hampton, with the expectation that the college would soon provide housing so Raymond and her mother could join her. The college did not—and so after finishing out the fall semester in 1958, Mrs. Parks returned home to Detroit for the holidays and stayed.

In the aftermath of the boycott, many people's roles had been overlooked as the lion's share of public attention had focused on King. According to E. D. Nixon, neither he nor Mrs. Parks had been invited to the third anniversary celebration of the Montgomery bus boycott's victory. The coverage Parks received in the black press during this period began to highlight how she had been "forgotten" and not given her due. In April 1958, announcing a talk she was giving in Pittsburgh, the reporter observed, "While the remarkable leadership ability of the Reverend Martin Luther King has been hailed throughout the world, there are many of us who have lost sight of the fact that it was the quiet unassuming seamstress whose courage set the boycott in motion." In a curious way, being forgotten had become part of Parks's appeal, demonstrating her modesty and humility.

JOBLESS IN DETROIT

The period after her return to Detroit from Hampton was a difficult one for Parks. She saved $1,300 while at Hampton, but that was quickly spent. Her nieces and nephews dubbed her "Recycling Queen" and "Mrs. Thrifty" because she conserved everything. No food was ever wasted, and Rosa's mother "knew how to prepare a meal from nothing." Having been ill in January and February, Parks wrote Septima Clark in May that she was feeling better now, but Raymond was out of work and "unhappy and wants to leave here." She was sewing for a shop and doing piecework at home. "I hope things will get better, or I don't know what we will do." After decades of barbering in Alabama (which didn't require barbering licenses), Raymond found Michigan's training and licensing requirements dispiriting and remained unemployed for most of 1959, but ineligible for unemployment compensation. Physically unwell and worried about money, Parks was making do with clothes donated to her, having not bought material for a new dress since March 1957. They tried to buy a new refrigerator only to be told their credit "hadn't gone through." They supplemented with food grown in

Sylvester's garden, and her cousins also pitched in to help.

In May 1959, the *Michigan Chronicle* published an article on Parks's difficult economic situation, entitled "Alabama Boycott Heroine Can't Find a Job!" "We're not sorry" about the move, Parks told the interviewer. "It's just that work is hard to find." In her understated way, Parks highlighted the discriminatory job situation blacks faced in Detroit—which, in her case, was compounded by the ways her own activism certainly did not make her a sought-after employee. Indeed, black women migrants tended to fare less well economically than black men in the North. And there had been no welcome wagon from white liberals for a woman activist fleeing the South.

Upon moving to the city, the Parkses had lived with various family members before renting an apartment on Euclid. In June of 1959, Parks wrote to Clark that she needed to "move to a cheaper place but rent is so expensive if a house is fit to live in. I can not pay the down payment on a house because I do not earn enough to pay for just living expenses." Housing segregation in Detroit drove up rents for black families compared to white families and drove down upkeep by landlords, as black people continued to be crowded into certain neighborhoods. Clark wrote Parks in September urging fortitude:

"Rosa, a leader must have personal strength to withstand all the destructive . . . Things are hard at times but just keep working and something is bound to give."

Forced to give up their seventy-dollar-a-month apartment in October 1959 because they could not afford it, the family moved into two rooms at the Progressive Civic League meeting hall. The PCL was a west-side Detroit group comprised largely of black professionals, and a forerunner to the more active civil rights groups in the city that sprang up in the 1960s. The rent was forty dollars, with Raymond serving as the caretaker and Rosa the treasurer manager of the PCL's credit union and house manager for the owner.

As in Montgomery, the civil rights community (white and black) didn't offer her any employment. "I didn't get any work," Parks noted, "but I went to a lot of meetings and sometimes . . . they would take up contributions, but that was never high." Disregarded by many white employers and unknown to many white liberals who had become transfixed with King's leadership, Mrs. Parks found a relatively closed labor market in her new Northern home. She also sat at the fissures of class, education, and age within the black community. With decades of political experience and administrative skill, the middle-aged Parks was no acolyte. Given her long political history and her fame from the boycott, and even despite her reserved personality, she would not blend into the background of an organization. She had been one of the MIA's best speaker/fund raisers and had brought in considerable money and membership for the NAACP. Yet curiously, in the first years following their move to Detroit, Parks seemingly was never asked to address the Detroit NAACP. Daisy Bates came in May 1958 and spoke to an overflow crowd of more than 1,800 people.

Additionally, Mrs. Parks did not have a college education at a time when the NAACP and other black organizations often required one for salaried positions. And she was a woman when much of the prominent civil rights leadership consisted of men. All this may have blinded many black leaders to Parks's employment needs and the skills she would have brought to any organization. Correspondence between the Detroit chapter of the NAACP and the national office reveals Parks's dire situation (and organizing talents) were simultaneously acknowledged and erased. In late 1957, Herbert Wright of the national office requested that Detroit organizers invite Parks for the youth conference being planned by the Detroit branch. The NAACP leadership was thus not only aware that the Parks family had moved to Detroit but also cognizant of her background organizing young people. In the years following the Parks's move, the Detroit

NAACP did not sponsor an event in her honor or help secure employment for her or Raymond, though they did make inquiries for other NAACP stalwarts or Southern civil rights exiles. Even though her troubled situation became the focus of a *Chronicle* article in May 1959, it would be another eighteen months, late in 1960, before the NAACP stepped in to help.

By the winter of 1960, Parks's health had deteriorated, though Raymond was feeling better, working at the Magby Barber Shop and moonlighting at another shop, usually earning between fifteen and twenty dollars a week. "He is much stronger and taking the family responsibility since my illness is so prolonged," Parks wrote to Clark. "He does not earn much money but does the best he can under existing conditions." Rosa had lost thirty pounds. Hospitalized in December at the Lakeside Medical Center, she had an operation for the ulcer that had been plaguing her since the boycott. But they did not have the money to pay the $560 medical bill, and a large portion went into collection. They slowly chipped away at the bill, $10 a month. Moreover, Parks had a tumor on her throat that needed to be surgically removed. This was a bleak time.

In March 1960, hearing of King's arrest on tax charges, Parks wrote him a letter praising his continued efforts in spite of segregationist attempts to "intimidate and embarrass you." She explained that she was "not well but better than I was sometime ago." King seems to have alerted the MIA because the organization sent her a donation in March. Surprised at the severity of Parks's situation, the MIA's September newsletter noted, "All freedom fighters should know that temporary relief will not meet the great need of Mrs. Parks. There must be some long-term planning." It also pointedly observed, "there was no person more loyal to the NAACP than Mrs. Parks while it operated in the State of Alabama"—the implication being that her plight was the responsibility of the NAACP, not the MIA, which the NAACP took note of in private correspondence between Gloster Current and Roy Wilkins.

In May, Parks wrote Clark to tell her that she was feeling better. Keeping "very busy," she was "quite confined here at the place where I live" but still planned to attend the upcoming workshop at Highlander at month's end. Highlander had announced a May meeting focused around the black student sit-ins rippling through the South. The point of this workshop—entitled "Are White Southerners Wanted in the Negroes' Current Struggle for Justice?"—was to discuss the position of whites, as well as black adults, in the burgeoning sit-in movement. The student lunch counter sit-in movement had been ignited on

February 1, 1960, when four college freshmen in Greensboro, North Carolina, sat down at a segregated Woolworth's lunch counter and asked to be served. Within days and weeks, these sit-ins, spearheaded by black college students, grew and rippled across the South. Many made the connection between Parks's action and these direct-action protests.

Parks attended the Highlander meeting in May 1960, explaining the inspiration the student sit-inners provided: "We decided with these setbacks and reprisals, we still cannot afford to give up . . . we couldn't consider it a lost cause because out of [these difficulties] . . . there comes a new and young fresh group of people who have taken this action in the sit-in demonstrations and [it] seems that they have put more pressure to bear than many of us have done in the past." Like Ella Baker, Mrs. Parks found the militancy of these young people refreshing.

Parks repeatedly stressed perseverance and highlighted the importance of reaching out to the mainstream (white) press so they "will not have the excuse of saying that you never complained or you never told us what you want and therefore we took for granted that you were satisfied." By this point, Parks had been doing this sort of press work for more fifteen years, laboring to get a white media to take white brutality against blacks and the violation of black rights seriously. "No cause is lost" she explained to those gathered, if it "destroy[s] the myth of the validity of segregation in South." But she did not think they should expect to win immediately. "We'll have to keep on going back again and again and again." Certainly her talk of perseverance was laced with her own troubles and her determination to persist in the midst of them.

She also spoke about the backlash against these efforts, referring to the tendency to call civil rights activists socialists as a way to silence them. Parks also stressed that eventually everyone should "[work] together for peace, world peace and disarmament and do away with war." Parks continued to be undeterred by the charges of Communism that followed people who advocated desegregation and disarmament in 1960. After the workshop, Clark sent her a check, clearly aware of the Parks's financial situation. Like Durr, Clark also tried to help raise money and call attention to Parks's financial situation.

Since the fall, the Parkses had been living at the Progressive Civic League apartment. That spring, the PCL held a program to call attention to Parks's recent medical costs, raising $153.20 for Parks and her family. Parks's precarious situation began to draw coverage in the black press. Given how private Parks was, this media attention to her personal troubles must have been embarrassing and saddening. It speaks to her sense of desperation regarding their situation that she gave specifics in these interviews. Perhaps also she took pleasure in the ways others were outraged on her behalf. Having always found it easier to have others advocate for her, telling her story and letting others draw the conclusions and express the indignation may have been the only way she was comfortable testifying to her imperiled situation.

Jet magazine ran a vivid and damning article in July 1960 on the "bus boycott's forgotten woman." They described Parks, whom they'd interviewed earlier, during the boycott, and now again in Detroit, as a "tattered rag of her former self— penniless, debt-ridden, ailing with stomach ulcers and a throat tumor, compressed into two rooms with her husband and mother." The article detailed the poverty the Parkses were facing, while noting that she had helped raise thousands of dollars for churches and the NAACP during the boycott. "If I had it to do all over again," Parks explained to the reporter, "I would still do it even though I know what I know now." Parks had written to tell Clark that *Jet* was doing this piece on her situation and "need of financial help." She certainly understood that a piece in *Jet*, the most widely read black magazine of the time, was a powerful act—and perhaps she was glad for the ways she could speak her own truth.

In July 1960, the *Pittsburgh Courier* ran an

article entitled "Rosa Parks Forgotten by Negroes: Montgomery Heroine in 'Great Need.'" The piece asked people to send money to Parks directly or to the Southern Conference Educational Fund (SCEF) run by Ann and Carl Braden. During this period, SCEF, like Highlander, was red-baited by the federal government, termed "a communist transmission belt for the South." Still, it is revealing that it was left organizations (in part through Durr's influence), rather than the SCLC or NAACP, that put out a broader call regarding the Parks's need. The call was picked up in the *Los Angeles Sentinel* and the *Los Angeles Tribune*, which explained that she had been "hospitalized for long and expensive treatment" and "has not recovered her strength sufficiently enough to work." Subsequent articles in the *Sentinel* and *Tribune* self-servingly praised local efforts at fund-raising for Mrs. Parks. She received $200 from a *Southern Patriot* article. In July 1960, the King Solomon Church in Detroit honored Parks as "The Forgotten Woman" in an event with representatives from twenty other churches around Detroit. A series of big and small donations rolled in. Parks's situation had drawn the concern of many ordinary people throughout the country. As compassionate as this help was, it still did not result in stable employment.

Over the summer, union activists of the more militant River Rouge-Ecorse NAACP branch wrote the national NAACP office of their plans to co-sponsor a fund-raiser for Mrs. Parks. River Rouge-Ecorse was a bedroom community of Detroit, abutting the Ford Motor Company's River Rouge complex. The branch, which counted numerous autoworkers and other members who lived in Southwest Detroit, wanted to raise money for Mrs. Parks as part of a fund-raiser for Local 600's Carl Stellato's bid for Congress. The September rally at Ecorse High School stadium, which honored Parks, drew two hundred people and collected $387.21 (with $100 from Local 600 itself). There, Parks gave a moving account of the boycott.

River Rouge NAACP branch president Lasker Smith (also of Local 600) explained to Gloster Current, director of branches, that Parks was "experiencing acute financial hardships stemming from her sparking the Montgomery, Alabama bus boycott," that she had been of service to the branch, and that they felt "an organized effort to aid Mrs. Parks is a responsibility which cannot be evaded." Indeed, it was the militant trade unionists of this little branch that forced the Detroit and national NAACP offices to address Mrs. Parks's plight.

The River Rouge-Ecorse NAACP branch under Smith's leadership had cut a far different path from the larger, more middle-class Detroit branch. The branch had drawn controversy in

1959 for boycotting the River Rouge Savings Bank because of its refusal to hire black people. The national office disapproved of the boycott. Smith, a self-described militant autoworker, was elected branch president in 1960. Under his leadership, the branch invited militant NAACP leader Robert F. Williams to speak and—to the chagrin of the national office, which asked them to retract—sponsored a resolution decrying the assassination of Congo prime minister Patrice Lumumba and calling on the national NAACP to condemn the murder. Smith alludes to Parks's participation in various branch events, though it is unclear from public records which ones she attended. However, River Rouge's activism likely corresponded more to her political sensibility than the Detroit branch did in this period.

In November 1960, long after Mrs. Parks had been hospitalized with ulcers, after numerous articles had run in the black press about her situation, and after the hospital bill had gone into collection, the national NAACP finally responded to her need. Current asked Smith to look into Parks's situation. Smith wrote that Parks was seeking employment, "however, at present, her health is a definite threat to her ability to undertake any type of permanent employment," and concluded, "Mrs. Parks is experiencing a number of anxieties, but she has a great reticence for making a major issue of her needs; she is reluctant to become the 'charge' of any group or agency. . . . Because of her reservations to discuss these things we did not get into matters such as the present extent of her indebtednesses or estimates of the cost of her present medical needs." Smith finished his report, dutifully adding that Parks thanked Current for his concern.

Current followed up, asking Smith to arrange a meeting with Parks to talk about her situation in person. Dismayed by Parks's troubled situation and angered by the media coverage, Current wrote privately to Wilkins after seeing the *Jet* article, "This case may well plague us in the future." For his convenience, Current met Parks at Detroit's Metro Airport, avoiding going out to her apartment. There he assured Mrs. Parks "that the NAACP was interested in her welfare and that of her husband; that we have always been interested in those who have worked with us, and who because of no fault of their own were victimized by experiences such as her own." Current sought to avoid future scandal, and apprised Wilkins that he had informed Parks that the NAACP wanted to hear from her directly if she experienced financial difficulties so they could be helpful. Having communicated to Parks that the organization was not happy with the publicity, Current wrote Wilkins:

She agreed that the publicity had not been helpful, but it grew out of the desire on the part of some individuals to raise money to help her. . . . She did not in any manner wish to cause the NAACP any embarrassment, but the newspaper reporters and Jet, which picked up the story from the Chronicle, had made more of it than perhaps they should have. Mrs. Parks is not a mean or vicious individual, but I suspect that the reporters led her on to making assertions which, in cold objectivity, can reflect upon the Montgomery Improvement Association, and even upon the Association.

To counter Current's displeasure at this publicity, Parks seems to have invoked the distress of others over her situation as the justification for these articles; once again she articulated her own need through other people's attention, perhaps implicitly noting the lack of urgency or care over her situation by the national NAACP office.

Current appears more concerned with protecting the NAACP's reputation than for Parks herself. Skipping over her decade of able service as the secretary of the Montgomery and Alabama chapters and the considerable fund-raising that Parks had done for the organization in 1956 and 1957, Current acknowledged her "useful qualities as a receptionist, insurance agent or worker," noting "of course she cannot actually go out in the field and sell insurance because of her health." He also sent a letter to the executive secretary of the Detroit branch, Arthur Johnson, about Parks's need and mentioned that she "would appreciate" steady employment. Current informed Johnson that the national office would pay the rest of the hospital bill "so that Mrs. Parks will not have this matter to worry her" and arrange dental visits for her and Raymond. But the local branch was supposed to look after her employment needs—either, Current suggested, a sewing job or an office job. Curiously, there was no suggestion that the NAACP could hire her. While records reveal that Current (who hailed from Detroit himself) sought jobs for people in need in Detroit—for other activists fleeing Southern tyranny or for those who had performed invaluable service for the organization—the Parkses seemingly were never beneficiaries.

By the spring of 1961, Parks's health had improved, and she and Raymond had found more steady employment. They had moved into a downstairs flat on Wildermere and Virginia Park in the Virginia Park neighborhood. Raymond was working around the corner at the Wildermere Barber Shop. Vonzie Whitlow, who apprenticed for Raymond there from 1961 to 1963, recalled long hours at a shop filled with talk, from baseball to politics, and Raymond's "excellent" skills: "Raymond bragged on his razor—'It could shave a baby's face' he would say." Rosa had found a job at the Stockton Sewing Company, a storefront factory crowded with sewing machines and ironing boards. The work was difficult and exhausting but steady. She made seventy-five cents a piece and worked ten hours a day.

Typical of her understated political edge, she told Septima Clark she was sending "several pieces of clothing to the 'victims of eviction' in Tennessee" (Highlander had just been evicted from its buildings in Monteagle). In 1962, Parks displayed her time-tested resolve when she agreed to be a Highlander sponsor, as did Reinhold Niebuhr. Faced with the repressive atmosphere of the Cold War and the direct targeting of Highlander, many people were unwilling to associate their name publicly with a "red" organization. But she wrote Horton that she was "very willing and also happy to be asked."

The coverage of Parks ricocheted through the black press. In December 1961, the *Baltimore Afro-American* ran an article entitled "Alabama Bus Boycott Heroine Now Living Quietly in Detroit." Underplaying her political commitments, the piece claimed Parks was living "a quiet and practically secluded life" and briefly mentioned that work for her was "scarce." A recurring sense of shame also ran through the coverage of Parks's situation in the black press. In 1963, *Chicago Defender* columnist Al Duckett described a recent collection taken for Mrs. Parks. "I do not know whether the collection taken for Mrs. Parks was an appreciation, gesture, or aid to her in time of need. All I can say is that if this race of mine is so ungrateful as to allow a Rosa Parks to be in need, then we don't deserve freedom." Still Parks's meager situation and simple life underlined her righteousness—and by extension the movement's—and so over the years, Parks's overlooked difficult situation almost became a trope in the black press to demonstrate the purity of the struggle. And perhaps for Parks herself, this became a catch-22, her own righteousness linked to her quiet suffering.

Over the years, Parks came to gloss over this difficult decade. All her autobiography mentions is work for a seamstress friend and then later in a clothing factory—and moving to a lower apartment on Virginia Park. But she included nothing of the deep suffering of this period. Following Parks's lead, historian Doug Brinkley claims that upon returning from Hampton, "Parks had little trouble finding a job . . . [and] was grateful for the grueling job [at Stockton's] and the steady income it provided to support her husband and mother." Allowing her troubles to be seen in public ran counter to her sense of decorum. The attitude evidenced in the NAACP's dealings with her—as they sought to contain the damage of the *Jet* article to the organization and manage her case—likely hurt and embarrassed her. While she might have been compelled to speak about her situation when her family's need had been so dire, there was no point in revisiting it.

POVERTY AND GLORY:
A MASS MOVEMENT FOR CIVIL RIGHTS

The Parks family's suffering occurred against the backdrop of a growing mass movement. Indeed, as her family struggled to regain its economic and psychic footing, the movement she loved and had helped to cultivate was growing in size and stature. In the spring of 1963, the campaign by King and the SCLC against downtown segregation and white violence in Birmingham had successfully drawn action from the Kennedy administration. In May, Kennedy sent a civil rights bill to Congress. The SCLC considered Parks an honorary member and called on her periodically to aid in their work or attend their events. By 1963, the SCLC had also named an award in Parks's honor. According to Diane McWhorter, Parks "had moved into the secure haven of 'legend,' her actual service as a Movement figure having been abridged by the Big Boys in the Montgomery Improvement

Association." Despite the regard it showed for Parks, this award didn't actually help with her difficult financial situation or recognize her considerable political and organizing talents. (Parks herself would not be awarded the Rosa Parks Award until its tenth year in 1972.)

Parks was also asked to come to Washington, DC, in August to be part of the March on Washington. Seventy-three-year-old A. Phillip Randolph had put out the call for the march to commemorate the one-hundred-year anniversary of the Emancipation Proclamation and the social and economic inequities that still wracked the nation. Randolph enlisted longtime organizer Bayard Rustin to help him organize this march for jobs and justice, which called for the passage of the Civil Rights Act, integration of public schools, a fair employment practices bill, and job training—and massive civil disobedience. The choice of Rustin as organizer was a controversial one. A gay socialist and pacifist, Rustin had briefly been involved in the Young Communist League in the 1930s (quitting in 1941), gone to jail in opposition to military service in World War II, and been arrested with a male lover on a "morals charge" in the 1950s. He was under scrutiny from the FBI and criticized by other civil rights leaders. Still, Randolph refused to bow to pressure to get rid of Rustin.

In order to get the National Urban League and

the NAACP to join, Randolph and Rustin gave up their plans for civil disobedience. President Kennedy feared that the march would be too radical and too critical of the federal government and that his civil rights bill wouldn't pass. He began putting pressure on the march's organizers to cancel it, and when they refused, Kennedy began lobbying for them to soften the message and succeeded in getting the march's themes changed to unity and racial harmony, a cry to "pass the bill," and no civil disobedience. Many in SNCC disagreed with this shift. According to SNCC chairman John Lewis, "a protest against government neglect was being turned into a propaganda tool to show the government as just and supportive." Not all civil rights activists accepted these compromises; Malcolm X was in DC during the march but termed it a "farce on Washington" for the concessions the leadership had made to placate the Kennedys.

The march itself now is remembered in a nostalgic glow as an inspirational and quintessentially American event, but at the time, it was dreaded and feared by many white Americans. In a *Wall Street Journal* poll taken in the days leading up to the march, two-thirds denounced the idea as "un-American." Most newspapers, as well as many politicians, predicted violence, and Washington, DC, police were on highest alert. NAACP president Roy Wilkins remembered that

Washington "seemed paralyzed with fear of black Americans" and the Kennedy administration "had the army preparing for the march as if it were World War II." Even when the fears of violence proved unfounded, the *Wall Street Journal* remained critical: "This nation is based on representative Government not on Government run by street mobs, disciplined or otherwise."

Despite public disapproval, the march was glorious and peaceful. On August 28, 1963, over 250,000 people came on freedom buses, cars, and trains to participate—some estimated the crowd numbered as many as 400,000 people. A coalition of religious, civil rights, and labor groups, black and white, packed the Mall that day. Dressed formally in a white jacket, black dress, gloves, and hat, Rosa Parks sat up on the dais that August afternoon. Her niece recalled staying up the night before Parks left working on the outfit.

As magnificent as the day was, the lack of recognition for women's roles was readily apparent, and Parks was increasingly disillusioned by it. No women had been asked to speak. Seeing how the program had emerged, Pauli Murray had written A. Phillip Randolph criticizing the sexism. Anna Arnold Hedgeman had also objected, asserting that the march should really be called "Rosa Parks Day" since Parks had started it all. Dorothy Height, president of the National Council of Negro Women, pressed for a more substantive inclusion of women in the program. Their criticisms were rebuffed as demands for inappropriate, sex-specific recognition, at odds with the spirit of the event. Plus, march organizers worried about how to pick one woman; the idea that multiple women might speak was too far-fetched to contemplate.

As a result, a memo was circulated, explaining Rustin and Randolph's proposed resolution to the problem:

> The difficulty of finding a single woman to speak without causing serious problems vis-à-vis other women and women's groups suggest the following is the best way to utilize these women: That the Chairman would introduce these women, telling of their role in the struggle and tracing their spiritual ancestry back to Sojourner Truth and Harriet Tubman. As each one is introduced, she would stand for applause, and after the last one has been introduced and the Chairman has called for general applause, they would sit.

This "Tribute to Women" would highlight six women—Rosa Parks, Gloria Richardson, Diane Nash, Myrlie Evers, Mrs. Herbert Lee, and Daisy Bates—who would be asked to stand up and be recognized by the crowd. No woman would give an address to the crowd.

Led by men, the main march, with Randolph at the head and King and others a few paces behind, processed down Constitution Avenue to the Lincoln Memorial; the wives of the leaders were not allowed to march with them. The five women honored (Myrlie Evers had made a previous commitment to be in Detroit) led a small side march along Independence Avenue to the Lincoln Memorial. They sat silently on the dais. Fellow activist Gloria Richardson recalled that the gendered treatment began before the event began. The NAACP had called Richardson beforehand, instructing her not to wear jeans but instead a hat, gloves, and a dress. Richardson did not appreciate the dress code requirements and scoured the Eastern Shore of Maryland till she found a jean skirt. Then, on the actual day of the march, Richardson got left behind in the march tent, and her seat in the front row was taken.

Daisy Bates introduced the tribute to women, a 142-word introduction written by John Morsell that provided an awkwardly brief recognition of women's roles in the struggle for civil rights. She began, "Mr. Randolph, the women of this country pledge to you, Mr. Randolph, to Martin Luther King, to Roy Wilkins, and all of you fighting for civil liberties, that we will join hands with you, as women of this country."

Randolph himself seemed flummoxed during this portion of the program, at one point forgetting which women were actually being recognized.

"Uh, who else? Will the . . ."

[Someone says, "Rosa Parks"]

Randolph continues, "Miss Rosa Parks . . . will they all stand."

Parks stood up and offered eight words of acknowledgment: "Hello, friends of freedom, it's a wonderful day." Right before King was about to speak, Richardson found herself put in a cab along with Lena Horne and sent back to the hotel. March organizers claimed that they were worried the two would get crushed. No one else was sent back to the hotel. "They did this," Richardson believed, "because Lena Horne had had Rosa Parks by the hand and had been taking her to satellite broadcasts, saying, 'This is who started the Civil Rights Movement, not Martin Luther King. This is the woman you need to interview.'" Richardson started helping Horne bring reporters to talk with Mrs. Parks. "We got several people to interview Rosa Parks. The march organizers must have found that out."

After the rally's completion, no women got to be part of the delegation that met with members of the Kennedy administration. Dorothy Height observed, "I've never seen a more immovable force. We could not get women's participation taken seriously." Mabel Williams, wife of the militant Robert Williams and herself a radical, recalled the outrage many felt that while King was being promoted as the great leader, Mrs. Parks was not getting her due. "I don't think she was too concerned about that. But people who were concerned about history were. . . . A lot of the male chauvinism that went on, we talked about that. But she was not bitter. . . . She wasn't fighting anyway for credit."

Given the iconic view of Parks, there is a tendency to believe that she was simply happy to stand on the dais that August day and did not notice the ways women were being relegated to a lesser role. But Parks did notice the way women were being marginalized, telling Bates that day how she hoped for a "better day coming." And in her autobiography, Parks describes the March as "a great occasion, but women were not allowed to play much of a role." Parks, according to Brinkley, "couldn't believe that she and Septima Clark were being treated like hostesses and was downright floored that dancer Josephine Baker was not even asked to speak." Coretta Scott King too highlighted how "not enough attention" was focused on women's roles in the movement in a feature article in 1966, making clear to the reporter that "it was a woman who triggered the whole movement." Scott King mailed an autographed copy of the piece to Parks.

The SCLC still sought Parks's participation in their ongoing work. But when Martin Luther King won the Nobel Prize in the 1964, though many in the SCLC journeyed to Oslo for the award, Parks did not, unable to afford the trip. Clark thought "they should have really offered Rosa Parks her transportation and everything over there, but you know, they didn't." King accepted the award on behalf of "those devotees of nonviolence who have moved so courageously against the ramparts of racial injustice. . . . These are the real heroes of the freedom struggle: they are the noble people for whom I accept the Nobel Peace Prize." One of those heroes certainly was Rosa Parks.

Parks's associates had a sense of her continuing financial difficulties. In 1965, Horton tried to put together a fund-raising campaign for a tenth-anniversary commemorative gift to Parks. He sought King's help but King never responded. Similarly, in Detroit, the Women's Political Action Committee run by Parks's friend Louise Tappes (and of which Parks was a member) decided to throw a testimonial dinner in her behalf. A 1964 WPAC newsletter explained:

> She has received many, many plaques and awards of merits, etc. from citizens all over the country, but as meritorious as they are, they do not compensate for Mrs.

Parks having to move away from her home for fear of loss of life, and neither do they compensate for the great financial loss of adequate income. WPAC members felt that to honor Rosa Parks in a very material way, would in some measure, say THANKS, for spearheading our nation-wide push for freedom, out of which, has emerged the great leader, Dr. Martin Luther King Jr.

On April 3, 1965, along with prominent church, community, and labor leaders, Coretta Scott King and Ralph Abernathy journeyed to Detroit to honor "a woman of bold and audacious courage."

Arriving an hour late to the festivities, Mrs. Parks received a thunderous standing ovation from the thousand people gathered at COBO Hall. Coretta Scott King honored "one of the noted women of the time [who] has been classified as an agitator by the Governor," reminding the audience that "at the time [Mrs. Parks] took the stand it was much more unpopular than now to speak out for our rights." Scott King spoke of the need for assistance to aid voter registration in the "Black Belt," condemned the aggressive actions of many Southern law-enforcement officials, and then led the crowd in singing "We Shall Overcome." At its annual convention in Birmingham in 1965, the SCLC also honored Parks. Lawyer Constance Motley gave the address praising Parks as a "freedom fighter": "Yours is the kind of courage and determination and nonviolent spirit we all need for the future."

But it was John Conyers who fundamentally shifted the Parks's family's economic situation. Parks had been a dedicated volunteer in Conyers's long-shot campaign for Congress. Elected in November 1964, Conyers became Detroit's second black representative to the House. In March 1965, the newly elected congressman hired Rosa Parks to work with constituents as an administrative assistant in his Detroit office. Recognizing her need, skills, and value to his own emerging political base, Conyers put an end to a decade of economic insecurity for Rosa Parks. With this position, Parks now had a salary, access to health insurance, and a pension—and the restoration of dignity that a formal paid position allowed. Political activist Mabel Williams recalled talking with Parks about "the hard, hard times" the family had encountered, and how if it had not been for John Conyers they might have perished. "John was a real hero to me and others who knew [what he did]," Williams explained.

Conyers, who became the sixth black congressman in the House at that time, was in a position to aid Mrs. Parks and also to benefit from her considerable personal and political skills. With her political acumen and decades of organizing experience, commitment to social justice, and ability to recognize people's needs—as well as her volunteer work on his campaign—she could play an important role at his Detroit office. With her history working at the grassroots, she would bring her experience from the back roads of NAACP organizing in Alabama to take on the social issues facing blacks in Detroit. Emblematic of a new black political power, Conyers also recognized and was not threatened by Rosa Parks's symbolic value in his office. Indeed, having this Southern heroine greet constituents in his office, attend community meetings, or stand beside him at public events embodied the mix of old and new black politics that Conyers was attempting to bring to the national stage. He saw her as the most important civil rights activist in the state. And so Mrs. Parks came to work for him.

Parks's decade of deep economic insecurity was drawing to an end. Her own political work in Detroit, however, was on the rise. Times were changing, and Mrs. Parks was now in a better position to take on Northern racism.

CHAPTER SIX

"The Northern Promised Land That Wasn't"
Rosa Parks and the
Black Freedom Struggle in Detroit

A YEAR BEFORE MOVING TO Detroit, Parks had visited the city on the invitation of Local 600 to speak to the membership about the boycott. Since 1949, Local 600 had emerged as a site of interracial militancy and dissent in the autoworkers union, as Walter Reuther consolidated his influence as UAW president. After public hearings investigating the Michigan Communist Party in 1952, white workers raged through the plants (as they had in the 1940s when blacks were hired in larger numbers in the auto industry), engaging in sit-down strikes and "runouts" to remove black activists who had been named as Communist sympathizers. The UAW did nothing to stop these hate attacks. Rather, shortly afterward, Reuther purged the leadership of Local 600 and placed its leadership under an international union administrator.

This did not obliterate the feistiness of many Local 600 members. They wanted to bring Rosa Parks to address the local, though Reuther did not. Reuther's continuing distrust of the local, and the controversial nature of the boycott, may have influenced Reuther's opposition to her visit. Undaunted by Reuther's lack of support, the local raised the money to bring her themselves and warmly welcomed her visit. Parks was no stranger to militant trade unionism herself, having aided Nixon's work with the Brotherhood of Sleeping Car Porters. While visiting the local, Parks likely made an important connection to the Tappes family. Sheldon Tappes worked at the River Rouge plant and rose through the ranks of the UAW; his wife, Louise, an active NAACP member and future leader of the WPAC, would become a close friend. Members of Local 600 put Parks up at the Garfield Hotel in Detroit's Paradise Valley, because in 1956, Detroit's downtown hotels were not open to black guests.

Motown was rife with segregation. Detroit's inner suburbs like Dearborn, Redford, Ferndale, and Warren swelled with whites fleeing black migration to the city and proudly asserted their racial exclusivity. Many of these suburban migrants condemned the city as decrepit and dangerous. And during the Montgomery bus boycott, the mayor of Dearborn, Orville Hubbard, boasted to the *Montgomery Advertiser* of his support of "complete segregation, one million per cent. . . . Negroes can't get in here. . . . These people are so anti-colored, much more than you in Alabama." Meanwhile, within the city limits, neighborhood associations had flowered like weeds following the black migration and racial tensions of the World War II era, as many white homeowners sought to prevent black people from moving into "their neighborhoods." Though they did not post signs, many Detroit restaurants nonetheless refused black people service; the acclaimed Joe Muer's Seafood served black customers in the back, wrapping their fish dinners in newspaper. Detroit hospitals separated black and white patients, with some even maintaining segregated wards, and the Arcadia skating rink, centrally located on Woodward Avenue, didn't allow black skaters.

Southerners had reacted to the double standard of being singled out for practices also happening in the North. Montgomery's police commissioner Clyde Sellers had decried the hypocrisy of Northern outrage during the boycott: "The northern press wants to play up things going on in the South, but they don't want to publicize segregation in their own cities." And in her talk to Local 600 and in others across the North, Parks explicitly linked Northern and Southern struggles against racial injustice, and framed racial discrimination and segregation as a national problem, not just a Southern flaw.

In 1961, the Parkses were able to leave their two rooms in the Progressive Civil League building. They moved to the ground floor of a brick flat in the Virginia Park neighborhood—a segregated neighborhood, as Parks described it to an interviewer, "almost 100% Negro with the exception of about two families in the block where I live. In fact I suppose you'd call it just about the heart of the ghetto." Virginia Park boasted a wide cross-section of black people—union activists, schoolteachers, families on AFDC, and some militants, according to resident Ollie Foster. The area, which would later become the epicenter of the 1967 rebellion, had grown increasingly crowded as black migrants were corralled into certain neighborhoods on the west side due to urban renewal and highway construction.

For the next four decades, Rosa Parks made Detroit's near west-side her home. Referring to the city as "the northern promised land that wasn't," Parks saw that racism in Detroit was "almost as widespread as Montgomery." Because the apparatus of racial inequality in Detroit was more covert, the daily humiliation of separate drinking fountains, elevators, buses, movie theaters, and lunch counters was thankfully gone. Still, Parks did not find "too much difference" between race relations in Detroit and Montgomery. Like Montgomery, the city offered a decidedly second-class citizenship for blacks. The systems of racial caste and power in Detroit denied people of color equitable education, safe policing, real job opportunities, a responsive city government, regular quality sanitation and health services, and due process under the law.

Segregation operated somewhat differently in Detroit than Montgomery. While she cherished Detroit's more integrated public spaces and a lessening of daily fear, Parks found "problems here . . . especially in the school system. The schools would be overcrowded. The job situation wouldn't be none too good." Housing was acutely segregated, and the differences in public services and policing that followed those boundaries made that segregation even more vicious. And many public spaces, while not explicitly marked "for whites only"—like Detroit's hotels, restaurants, and hospitals—practiced that just the same.

Looking at Rosa Parks's life in the North provides a different view of the racial landscape of postwar America and her direct experiences of Northern, as well as Southern, racism. Parks is so associated with Montgomery, so intertwined in the public memory with the racism and segregation of the Deep South, that the fact she spent more than half her life in an also-segregated Detroit hardly enters into our understanding of her life and legacy. Her description of the city as "the promised land that wasn't" is a palpable reminder that Northern migration didn't necessarily produce salvation and that racial inequality was a national plague, not a Southern malady. The civil rights movement was not simply a struggle between the liberal North and a redneck South, as the fable of Rosa Parks too often suggests.

In many of the memorials and descriptions of her life, Parks's migration north and her work in Conyers's office is treated like a postscript—the happy ending to a difficult life in the South and a respite from Montgomery's racial injustice. But the racial inequality that characterized Montgomery—jobs, housing, and school segregation, police brutality, negligible protection for black people under the law, limited black political power—was also endemic in Detroit. And thus Parks's own activism was not limited to the Cradle of the Confederacy. A decade before the 1967 riot and the black militancy that would make Detroit famous in the racial imagination, Parks moved to the city and joined a burgeoning civil rights movement there. She would spend the rest of her life, nearly fifty years, in Detroit—as a churchgoer and an aunt to her thirteen nieces and nephews, as a staff member for liberal congressman John Conyers and a political activist drawing attention to the racial inequalities of the liberal North. Yet her sustained critique of Northern racism and her half century of political work and community life in Detroit are largely unexplored.

The historical connotations of black freedom in the "promised land" (runaway slaves, the Harlem Renaissance, and black migration during the two world wars) have made it difficult to envision Rosa Parks as part of a struggle for black freedom in the North. America's race problem is often framed as a relic of a premodern system entrenched in the South and embodied in the form of bus driver James Blake, Montgomery's intransigent city leaders, and its burgeoning White Citizen's Council. The idea that Southern civil rights workers might also become Northern activists disturbs the easy oppositions embedded in these popular notions. Yet both Parks and King stressed the national character of racism. "The racial issue that we confront in America," declared King in a 1960 speech in New York, "is not a sectional but a national problem. . . . There is a pressing need for a liberalism in the North that is truly liberal, that firmly believes in integration in its own community as well as in the deep South." Parks too questioned the hypocritical silences of Northern liberalism, seeing Detroit's 1967 riot as "the result of resistance to change that was needed long beforehand."

The depth of racial injustice in the North combined with the feign of Northern innocence proved frustrating for the "mother of the movement." Parks continued to receive hate mail and menacing phone calls well into the 1970s in Detroit. She and King were called Communists, not only for their work in the South but also for their support of open housing and desegregated schools in the North. As Gunnar Myrdal had observed in *American Dilemma*, "The social paradox of the North is exactly this, that almost everybody is against discrimination in general but, at the same time, almost everybody practices discrimination in his own personal affairs." The terming of Northern segregation as "de facto" was a misnomer to appeal to Northern sensibilities, according to historian Matthew Lassiter, "despite ample historical evidence of comprehensive state action in producing deeply entrenched patterns of residential and educational segregation."

While offering them the opportunity to get away from the difficulties of Montgomery and a chance to be near family, Motown was not a land of milk and honey for the Parks. There was the blessing of extended family. Residing in Southwest Detroit, Sylvester and his wife, Daisy, had thirteen children, whom the Parks family now got to watch grow up. And her cousins Thomas Williamson and Annie Cruse and their families lived there. She saw them regularly. "They would make us clothes all the time," cousin Carolyn Green recalled. "I loved going over," niece Rhea McCauley concurred.

But the family still struggled economically. Being a notorious black woman did little to improve her job prospects in Detroit. Its racially segregated employment structure created financial problems similar to those in Montgomery, and steady, well-paid work proved elusive. In the years before Conyers hired her, Mrs. Parks took in piecework, sewed in the home of a seamstress friend, and then got a job sewing aprons and skirts ten hours a day at the Stockton Sewing Company.

In many ways, the fable of Rosa Parks with its much simpler tale of good guys (moral, upstanding Southern blacks and their Northern white allies) and bad guys (racist Southern whites and alienated Northern blacks) has obscured this history of Northern struggle. The treatment of the race problem as a Southern—not national—issue was a strategic formulation of that era, meant to appease Northern sensibilities and Cold War imperatives. To acknowledge Parks's comparison of Northern and Southern racial inequality would have disrupted this politically convenient binary. Framing racism as a Southern relic, Northern liberal politicians held up the Southern movement as proof of the perfectibility of American democracy and treated Northern movements and activists as dangerous and deviant. The media followed suit. In the liberal imagination, as the Southern civil rights movement increasingly captured national attention, a Southern sharecropper activist could be endowed with a righteousness that a protesting

Detroit autoworker or public housing resident could not. And so, to associate Mrs. Parks with Northern militancy and ghetto struggle appears to put a blemish on the mother of the movement.

As with many Southern migrants, Parks's political activities did not end when she left the South. But the image of Parks on the bus in 1955 is fixed in the popular imagination partly because she left the South as the civil rights movement she helped spur was blossoming. As her comrades in Montgomery and across the South fomented a nonviolent revolution increasingly captured by the national media, Parks had a new political base. Though she remained personally close to many Southern movement people and attended some events, she wasn't a daily participant—and so became frozen in time, heralded for starting it all but largely unrecognized as an ongoing political actor. Simultaneously, with the nation's eyes focused on the South, Mrs. Parks's political activities and those of her comrades in Detroit were treated differently than parallel movements evolving in the South.

Many of the interviews with Parks—including more extensive oral histories on the civil rights movement—took place in her home or in Representative John Conyers's Detroit office. Despite sitting with her in Motown, interviewers barely asked about her Northern activism or the racial landscape of the city (except for a question or two on the riot). They hardly seemed to notice her continuing involvement in the struggle for racial justice in Detroit. Much of the corresponding media attention to her in the 1960s and 1970s focused on Southern-based events—Mrs. Parks attending the Selma-to-Montgomery march, or the anniversary of the bus boycott, or King's funeral. On the tenth anniversary of the boycott, reporters descended on Mrs. Parks. In numerous interviews, she made clear she "would do it again," but she also noted, "I can't say we like Detroit any better than Montgomery." No one cared to probe that response, and Mrs. Parks didn't elaborate.

The Southern focus of Mrs. Parks's interviewers reflected a broader blindness among liberal commentators and subsequent historians to the parallels between Southern and Northern racism and anti-racism struggles. By the early 1960s, the national media (based outside of the South) had grown increasingly sympathetic to the nonviolent Southern struggle. Conversely, while Northern protests often made front-page news, they were not framed through the same righteous lens used for the Southern movement. In cities like Detroit, public officials regularly refuted black demands with the charge that "this is not the South" and repeatedly expressed their shock at rising militancy and the uprisings of the late 1960s—willfully forgetting that decades of black struggle had produced negligible change. Detroit's white officials thought they had solved the city's racial problems with interracial commissions, liberal proclamations, nominal desegregation, and token hires. And the media picked it up wholesale, particularly after the 1967 uprising, when few stories looked back on this decade of frustrated activism that had laid the foundation for the anger that would explode. Time and again, news articles expressed "surprise" over the riots.

Even when interviewers in the 1960s and 1970s asked her questions on contemporary race relations, they often inquired about the current racial situation *in the South*. Parks was almost never asked about whether things in Detroit had changed, about the Kerner Commission report, Northern school segregation, Nixon's welfare policies, police brutality, or the war in Vietnam— despite her considerable attention to these matters. In an interview in 1970 in Conyers's office, when asked about her decision to leave the South and her civil rights work there, Mrs. Parks pushed back. "I don't know whether I could have been more effective as a worker for freedom in the South than I am here in Detroit. Really the same thing that has occurred in the South is existing here to a certain degree. We do have the same problems."

Notably, this interview took place inside Congressman Conyers's office at a time when the office was a hotbed of local and national black political organizing. Parks was intimately involved in this push to elect more black public officials and cognizant of the needs of black Detroiters, yet few interviewers valued her insights about contemporary Northern black politics. Had Parks been a male civil rights pioneer turned congressman's staff assistant, it seems inconceivable that these interviewers would not have probed for insights into Detroit's race relations and directions for the congressman's agenda. A related omission occurred as Parks worked on her autobiography with Jim Haskins in the late 1980s. Haskins had family roots and activist connections in Alabama, having been a student at Alabama State during the boycott, so much of their detailed conversation was spun out from this shared background. Moreover, Haskins brought numerous articles and other memorabilia to help jar Mrs. Parks's memory and push her to clarify and nuance these accounts. But those articles tended to replicate a Southern focus—on the boycott, the political landscape of Alabama, and the various movements that led up to it. So Haskins and Parks concentrated on correcting and improving those accounts. However inadvertently, Haskins's Southern focus indelibly shaped the structure of *Rosa Parks: My Life* and the extant historical record.

Despite these interviewers' blinders, Rosa Parks recognized that the "same problems" beset her new hometown and, as she had for decades, set about seeing what she could do to challenge them. Parks was thus in on the ground level as a rising black politics—of grassroots activism and black electoral strategies—took hold in Detroit.

AN AMERICAN DILEMMA: RACIAL INEQUALITY IN THE ARSENAL OF DEMOCRACY

Black migration to Detroit swelled in the twentieth century. Half a million Southerners came to the city during World War II, most of them black, and the numbers of black migrants continued to swell in the decades after the war. Indeed, Detroit's black population doubled between 1940 and 1950. The Parks family thus joined a heavy stream of black migrants to the North. By the 1960s, the majority of black people would live in the North. As historian Hasan Jeffries has documented, people who had moved from Alabama's Black Belt to Detroit formed a key source of information and support for Motown's migrant pool: "It was possible for a Detroit factory worker to earn ten times as much as a Lowndes County [the neighboring county to Montgomery] farmhand. At the same time, they were always the last hired and the first fired, and housing was just as cramped and crowded as it was in southern cities." As in Montgomery, black women in Detroit were largely trapped in low-wage service labor.

Another demographic shift was afoot. Armed with home loans and new highways, white Detroiters migrated to the suburbs. Between 1950 and 1960, while the black population grew by 60 percent, the white population of the city shrank by 23 percent, or 350,000 people. A rating system developed in the 1930s by the Home Owners Loan Corporation and continued by the Federal Housing Authority to reassure banks and promote home ownership gave the best ratings to racially homogenous white neighborhoods still prime for development. Detroit's expanding suburbs were given high ratings, which spurred this white migration, whereas 50 percent of all city homes were "redlined" and deemed unsafe for investment, even in solidly middle-class black neighborhoods. This sped up the decline of the city as federal home loan programs made investment in the city's inner core sparse. With plentiful GI Bill loans significantly more accessible to returning white GIs than their black counterparts and millions of dollars for federal highway construction, Detroit's suburbs proliferated with white families, while black neighborhoods within the city grew more crowded. Many white suburbs were hostile to black people moving in. Thus, the twin weapons of state bureaucracy and white vigilantism conspired to keep most black families jammed into increasingly crowded city neighborhoods while rewarding white families moving to Detroit's white suburbs.

In 1948, the Supreme Court took up four cases of black homeowners, including Detroiters Orsel and Minnie McGhee, to rule unanimously in *Shelley v. Kraemer* that courts could not enforce restrictive covenants, which proscribed home owners from selling their property to certain groups of people. Indicative of how entrenched such discriminatory practices were in American society, three Supreme Court justices recused themselves from the case likely because they had restrictive covenants on their own properties. The Supreme Court's decision did not prohibit the covenants, just the court's enforcement of them—which provided an ample loophole for home-owners, public officials, and realtors to maintain such practices. And so Northern metro areas continued to be as segregated in 1960 as in 1940, in part because the FHA continued to support racially restrictive development.

Despite the jubilation in the black community over the Court's decision, Detroit authorities refused to enforce it and developed strategies, along with banks and realtors, to maintain these discriminatory practices, as white officials and businesspeople did across the country. "Detroit newspapers," according to Detroit's NAACP executive secretary, Arthur Johnson, "wrote detailed articles instructing and encouraging white homeowners to circumvent the law and keep blacks out. This was indicative of how the mainstream media in Detroit was but an extension of the white institutional power structure." Between 1945 and 1955, about 100,000 private units were constructed on vacant city land, but only 2 percent of those were available to black people—and while the waiting list for public housing was six thousand deep for blacks, there was barely a wait for white families.

Much like it was in Montgomery, state-funded urban renewal, slum clearance, and highway construction blazed through Detroit in the decades after World War II. The Detroit Plan crafted in 1946 promoted slum clearance, including razing 129 acres in the Black Bottom. Between 1949 and 1971, the state and city began twenty-seven urban renewal projects at a cost of $263 million. Detroit's Paradise Valley fell prey to the Oakland-Hastings portion of the I-75 freeway (later renamed the Chrysler Freeway), as did the bustling Hastings Street with its black-owned businesses and music clubs. These urban renewal projects often resulted in black removal, and many community activists criticized them for focusing on attracting white suburbanites back to the city rather than improving housing for its black residents. Most black families forced out by renewal projects had difficulty finding other decent, affordable housing, and the city provided little assistance, often engaging in questionable removal practices. By 1962, almost 15 percent of the city had been cleared for urban renewal. In March 1963, the Detroit Commission on Community Relations reported that ten thousand structures had been razed or were scheduled for demolition, displacing 43,096 people, 70 percent of them black. The impact of urban renewal touched black life immeasurably.

One facet of residential segregation was that black residents (who were poorer on average than their white counterparts) paid more for housing than white Detroiters in the metro area because they were restricted to increasingly over-populated parts of the city. Yet, half of the housing black people inhabited was substandard, in part because of the difficulties in getting loans for upkeep. By 1967, Detroit boasted the highest rates of black home ownership rates in the nation, but the quality was far worse and the percentage of blacks owning still considerably lower than for whites in the city. Fires were common, particularly because many of the buildings were old and made of wood. Moreover, the city only picked up garbage once a week, which meant that in crowded neighborhoods, garbage overflowed. Thus, when Parks said she lived in the heart of the ghetto, this pattern of structural neglect was in part what she was referencing.

Inequality was not confined to Detroit's housing market. Detroit's economy was also being transformed in ways that bore heavily on black migrants. The auto industry, which had attracted many black workers to the city, restricted blacks to certain jobs and rarely hired them in supervisory positions. At the very point that large numbers of blacks were coming to the city, automation was transforming the auto industry, shrinking the number of jobs. Detroit-based auto companies like Hudson, Nash, Fraser, Briggs, Kaiser, and Packard didn't survive and were bought out and phased out amidst the downturn. The city experienced four recessions during the 1950s, and black Detroiters were disproportionately hard hit. Jobs fell from 338,000 in 1947 to 153,000 in 1977, while Detroit's black population rose from 300,000 in 1950 to 759,000 by 1980.

Schools in Detroit were also separate and unequal, with inner-city black students often viewed by teachers and administrators as uneducable and tracked toward vocational education. In 1962, *Ebony* reported in a lengthy feature, titled "School Segregation Up North," on the pattern of school segregation across Northern cities—45 percent of black students in Detroit attended schools that were more than 80 percent black. The curriculum was out of date and filled with racial stereotypes, and almost no attention was paid to African American or global history or literature. In 1963, when Northwestern High School students protested the lack of black history in their textbook, some teachers responded, "Black people didn't do anything." This meager schooling produced a dropout rate nearing 50 percent among black youth, while the unemployment rate for blacks under twenty-five hovered between 30 and 40 percent. And black high school graduates in the city still earned an average of $1,600 less than white graduates, in part because blacks also were locked out of skilled training schools.

Yet city officials denied these patterns of systemic racial inequality in housing, schools, jobs, and public services. Casting themselves as "color-blind," public officials often castigated sectors of the black community as lacking the values, work ethic, and cultural skills necessary for success and attributed inequities to larger cultural deficits within the black community. This "culture of poverty," as it would be known by the mid-1960s, accounted for these racial differentials, not governmental action. Similarly, many white Detroiters asserted their rights as property owners and parents to advocate racially discriminatory practices because of the deficits of black parents, homeowners, and renters, while still professing a generic commitment to equal treatment and civil rights.

The claim of a color-blind city rang hollow to most of Detroit's black community, including Parks. Disappointed by the caution of the NAACP Detroit chapter, local activists called for a mass march to highlight the second-class citizenship of blacks in the city. Reverend C. L. Franklin explained to the *Detroit News* that the march would serve as a "warning to the city that what has transpired in the past is no longer acceptable to the Negro community." On June 23, 1963, Parks joined King at the front of Detroit's Great March to Freedom. Held two months before the March on Washington, this march drew nearly 200,000 Detroiters, rivaling the numbers of the people that would journey to DC in August. Dressed in their Sunday best, "a mighty sea of black faces," according to marcher Reverend Malcolm Boyd, spilled down Jefferson, filling block after block after block. The march was nearly all black in composition. "We didn't have to walk," recalled Detroit labor activist General Baker, "but were pushed up Jefferson." Conceived as an act of solidarity with the SCLC's Birmingham campaign, the march highlighted the severe inequalities in Detroit and helped to accelerate a rising black militancy in the city.

At the finish, in front of a packed Cobo Hall, Reverend Albert Cleage hammered home the problem of northern racism, calling on those gathered to challenge racial inequities in Detroit. King did the same, as Parks recalled, "remind[ing] everybody that segregation and discrimination were rampant in Michigan as well as Alabama." She found his speech that June day the best she had ever heard him give. Calling the march the "greatest demonstration for freedom ever held in the United States," King condemned racial injustice as "a national problem," asserting "that de facto segregation in the North is just as injurious as the actual segregation in the South." Criticizing gradualism as "little more than escapism," King told the crowd that "to help us in Alabama and Mississippi and over the South, do all that you can to get rid of the problem here." Curiously, despite Parks's position at the front of the march, she remained unnoticed by the press that wrote about the event, including the *Michigan Chronicle*, the local black newspaper that covered the event extensively. To mark the occasion, Motown put out its first spoken-word record, which featured King's speech at the Great March, recorded by Parks's friend Milton Henry. Parks loved the recording and played it all the time.

That same week, Parks spoke at a luncheon honoring Daisy Bates and Birmingham black businessman A. G. Gaston. There again she made the comparison between what they had done in

Montgomery and what people were doing in Detroit to protest housing discrimination. "We had seen Negro children yanked from seats in the white section of the buses as if they were animals and I for one had just had enough of it." Blacks in Detroit experienced the same "tiredness" around the persistence of housing segregation, Parks argued, that black Montgomerians had felt around the inhumanity of bus segregation. They had "had enough" of the liberal inequality that Detroit proffered its black residents. Parks joined the fight around open housing. Open housing advocacy in the early 1960s drew "all sorts of threats, violence," recalled Detroit City Council member Mel Ravitz. On July 27, the Detroit Branch of the NAACP led a crowd of two hundred people to protest housing discrimination in Oak Park. Parks marched at the front and was one of the featured guests along with Myrlie Evers, whose husband, Medgar, had been assassinated a month earlier in Jackson, Mississippi.

Despite her participation in certain NAACP events, there is no record that Mrs. Parks joined or was active in the Detroit NAACP branch when she first moved to the city. Indeed, fellow SNCC activist Martha Norman says that Parks definitely did not join the chapter initially, viewing it as too conservative in this period. When the Parks family moved to Detroit, the local branch was the largest in the nation, setting a record membership level in 1956, but quite anti-Communist, moderate, and middle-class focused.

Along with housing segregation and urban renewal, police repression was a constant affront to black life in the city. As James Baldwin had observed in 1962, "The only way to police a ghetto is to be oppressive." The *Michigan Chronicle* recorded a steady litany of police abuse and harassment of black Detroiters. For a decade, the Detroit NAACP had called attention to the systemic nature of police brutality and malfeasance in the city. In 1958, after presenting records of 103 complaints from January 1956 to July 1957, they praised the city for finally convening the Citizen's Advisory Committee on Police Community Relations but nonetheless highlighted the "flagrant violations of citizens' rights" and "improper and abusive police conduct" that needed to be addressed. In 1960, branch executive secretary Arthur Johnson again lambasted the "chronic" nature of police brutality, citing their own records of more than 244 complaints against police over the past five years. Noting "discrimination in all areas of community life," Johnson explained, it was law enforcement "where Negroes are daily made openly and painfully aware of their second-class status in the community." In forty-seven cases known to the NAACP, the beatings were so severe they led to hospitalization. Yet, Detroit's major newspapers "had a standing arrangement not to cover incidents of police brutality," according to Johnson; the NAACP would often send press releases with photos of a new incident to all the major papers, but only the *Michigan Chronicle* would run a story. The public silence about this treatment exacerbated this repressive climate.

Thirteen days after Detroit's Great March, a police officer killed a young black woman, Cynthia Scott. Cutting an impressive figure at six foot four, Scott, a sex worker, was shot twice in the back and once in the stomach by police officer Theodor Spicher. Three days later, the prosecutor ruled that Spicher had shot the "fleeing suspect" in self-defense. While the police claimed that Scott had pulled out a knife, the acquaintance who was with her recounted that she didn't have a weapon; rather, the police had been harassing her, and when she walked away from them after telling them they had no grounds to arrest her, they shot her. Many in the black community were outraged. Richard Henry, whose brother Milton served as the lawyer on Scott's case, and Reverend Cleage helped organize a picket line outside police headquarters a week later. Five thousand people demonstrated, yelling "Stop killer cops" and threatening to storm the police building. Petitions were circulated to recall the prosecutor. Hundreds of people picketed and sat in at police headquarters, and the case became a touchstone for young activists in Detroit and the emergence of the Freedom Now Party.

Just as the humiliating bus treatment built to a breaking point in Montgomery, the disrespectful treatment of blacks by police in the city was becoming too much to bear. In 1964, the head of the NAACP, Roy Wilkins, noted how police relations had worsened in Detroit. In December 1965, Conyers warned about the city's cockiness in praising itself for getting through the summer without major incident, unlike Watts, or Harlem the previous year: "That just means that the wrong citizen and the wrong policeman didn't happen to get together." In some public appearances, Parks also made the point of comparing police treatment in Alabama and Michigan.

Yet, Detroit city officials refused to make any systematic change, preferring to study the problem and convene meetings, just as Montgomery officials had done around bus segregation in the mid-1950s. Indeed, following the 1965 Watts riot, Detroit police grew more aggressive, using new federal funds to create a Tactical Mobile Unit, for "crowd control," which many black residents viewed as using Gestapo-like tactics. And Detroit's main newspapers paid little attention to police brutality in their own backyards, despite their attention to police dogs and fire hoses in Birmingham and other Southern police aggression.

"I HAVE BEEN AN UNCLE TOM AND I REPENT": BLACK CHRISTIANITY IN DETROIT

Southern migration, a growing racial consciousness, and a rich black-nationalist tradition transformed the religious landscape of the city in the decades following World War II. Black Detroiters had a rich and varied religious life. Similar to Montgomery, postwar Detroit was home to a handful of activist ministers who challenged the complacency of their white and black peers. Reverends Horace White, Charles Hill, and C. L. Franklin would inspire a new group of ministers to make an independent Christian witness in the city that was not tied to the priorities of city elites. In the prewar years, Detroit's major black churches maintained an alliance with the car companies, particularly Ford Motor Company, which stifled criticism of the systematic inequality endemic in the auto industry. Ford had required a letter from a minister attesting to an applicant's "uprightness" and "reliability" in order to hire black men. They rewarded the ministers with gifts and well-paid congregants. White and Hill, among others, would break this alliance in their commitment to building a union for black auto-workers.

Inspired by their precedents but also influenced by Malcolm X and the Nation of Islam, Reverend Albert Cleage would become the leading Christian voice of black nationalism over the decade. Believing the church to be foundational to the black struggle and the black nation, he challenged his fellow Christians to realign their priorities—"I have been an Uncle Tom and I repent"—and commit to the struggle. Raised in Detroit, Cleage had attended Oberlin and the University of Southern California, returning home in 1954 to pastor St. Mark's Presbyterian Church. When that proved stifling, Cleage led part of the congregation in forming a new church, Central Congregational Church. In 1957, the church purchased a building on Twelfth Street. In the early 1960s, Cleage joined with Richard and Milton Henry to build the Group on Advanced Leadership (GOAL), an all-black organization designed to be a "chemical catalyst" in the struggle for racial justice "because something more needed to be done about police brutality, Negro-removal disguised as urban renewal, Negro-hating textbooks and the lack of black business." Urban renewal proved the radicalizing factor for Richard Henry and other black nationalists in the city. These Detroit radicals joined with others throughout the country to found the Freedom Now Party, a political party separate from the Democratic and Republican parties to promote the interests of black people. The Henrys, who would become some of the leading black militants in the city, worshipped at Central. From 1961 to 1965, they published the bimonthly *Illustrated News* on pink newsprint; it became a venue for an emerging black nationalism in the city. Rosa Parks read it carefully.

Parks too had found a deep connection between her racial activism and her Christian faith. When she got married, she had stopped reading the Bible, perhaps because her husband's politics were less faith-based. But she had long since returned to a rich and active worship, first in Montgomery and then in Detroit. Parks joined St. Matthew's AME Church on Petoskey, a small church with only about two hundred members, because her cousin Annie Cruse and friend Mary Hays Gaskin went there. By 1965, she had risen to the position of deaconess, the highest rank a woman could attain. The deaconesses held responsibility for promoting the general good of the church and ministering to the needs of its congregants. Faithful in her Sunday attendance, she often came by during the week to pray or help with the church program or other needs.

But while St. Matthews remained her religious home, she often attended events at Cleage's

Central Congregational Church. According to SNCC comrade Martha Norman Noonan, Parks gravitated toward political events held at Cleage's church, choosing to align herself with the more radical elements in Detroit. Central Congregational held numerous programs on the black struggle and black consciousness that interested her—and the church was close to her Virginia Park home. Historian Angela Dillard writes about how Cleage's church blended "theology, social criticism, and calls to action, during the late 1950s . . . attract[ing] a core of activists who would become influential in the theory and practice of black nationalist politics in Detroit." One speech Parks attended there featured black sociologist Nathan Hare speaking on "The Psychology of Uncle Tom[:] 'White on the Inside,'" another featured Stokely Carmichael talking about Black Power. Hare recalled the first time he met Mrs. Parks was after a speech he gave at Cleage's church; she seemed "in her element," he recalled, and came up afterward and told him how much she liked his talk.

Parks, like Cleage, was a staunch and devout Christian—and the mix of black activism and Christianity that developed in Detroit resonated with her. She saw no contradiction between religious belief and political militancy. Serving God necessitated collective action to address the needs of her fellow men and women. To Mrs.

Parks, God stood with the oppressed and did not take kindly to complacency. As her Mississippi comrade, Fannie Lou Hamer, also a devout Christian activist, explained, "You can pray until you faint. But unless you get up and try to do something, God is not going to put it in your lap!" Certainly as her interest in slave resistance and the Underground Railroad grew, Mrs. Parks saw the deep roots of Christian militancy in the struggle for racial justice in America. That faith also underwrote her courage. She often carried her Bible, and many times, particularly in difficult situations, would take it out to read and pray.

As in Montgomery, class, ideological, and religious differences ran through Motown's black churches and black Detroiters' attempts to draw attention to the city's racial inequality. In November 1965, Detroit hosted two civil rights conferences, providing a preview of the black militancy that the media would discover in 1966 with Stokely Carmichael's calls for Black Power. Hoping to capitalize on the tremendous energy of the summer's Great March, organizers wanted to start a Northern counterpart to the SCLC—an NCLC—and planned a fall conference. Differing on whether to include militants and black nationalists like Malcolm X in the conference program, Reverends Cleage and Franklin, reflecting tensions in Detroit's activist community, parted ways. Cleage decided to organize a rival conference, the Grassroots Leadership Conference. The NCLC held its three-day convention at Cobo Hall, but the attendance was disappointing; about fifty people participated in the work-shops, and only three thousand came to Adam Clayton Powell's keynote address. Between three hundred and four hundred activists attended the Grassroots Leadership Conference and heard Malcolm X's keynote, titled "Message to the Grassroots" and recorded by Milton Henry. While Parks started out at the NCLC, she also attended the Grassroots Leadership Conference.

JOHN CONYERS

The Supreme Court's 1962 decision on urban voter underrepresentation in *Baker v. Carr* led to the redrawing of Michigan's congressional district boundaries. The creation of Michigan's First Congressional District on Detroit's north side opened up the possibility for Detroit to send a second black representative to Congress (Charles Diggs represented Detroit's east side). Even before the boundaries were finalized, the firm of George Crockett and Maurice Sugar had encouraged a young civil rights attorney, John Conyers Jr., to enter the race against the incumbent, white congressman Lucien Nedzi. Conyers's campaign thus commenced before that of his closest challenger, black Democrat Richard Austin.

In early 1964, Rosa Parks took an interest in Conyers's long-shot campaign. Having met Conyers through his work on behalf of voting rights in the South, she volunteered in his campaign for "Jobs, Justice, Peace." Born on May 16, 1929, in Highland Park, the thirty-five-year-old Conyers had been educated in Detroit public schools and attended Wayne State University, where he obtained his undergraduate and law degrees. He served in the army during the Korean War. In 1963, Conyers had gone to Selma as a legal observer. Conyers's father, John Conyers Sr., had been an official in the UAW until he was ousted by Walter Reuther along with Coleman Young, George Crockett, and Walter Hardin for ties to the CP and CP activists. Before running for Congress, John Conyers Jr. had served as a legislative assistant with Congressman John Dingell and worked for the Michigan workmen's compensation department. Because of his work with Dingell and his father's union work, Conyers was known politically throughout the state.

An early opponent of U.S. involvement in Vietnam, Conyers had received support from the emerging antiwar movement, civil rights advocates, and portions of Detroit's labor movement. Parks began attending campaign meetings, rarely saying anything but willing to help with campaign tasks. "Everyone was frozen in their tracks," Conyers recalled. "Rosa Parks is supporting Conyers." Many people, including the candidate himself and King's nephews who lived in Detroit, wanted Dr. King, who had purposely chosen to steer clear of any political races, to come to Detroit on Conyers's behalf and had reached out to him. But Conyers credited Parks's efforts as the decisive factor in convincing King to come. Parks called King and implored: "You've got to come to Detroit and embrace Brother Conyers. We need you." King could not say no.

Over Easter weekend, King came to Detroit, where he gave a moving speech at Central United Methodist Church and then endorsed Conyers's campaign, the only political endorsement he made. According to Conyers, "Boy that really zoomed me right up." King's visit "quadrupled my visibility in the black community. . . . Therefore, if it wasn't for Rosa Parks, I never would have gotten elected." Conyers faced considerable opposition in the crowded primary, particularly from Richard Austin. Older and more well known, Austin was an accountant with many influential white and black supporters as well as ample ties to the labor movement and the Democratic Party. According to Conyers, once Austin entered the race, "people were told to take my bumper sticker off their car." Initially the UAW had come out for Conyers; when Austin entered the race, they equivocated, as did the Trade Union Leadership Council (TULC). Formed to be an independent voice for blacks in the UAW after Reuther purged militants, the TULC had played a crucial leadership role in black politics in the late 1950s and early 1960s, pivotal in the election of Jerome Cavanagh as mayor in 1962 and in various local efforts around school segregation and urban renewal. Conyers was legal counsel to the TULC, and his father had a long and strong relationship to the UAW. This decision to support Austin split the TULC's leadership and membership and weakened relations between the pro-union Conyers and the UAW.

Conyers was seen as more progressive and more independent, making him the choice of many politically minded black people like Rosa Parks—and backed, according to the *Los Angeles Sentinel*, with the "largest volunteer organization ever seen in Michigan." Thousands of volunteers—along with the candidate himself—stumped at churches, supermarkets, and block clubs. Women played a crucial role in this grassroots support; many felt, according to Ida Murray, that "John was a candidate of the people," whereas "labor was picking your candidate" with Austin. Many saw the young Conyers as a David going up against the Goliath of the Democratic Party and union establishment.

One lucky break for the campaign was that Detroit's two main newspapers were on strike; had they not been, Conyers believed, they certainly would not have supported his upstart candidacy and Austin might have benefited.

In September, Conyers won the Democratic primary in a field of eight candidates by a slim margin and the recount narrowed the win to forty-three votes ahead of Austin. The September 1964 election was not a mandate for progressivism, however. Faced with a rising open-housing movement pushing to end the right of home-owners and realtors to discriminate, Detroit voters approved an anti-open-housing referendum allowing homeowners and realtors to "accept or reject any prospective buyer or tenant for his own reasons." California voters followed suit in November, passing Proposition 14, which repealed the recently passed Rumford Fair Housing Act. Most white people in Detroit and L.A. wanted to retain their right to discriminate in the sale and rental of their property. Thus, the white backlash against civil rights typically associated with the period after the riots in these cities was actually a frontlash that sought to thwart any real Northern desegregation years before the riots.

In the general election, Conyers ran against attorney Milton Henry (who lived in Pontiac, not in the district) of the Freedom Now Party and

Robert Blackwell of the Republican Party and executive secretary of the Michigan Labor Mediation Board (who later became the first black mayor of Highland Park in 1968). Because the First District was about half black and two-thirds Democratic, Conyers won handily. Conyers became the sixth black in the House of Representatives and the first black person ever to serve on the House Judiciary Committee.

On March 1, 1965, Conyers hired Parks for a position in his Detroit office, where she would work till she retired in 1988. Tellingly, after more than twenty years of dedicated political work, this was the first time Parks had held a paid political position. She would remain within a gender-appropriate role, answering phones, handling constituent needs, welcoming visitors, and coordinating the office. But her work was invaluable to the new congressman. Conyers would spend a great deal of the time in DC, so Parks helped hold down the fort in Detroit in an office on the third floor of the Michigan State Building. Indeed, for a time, Parks was Conyers's surrogate in the city, doing community work, keeping a pulse on the most pressing issues, and demonstrating the congressman's commitment to community struggles.

Traveling all over the city, she visited constituents at schools, hospitals, and senior citizen homes, attended community meetings and rallies, and kept Conyers grounded in community activism. Taking up various urban social issues, Mrs. Parks heard people's problems, gathered information about their concerns, and filled in for Conyers at public functions. Her job often focused on addressing constituent needs, particularly around welfare benefits, education, job discrimination, Social Security, and affordable housing. She sat in with the congressman in numerous meetings in Detroit, particularly in the first years. Adam Shakoor recalled that when he met with Conyers in the early 1970s on alternative treatments and community initiatives for addressing heroin addiction, Parks joined them.

She also traveled with Conyers to national black events and to support black candidates and often joined the congressman in meetings with community activists in Detroit. Conyers aides Leon Atchison and Larry Horwitz were adamant in later interviews, however, that Mrs. Parks made her own political agenda, and that she attended many black political events because of her own beliefs and moral compass, not because the congressman sent her or she was representing him.

The office was a busy place, filled with the cultural politics of the era. Above the desks, for instance, was a mimeographed poster, done by graphic artist Ron Cobb, of an older black man with a hoe bearing the caption: "Remember, Uncle Tom says—'Only you can prevent ghetto fires.'" People often came to Conyers with incidences of discrimination, particularly numerous complaints of race-based job bias. At some workplaces, Atchison recalled, they were able to get redress. At the IRS, black women were being discriminated against and not promoted. They went over and interviewed people on the spot. The office put pressure on them to get rid of the director of the local office. They had similar success at the Army Tank Automotive Command.

Thus, Parks was well acquainted with the needs of Detroit's black poor and working class. Housing, and particularly public housing, were among the issues closest to her heart. Housing for blacks in Detroit by the mid-1960s was decrepit, deeply overcrowded, unsanitary, and unequal. The density in black neighborhoods was often more than twice that in white neighborhoods. Having lived in public housing herself in Montgomery, she worked to get money for public housing in Detroit. Particularly as President Johnson's Great Society programs opened up funding for city needs, Parks tried to get a piece of that money for Detroit. Part of her job was to listen to what people needed and then report this back to the congressman.

Conyers's decision to hire Parks engendered

some outcry. "People called her a troublemaker," Conyers recalled. More than a decade after her bus stand, Parks continued to receive hate mail. This harassment increased after Conyers hired her, and her name was publicized. People sent rotten watermelons, voodoo dolls, and hateful cards and letters to the office. Many seemed to come from fellow Detroiters, as a rising white resistance had flowered in the city. They were "quite threatening," but she would listen and say, "Have a nice day," according to Atchison. "She was cool—and didn't seem stressed about it." A May 19, 1969, letter from Detroit read:

> We don't think John Conyers should be hiring a person of your low caliber Rosa, to work in his office. Maybe in his private home for purpose of scrubbing the floors as a domestic maid, perhaps—but certainly not doing office work. . . . John Conyers is a bad enough senator as it is, without his adding fuel to the fire by hiring an evil dame in his office to help him. Your two brains probably dig up plenty of bad ideas to bug us lawabiding serious minded hardworking taxpayers.

A March 8, 1971, letter carped, "People seldom complain but inside their hearts they are fully aware that it was YOU, Rosa, who is chiefly responsible for the unholy racial mess this nation is in today. By rights, you ought to be shot at sunrise, or otherwise appropriately taken care of, for your dastardly deed in Montgomery Alabama, and all the subsequent riots etc. You sure started a war, Rosa. Shame on you. Perhaps you are now getting what you deserve." A 1972 letter from Indiana made clear the writer's objections to her move north, "Why didn't you stay down South? The North sure doesn't want you up here. You are the biggest woman troublemaker ever." Thus, fifteen years after her bus stand, many whites outside the South regarded Rosa Parks as a "dastardly" troublemaker.

Some attacked Parks as a Communist. An April 1966 article in the Shreveport newspaper the *Councilor* featured the infamous photo of King, Parks, and Abner Berry at Highlander. The reporter began, "Here is proof that the secretary to a United States congressman hovered with top communists at a mountain retreat in Tennessee. She is Rosa Parks of Detroit. When I first heard that Rep. John J. Conyers, Jr. (D-Mich.) had hired Rosa, I could not believe he would be so brazen at a time when young Americans are fighting in Vietnam. I called Conyers's office in Michigan and a woman on the other end identified herself as Rosa Parks." The reporter then regaled readers with a minstrel version of his conversation with Parks:

She denied, however, that it was a Communist school.

"Then, why were top level communist officials present in such numbers, Rosa?"

"I jes don't know, Mr. Touchstone, you'll have to ask Mr. Myles Horton who run the school," she replied.

While most Americans would not have sent hate mail to Rosa Parks, equating civil rights activism with Communist subversion was not a fringe position. Many Americans worried about the Communist influence on the civil rights movement and viewed the black freedom struggle with fear. In a Gallup poll in the days before the March on Washington, two-thirds of Americans surveyed viewed the march as "un-American," and in a 1965 national poll, half responded that they thought Communists were involved "a lot" in the civil rights demonstrations. Support of open housing in the North was often attacked as a "Communist" attack on private property.

Regardless of the harassment, Conyers was awed by Parks's presence in the office. Horwitz described Conyers and Parks's partnership, "She was a . . . presence. John gave her a job and economic security. She gave John prestige and stature. When he was very junior, after a bitterly divided primary, he needed this." According to the *Detroit Free Press*, "There were claims that

Conyers added her to his staff merely for the free political advertising that she generated." But Atchison, who was then in charge of Conyers's Detroit office, says that's only partially accurate. "There was that value there. But also there was a concern for her finances." Over the next two decades, busloads of schoolchildren came to meet her, and her position over the twenty-three years she worked there became more ceremonial. Jamila Brathwaite, who joined the staff in the mid-1980s, in the last years of Parks's work there, recalled, "Everything just stopped. We didn't want to answer the phones . . . to get that time to really talk to her. She gave us that time. If you wanted to talk, she would talk to you." Brathwaite recalled that one day, many weeks after a conversation they had had about the black freedom struggle, south and north, Mrs. Parks brought in a book for her. Brathwaite was surprised to see it was on Malcolm X.

Still, in the late 1960s, according to Horwitz, Conyers's white supporters who visited the Detroit office often didn't know who Parks was. "There was an absolute racial divide," Horwitz noted. "She was a heroine in the black community but not in the white community [at that point]." Many white liberals had fixated on King and didn't necessarily know who Rosa Parks was.

Parks continued a busy community schedule—making public appearances and speeches at scores of church programs, women's day events, and schools, traveling to political affairs and mobilizations, often apologizing to Conyers for having to leave the office. Calling her "a true activist," Conyers recalled the variety of issues Mrs. Parks was involved in, particularly "ones that didn't get the media attention." However, she tended to underplay this work in interviews from the period. In a 1967 interview, Mrs. Parks was asked why she had chosen not to be active in the civil rights movement in Detroit, to which she responded, "I have considered myself as active as I could be. . . . But I haven't been aggressive enough to try and take over any organization or be too much in the foreground. In fact, I wasn't that way in Montgomery. . . . I worked quietly and tried to do whatever I could in the community without projecting myself. And as far as I am concerned, I haven't changed. I'm just the same as I was in Montgomery." While not directly challenging the interviewer, her quiet rejoinder attests to her continuing active role in Detroit. She had long been someone who did the behind-the-scenes work necessary for political mobilization—in Montgomery *and* Detroit.

Many of her associates attested to Parks's radiant kindness and deep empathy with people's suffering. Her commitment to meeting the socio-economic needs of black Detroiters extended to her personal practice. By 1966, according to friend Mary Hays Carter, she had "a private charity going. . . . She engages the business people that she is acquainted with [to assist with] the problems of those that are without gas during the winter or without electricity. She does her own investigating—she seems to know whether these people are 'putting her on,' and I have never known her to call me up and ask me to cook food for some hungry family or to help her find clothing for some unfortunate family that they were not genuinely in need." Parks took an active role in her block club, serving for a time in the 1960s as vice president. The block club worked on cultural and neighborhood improvement, sponsored a youth program providing recreation and job guidance to neighborhood teenagers, and held block festivals to build community.

In 1967, Conyers received the SCLC's annual Rosa Parks Freedom Award for his contribution to civil rights. The first African American on the Judiciary Committee, he had cosponsored the Medicare bill, sought more funding for the War on Poverty, particularly for education and housing, and opposed the war in Vietnam. Conyers was one of seven in Congress to oppose military appropriations in 1965 and to call for a peaceful resolution to the United States' role in the conflict—which led to considerable opposition from the UAW in his run for reelection in 1966. Parks helped present him the SCLC award.

One of Conyers's central priorities was to get more black people elected to public office. According to Horwitz, Conyers belonged to a new generation of black politicians "calling our own shots"—not opposed to labor or the Democratic Party "but [affirming that] 'we're not going to be taken for granted.'" Parks similarly embodied this "independent" spirit. Many of Parks's efforts on behalf of black candidates were centered in Detroit. She actively supported Coleman Young's initial run for Common Council in 1960, worked on George Crockett's run for Recorder's Court in 1966, on Richard Austin's unsuccessful campaign to become the city's first black mayor in 1969 and Coleman Young's successful one in 1973, and on behalf of Erma Henderson, who became the first black woman elected to Detroit's City Council in 1972. "Rosa was Black. No question about that. She supported Black candidates," observed Michigan State Representative Fred Durhal. Parks made appearances for the candidates, did mailings, made phone calls, and other office work. "One thing about Rosa Parks, she was an active participant, not a sideline person," attested Durhal, who recalled all the nitty-gritty work Parks did on behalf of black candidates. According to Atchison, Parks had crossover appeal in those years, "You could take Rosa into the white community and nobody gets upset. But she would energize the black community, [exhorting] 'now is the time.'" She also helped with the mayoral campaigns of Carl Stokes in Cleveland and Richard Hatcher in Gary, Indiana.

GOING SOUTH

In April 1965, moved by the photos of marchers being beaten on the Edmund Pettus Bridge in Selma, Parks decided to return to Alabama to join the march herself. She had marched down Woodward with other Detroiters to show her solidarity with the Selma marchers. She could not afford the trip, but through the intervention of Louise Tappes, the UAW helped pay her way. Parks traveled with the UAW from Detroit to Atlanta and then by bus to Montgomery, spending the evening with her friend Bertha Butler.

The next morning, as the march entered its final stretch into Montgomery, Parks joined the last four-mile leg. The air reeked of stink bombs. White Citizens' Council members had plastered the roads with huge billboards of the 1957 picture of her and King at Highlander, calling them Communists. Parks had not been given a vest to denote her as an official participant, and many of the young people did not know her. Because she did not have an official jacket, the police kept pulling her out and making her stand on the sidelines. Parks got shoved on the sidewalk. A marshal recognized her standing there. "I was in but they put me out," she explained. "It seemed like such a short time that I had been out of Alabama, but so many young people had grown up in that time. They didn't know who I was." She marched for a bit with Dick Gregory's wife, Lillian, and also for a time with blues-folk singer Odetta, but she could not keep up and would end up on the sidelines to wait for someone else to spot her and pull her back in. Indeed, this sense of being "put out of the march" would be the most indelible image of the experience for Parks. Nixon did not march, Parks recalled, but stood on the sidelines. A number of the whites in the crowd did recognize her, yelling, "You'll get yours, Rosa."

At the march's conclusion, a huge crowd gathered on the hill next to the capitol. Coretta Scott King looked over at Mrs. Parks as the speeches began and thought to herself, "We had really come a long way from our start in the bus protest, when only a handful of people . . . were involved." Parks—along with Dr. King and a number of other leaders—gave speeches that were broadcast nationally. Introduced as the "first lady of the movement," she was coaxed to the podium by thunderous applause from the huge crowd—"the most enthusiastic" reception of all the speakers, according to the *New Yorker*, with calls of "Tell! Tell! Tell!" In her remarks, she spoke about her personal history growing up under racism and her fear of KKK attacks: "My family was deprived of the land they owned." Telling the crowd, "I am handicapped in every way," she publicly affirmed her connection to Highlander and tried to counter "the propaganda" being circulated about the school's Communist ties. Refusing to be frightened by the billboards, she highlighted what she had learned from Highlander and disputed the idea that Dr. King was a Communist. As Horton recalled, she credited Highlander as the place where she learned "not to hate white people" and affirmed that she was "the one at Highlander, I was the one. I am the student, not Martin. He was just our speaker." She concluded with customary modesty by saying others could say it better than her.

Enjoying being back with old friends, Mrs. Parks felt Dr. King seemed "unusually shy" and "distracted." She did not see either Myles Horton or Virginia Durr. The Durrs had a large gathering of movement people over to their house that night and were disappointed, as was Myles Horton, "that you did not get in touch with them, but understood the situation." Returning to the hotel in Atlanta tired, Parks felt depressed. She had premonitions something bad was about to happen. That night she had a nightmare: standing in a field with a large billboard, she saw a man with a gun and was trying to warn her husband when the man with the gun aimed at her. She woke up shaken and was horrified to learn about the murder of Viola Liuzzo the night before. A white Detroiter who had journeyed south to join the march, Liuzzo was murdered as she drove marchers home. Members of the Klan, including an FBI informant, Gary Rowe, pulled up alongside Liuzzo's car, trying to force her off the road. They shot at her and the other passenger, nineteen-year-old African American Leroy Moton, who played dead when the Klan searched the car.

Back in Detroit, Parks visited the funeral home, attending the memorial service at the People's Community Church. At a mass meeting the night before the funeral, 1,500 people gathered to show their outrage over Liuzzo's murder. The crowd gave Parks a standing ovation. Sickened by the killing, Parks saw the need for further pressure on Johnson. "This was no time to be dormant," she declared in a testimonial dinner for the Women's Public Affairs Committee (WPAC). Following the murder investigation closely, she became disgusted by how Liuzzo was labeled immoral and a Communist to draw attention away from the killing. The Klansmen who killed Liuzzo were never convicted of murder—likely because of the FBI's involvement in the killing and their desire to protect informant Rowe.

Liuzzo's murder spurred Parks to be even more politically active, particularly in the WPAC, a black women's community and political action group headed by her friend Louise Tappes, and also in Detroit's Friends of SNCC.

FRIENDS OF SNCC

Mrs. Parks had been thrilled by the unfolding freedom struggle in the South, particularly the work of the Student Nonviolent Coordinating Committee. In the early 1960s, she became active in the Friends of SNCC (FOS) organization in Detroit. To Mrs. Parks, the 1960 student sit-ins picked up the bus boycott spirit. "Really it's the youth," she told a reporter in 1965, "keeping the civil rights movement going." Younger activists in Detroit, SNCC worker Martha Norman Noonan explained, were "conscious of how much she was with us. . . . We didn't have any sense of her as an icon. Just a fellow freedom fighter. . . . [We saw her] more like a comrade. We viewed her as a heroine but we were surrounded by heroines. . . . It wasn't like, 'Oh this is Mrs. Parks.' "

The Northern FOS organizations provided fund-raising and support infrastructure for SNCC's Southern work and helped Northern young people who wanted to be part of the movement also take on issues closer to home. The FOS served several functions, as fund-raising entities for the work being carried on throughout the South, information centers for spreading word of the Southern activities in the North, and independent organizing centers for protest campaigns to bring national pressure on the federal government. Indeed, by 1966, Parks and Dorothy Dewberry were basically a two-person operation running the Detroit FOS. Dewberry was a Detroit native, a former NAACP youth chapter member, a Northern Student Movement worker, and student at the Detroit Institute of Technology. Now key to maintaining SNCC's presence in Detroit, Dewberry later married Detroit activist Dan Aldridge. At the Detroit FOS office, Parks did mailings, collated goods to be sent south, and performed other office tasks.

From 1965 to 1967, Detroit FOS focused on supporting the independent political movement that had grown in Lowndes County, Alabama. Disillusioned by the Democratic Party's capitulation to segregationist interests at its national convention in August 1964, SNCC moved toward creating an independent political party. SNCC workers like Stokely Carmichael joined forces with a burgeoning local movement in Lowndes County, known for its racial hostility. At the beginning of 1965 none of the 5,122 voting-age African Americans there was successfully registered to vote. Black people made up the majority of the county, nearly twelve thousand of the fifteen thousand county residents, and fraud and corruption were so extreme that there were more white voters on the rolls than there were voting-age whites in the county. Black Lowndes residents began to build a movement to break the racial and economic caste system. When the Selma-to-Montgomery march traveled through the county, Carmichael and other SNCC activists built connections to these local activists and decided to come back to help organize. They helped local residents build an independent black political party separate from the Democratic Party, much like Detroit's Freedom Now Party, and ran their own black candidates for local office.

The Lowndes diaspora—many of whom had migrated to Detroit—responded with help and support. Detroit FOS helped to provide an important ballast to the Lowndes movement. Parks joined the Detroit Lowndes Christian Community for Human Rights. With FOS, she raised money and collected clothes, returning to Alabama in support of the Lowndes County Freedom Organization on a couple of different occasions.

On March 27, 1966, in the backwoods of Lowndes, five hundred county citizens and one hundred SNCC workers gathered for a mass meeting and "first anniversary" service of the Lowndes movement entitled "No More Chains or Sorrow." Hand-lettered programs listed the "mother of the civil rights movement" at the beginning of the program. Following the opening songs and introductions, Mrs. Parks praised the crowd gathered that night for their valiant organizing in this remote, oppressive part of her former home state. Loudspeakers broadcast her words to the overflow crowd outside.

Parks's legendary calm was in evidence despite the danger of these trips. Lowndes was a violent place. A white volunteer, Jonathan Daniels, had been killed in 1965. "We were always conscious of danger," Gloria House, a SNCC worker explained. Dorothy Dewberry Aldridge, who accompanied Parks on these trips to Lowndes, recalled the importance of these visits for local activists—Parks wanted to "lend her support . . . [and] everybody was so honored to have her." They would canvass, visit people's homes, and bring goods. According to Aldridge, on one of their trips to Lowndes, they were riding with Stokely Carmichael, who was notorious for his fast driving. Alarmed, Aldridge started to panic, thinking, "We're going to kill the mother of the civil rights movement." But Mrs. Parks was "as calm as can be. She had the effect of being able to calm people [by her composure]." Parks had been down this way before—not this particular road, but for decades now she had faced the fear to keep on organizing.

In October 1966, Carmichael came to Detroit for an address at Central Congregational.

Thirteen hundred blacks and about fifty whites packed into Cleage's church to hear Carmichael talk about Black Power. From the podium, Carmichael began by singling Mrs. Parks out in the audience and calling her his "hero." Interrupted at almost every sentence by applause, Carmichael spoke of the need for independent black economic advancement, decried educational inequality, saying we should "sue the country for segregated schools," and lambasted American involvement in Vietnam. He called on people to set aside individualism and be "black people first," rather than Democrats or Republicans, and spoke on the need for black pride. "We have to learn to love black and it isn't easy," Carmichael explained, decrying the use of hair straighteners and processes.

THE 1967 UPRISING

In 1967, the Parkses were still residing on the ground floor of a brick flat on Wildermere and Virginia Park. Raymond barbered around the corner at the Wildermere Barber Shop. The Parkses' flat functioned as a bit of a salon in Virginia Park, filled with robust discussion and debate. Many of the young men who came by greatly admired Malcolm X, like the Parkses did, and shared their feelings of the importance of continued struggle.

The Parkses were frequent visitors to Edward

Vaughn's bookstore, the only black bookstore in Detroit. Opened in 1959 and devoted to African American studies, Vaughn's soon became an epicenter of black militant activity. It was one of the only places in the city to buy books written by black authors, and activists would often meet to debate and strategize. Rosa and Raymond regularly went to Vaughn's to browse and discuss. "One of my best customers," Vaughn recalled, Mrs. Parks was "always very conscientious on issues of race." Vaughn remembered them as a "great couple," who "together were two of the quietest people you ever see." According to Rosa's cousin Barbara Alexander, Raymond was even "quieter than Rosie." It was Rosa, not Raymond, who tended to get involved in things, taking part periodically in the various discussion groups that met at the bookstore.

Presaging the development of a vibrant black arts movement in Detroit, these groups—called Forum 65, Forum 66, and Forum 67—were led by people like Albert Cleage and the Henry brothers. Many of these activists saw how urban renewal had wreaked havoc on black housing and commerce. The Parkses' neighborhood, Virginia Park, had been compromised by urban renewal and highway construction. One of the most attractive neighborhoods in the city, with beautiful homes and trees and high rates of home ownership, Virginia Park had grown increasingly crowded as more people, particularly poorer people involved in the underground economy, were pushed there because of highway construction in the Hastings area. Given the realities of Detroit's segregated housing market, landlords proceeded to subdivide properties into smaller apartments, and many families had to double or triple up.

Most black Detroiters faced similar conditions with overcrowding, inferior city services, unresponsive city government, and repressive policing. As in Montgomery, political and class tensions fissured Detroit's black community, as some benefited from the new political and economic opportunities of the city while most did not. Detroit's housing was still extremely segregated. Blacks were often met with violent reprisals by police and white vigilantes if they moved into some of Detroit's all-white suburbs or white sections of the city—while the majority of black people were crowded into underserved inner-city neighborhoods. Urban renewal had meant black removal, the disruption of neighborhoods, and increased tensions within the black community. The new interstate system sliced through the black community, isolating certain neighborhoods from the rest of the city. The civil rights movement in Detroit, as in most Northern cities, had garnered few substantive successes. This frustration with the lack of response to black grievances combined with persistent social and economic inequality triggered riots in nearly every major American city between 1964 and 1968. Many of the social issues, which Parks knew intimately from her own experiences in the city and her work with constituents, came to a head that July.

The force enabling this structural inequality was police repression. In Detroit, the demographics of the police did not reflect the city's population. Though the city was 35 percent black, there were only 217 black officers in a police force of 4,709. Three of the 220 lieutenants were black, and only one of the city's sixty-five inspectors. Patterns of police harassment and brutality by white officers on black Detroiters had been publicized for years. Many black Detroiters saw the police as an arm of state repression and harassment rather than a protective force. Police were often disrespectful and regularly took money and other items of value from black people they stopped. Any note of protest was likely to lead to a beating and a trumped-up charge of drunkenness, disorderly conduct, or resisting arrest. Indeed, police had expanded the practice of arresting black people simply on "investigation," constituting about a third of their arrestees.

Some of the tinder for the uprising came from the self-satisfaction of many whites who believed

Detroit was a place of robust opportunity for blacks. That Northern liberalism had become too much to bear as many black residents still experienced second-class citizenship. While activists had long called for state remedies to Detroit's segregated schools and housing, reform in police practice, and the opening up of job possibilities, little had changed. There had been little enforcement in Detroit of the *Brown* decision and little substantive adherence to the spirit of the Civil Rights Act. Indeed, Congress passed the 1964 Civil Rights Act only after its liberal Northern sponsors deliberately exempted northern schools by stipulating that "desegregation shall not mean the assignment of students to public schools in order to overcome racial imbalance." Detroit would not be forced to desegregate its persistently separate and unequal schools.

Still, many in the city, including the city's white political leadership, believed they could avoid the urban unrest that had swept Harlem in 1964 and Los Angeles in 1965. They saw the city as the apex of racial progress, with two black congressmen, a strong NAACP, a liberal mayor, and a prosperous auto industry that appeared to offer black and white workers economic security and opportunity. Detroit's riot, the *Washington Post* later lamented, was "the greatest tragedy" of all the uprisings because the city had been "the

American model of intelligence and courage." But many of Detroit's civic leaders in the years before the 1967 riot had turned a blind eye to mounting protest in the city, similar to Montgomery's white officials who had believed blacks were satisfied.

At 4 a.m. on July 23, 1967, police raided an illegal after-hours bar or "blind pig" at 9125 Twelfth Street, about a mile from the Parkses' apartment. Because many Detroit entertainment venues and restaurants had barred blacks, and black business owners had difficulty securing the capital and paperwork for an official establishment, many working-class black people socialized in such venues. Detroit bars closed at 4 a.m., so blind pigs also provided recreational spaces for factory workers who worked late shifts. In April 1967, a Department of Justice representative visiting Detroit cited police raids on blind pigs as "one of the chief sources of complaint."

Celebrating the return of two men from Vietnam, over eighty people had gathered when police roughly tried to close down the venue and began arresting all the patrons. The crowd that night refused to disperse and grew larger and more angry as morning dawned and the day went on. The police grew more forceful and violent as well.

Conyers arrived to try to disperse the crowd.

"We couldn't get people to disperse. . . . You could hear in the background sometimes windows being smashed and stores being looted. Houses were being set fire to. . . . People were letting feelings out that had never been let out before, that had been bottled up. . . . It was the whole desperate situation of being black in Detroit." The crowd did not react well to Conyers's entreaties, calling him an Uncle Tom and chanting "We want Stokely Carmichael."

At the height of the unrest, the riot encompassed fourteen square miles, a full two hundred square blocks, of the city. Governor George Romney requested federal help, and late on the 24th, President Johnson agreed to send in 2,700 army paratroopers. The police responded violently against all blacks, not just those engaged in criminal acts. Tanks rolled through the streets of Detroit, and police and National Guardsmen were given wide latitude to "subdue" the riot by any means necessary, which often meant indiscriminately intimidating, arresting, and mistreating black residents. As Conyers explained, "What really went on was a police riot." In a move that only served to increase the chaos, many officers shot out the streetlights. They raided apartments where supposed rioters were hiding, arresting and assaulting many uninvolved Detroiters.

During the riots, Vaughn's bookstore was

destroyed by police, who, according to historian James Smethurst, attacked it because it was a gathering place for black militants. Vaughn, out of town when the uprising started, returned the next day, feeling that "nothing would be wrong with my store, at least from the people, and of course I was correct." Two days later, the police destroyed the shop. Firebombing the building, they mutilated the artwork, damaged many of the photographs and books, and left the water running, ruining the vast majority of books. Police maintained their actions were necessary because they had reports that guns were stored in the bookstore, but witnesses maintained that the attack was a hate crime.

Over seven thousand people were arrested during the uprising. So many people were arrested that police turned Belle Isle Park into a jail and held people in buses outside the court. Judge George Crockett refused to set high bail for these misdemeanors, letting people go on their own recognizance, unlike many of his colleagues, who set bail at $10,000. Perhaps the most egregious event came when police killed three young men in the Algiers Motel. While the officers reported a gun battle, no weapons were ever found, and witnesses said the young men were deliberately murdered. At the end of five days, forty-three people were dead—thirty at the hands of the police. Hundreds were injured, including eighty-five police officers. Property damage was estimated at $45 million, with 412 buildings completely burned. City officials were quick to call it a riot, in part because insurance policies with extended coverage covered the "perils of riot and civil commotion" but not insurrections. But parts of the city would never be rebuilt. In Virginia Park, after the riot, the city cut down the trees that lined many of the blocks.

The Parkses home was near the uprising's epicenter. They could see some of the fires and looting from their apartment "because we live right in the heart of the ghetto." The uprising took a significant personal toll on the family. Raymond's barbershop was looted, his hair-cutting equipment stolen, and their new car vandalized. Raymond was "just beside himself," Parks recalled. "I had to spend most of my time trying to keep him as calm as possible." In a 1980 interview, Parks recalled, "It was hard to keep my husband in. I had to drive him to get a shot, a sedative to quiet him down. One of the troopers threatened to hit him on the head with a rifle. This was right at our house. He was trying to watch the barbershop. He had a knife that a judge whose hair he took care of in Alabama had given him. And the trooper took it. He said that he always regretted that. It wasn't something dangerous. That was pretty sad." In another interview, she described Raymond having a nervous breakdown similar to what had happened during the bus boycott.

Conyers's office, where Parks was working, became a crucial way station and complaint center during the uprising. Conyers recalled, "People were calling up reporting what the police were doing or did or reporting missing people, people wanting to file complaints. Fear [and] anger. Could this be happening in America." Parks participated in many meetings, viewing the events partly as an outgrowth of the frustration at the continuing inequities in a putatively liberal city.

Deeply saddened by the destruction, she attributed the uprising's origins to the long history of white resistance to civil rights demands and rising anger among black youth. "[King's] philosophy didn't accomplish what it should have because the white Establishment would not accept his philosophy of nonviolence and respond to it positively. When the resistance grew, it created a hostility and bitterness among the younger people, who worked with him in the early days, when there was some hope that change could be accomplished through his means." As one young black Detroiter explained, "For a change we have one voice saying that black people are not satisfied with the way that they have to live."

Mrs. Parks located the uprising in the context of

white resistance and deafness to black grievances in Detroit. Ed Vaughn echoed this sentiment. "Everybody who cared, white and black, told them. They did not listen." Historian Douglas Brinkley has argued that Parks believed the riot had "nothing to do with civil rights—it was pure hooliganism and she had little sympathy for its perpetrators." However, in a number of interviews in the years right after the riot, Parks seems to have a more complex view than Brinkley asserts. In an interview two months after the riot, Parks put forward a class analysis of what underlay the uprising: "It could be understandable how they would resort to doing these things because they just hadn't had the training and the background to feel that they should have patience when they see all of the wealth about them while they themselves are deprived of it. Everything now is geared to affluence, plenty, prosperity." Parks explained the uprising as resulting both from the exclusion of black people from America's postwar affluence and as part of a broader cultural ethos of consumption and accumulation that plagued American society in the 1960s.

Parks did not cast her years of activism or her protest on the bus as utterly distinct from the actions of the rioters. The city's leadership along with the federal government tried to downplay the concerns and structural inequalities that fueled these disturbances. While never condoning random violence or theft and not seeing how it "was going to accomplish any good," Parks could understand the uprising as "the result of resistance to change that was needed long before-hand." She saw the ways that "the establishment of white people . . . will antagonize and provoke violence. When the young people want to present themselves as human beings and come into their own as men, there is always something to cut them down." Emphasizing the ways that the violence of the riot had been "provoked" by systemic inaction, Parks stressed the ways that full American citizenship was tied to a decent standard of living and a publicly unbowed identity—which had been denied to these young men. In her reflections on the riot soon afterward, Parks thus was willing to contextualize people's anger.

Many tried to ascribe the riots to the growing Black Power movements throughout the nation, casting a rising black militancy as a threat to the legacy of the civil rights movement and blaming it for the violence on display in riots across the country. In a five-part series in the *Detroit News*, black journalist Louis Lomax fingered six activists in the city—James and Grace Lee Boggs, Reverend Cleage, Milton Henry, Richard Henry, and Ed Vaughn—as spearheading a dangerous Black Power militancy that bore partial responsibility for the climate that produced the riot. Parks, though, felt differently: "If you looked beneath the surface, we could see the frustration of some of these people. . . . I guess for whatever reasons it came about, I felt that something had to be wrong with the system." Dispirited by the riots, she nonetheless observed, "Regardless of whether or not any one person may know what to do about segregation and oppression, it's better to protest than to accept injustice." While many decried the violence as senseless and self-inflicted, Roger Wilkins of the U.S. Justice Department, who had gone to Detroit and was nearly killed by National Guardsmen, took a view similar to that of Parks. He saw the riots as "a jagged plea to the political system: Pay attention to us, we're left out, we ache. In a sense it was a hopeful scream."

In late August, Conyers publicly called for a Full Opportunity Act—a $30 billion aid program guaranteeing every citizen a job, raising the minimum wage, promoting massive construction of low-income housing, enacting a comprehensive college loan program, and stepping up enforcement of nondiscrimination in housing, schools, and jobs "both in the North and the South." The plan garnered little national support.

Locally, the Citizens City-wide Action Committee (CCAC) stepped into the fray. CCAC

441

was a grassroots, citywide movement of black militants and nationalists of various stripes chaired by Christian nationalist Reverend Cleage. Many black Detroiters were dismayed when the officers involved in the Algiers Motel killings escaped indictment. Angered by the police cover-up, young radicals led by Dan Aldridge and Lonnie Peek were inspired by H. Rap Brown's call for "a people's tribunal" when he addressed a crowd of five thousand at Detroit's Dexter Theater. They had hoped the city's newspapers would make a full inquiry into the events, but a sympathetic reporter, according to Aldridge, found his story quashed by his editors. So, in the absence of an indictment of the cops or substantive media attention to the case, they decided to hold a tribunal as a way to air a fuller version of the events to the community. "Watch accurate justice administered by citizens of the community," a CCAC flier announced. "Witness the unbiased, legal action of skilled black attorneys. Review and watch the evidence for yourself."

The "People's Tribunal" was held at Cleage's church on August 30, 1967. It had originally been scheduled for the Dexter Theater, but the theater backed out. According to Cleage, it was held in his church because there were fears that the police would attack any other place. The church's executive board made a public statement attesting to its reasons for holding it there: "We love our church and the building in which we worship. But even if granting permission for the People's Tribunal to be held here means the destruction of the building, as churches have been destroyed in Birmingham and all over the South, we still have no choice." The trial was held under an eighteen-foot image of the Black Madonna that Cleage had installed on Easter Sunday 1967. Painted by Detroit artist Glanton Dowdell, the portrait depicted a dark-skinned mother cradling an equally dark infant. Cleage explained the significance of the powerful image—to "have come so far that we can conceive of the Son of God being born of a black woman." Attendance at the church—which came to be known as the Shrine of the Black Madonna—skyrocketed after the uprising.

The tribunal gave a grieving black community a people's trial, which had been denied them by the compromised legal process. Those gathered heard the case against three white Detroit police officers, Ronald August, Robert Paille, and David Sendak, and a black security guard charged in what witnesses called the "execution" of three young black men—Carl Cooper, Aubrey Pollard, and Fred Temple—at the Manor House annex of the Algiers Motel on July 26, 1967, the fourth day of the uprising.

Over two thousand people packed the church,

with others trying to get in. Journalists from France and Sweden covered the event. Attorney Milton R. Henry served as one of the two prosecutors; Solomon A. Plapkin, a white attorney, and Central Church member Russell L. Brown Jr. acted as defense counsel. Kenneth V. Cockrel Sr., a recent Wayne law school graduate and future cofounder of the League of Revolutionary Black Workers (LRBW), was the judge and moderator. The stenographer was Central Church member Carolyn Cheeks Kilpatrick, who would later be elected to Congress. They called witnesses to the events to give accounts of what they saw; because the police sought to intimidate the witnesses, the organizers tried to keep them hidden until they testified.

Among the people selected to be jurors were African American novelist John O. Killens, Edward Vaughn, and Rosa Parks. Dan Aldridge had asked Parks to serve as a juror because of her reputation in the community as a person of integrity, and she had agreed. Mrs. Parks's willingness to take part in the Tribunal took great courage and fortitude, according to Dorothy Aldridge. They both knew Carl Cooper's family. So the police killings at the Algiers Motel were not just a community outrage but a personal tragedy for a family that Mrs. Parks knew. Shaken by Cooper's killing, Raymond's breakdown, and the destruction in her neighborhood,

Rosa Parks put aside her personal difficulties and maintained her composure in the service of this community hearing.

The jury found the officers guilty of murder. Cockrel urged that the sentence should be carried out by "the people." "There is no way to put down on paper the sheer horror of the recital of events," Cleage would write in the *Michigan Chronicle*. "It is hard to believe . . . that a group of ordinary white men could so hate ordinary black men." Given its organizers and leaders, Parks's participation in the People's Tribunal shows how she was located firmly in the midst of an emerging militancy in the city.

Right after the uprising, living so close to its epicenter, Mrs. Parks took part in the formation of the Virginia Park District Council to help rebuild the area and promote local economic development. The council helped facilitate the building of a shopping center, the Virginia Park community plaza shopping center, which broke ground in 1981, one of the only community-owned black shopping developments in the country. The Virginia Park block club focused on rehabilitation and affordable housing, with a commitment to rebuilding and empowering the neighborhood. Martha Norman Noonan and other friends formed the People's Food Co-op, which Parks joined immediately, supportive of cooperative buying. According to Aldridge, Mrs.

Parks was a locavore decades before its time and dedicated to healthy eating. Her brother kept a huge garden, where they cultivated fresh fruits and vegetables. Parks canned and preserved foods and, her niece recounted how her aunt often taught other people how to preserve food, so they might also stretch their food supply and not waste anything.

In 1969, Parks's friend Louise Tappes succeeded in getting Twelfth Street—"where the civil disturbances began"—changed to Rosa Parks Boulevard. The city council rescinded a law forbidding the naming of streets for living persons in order to honor Parks. The symbolic meaning of Twelfth Street would forever be linked to, if also transformed by, Rosa Parks.

The last time Mrs. Parks saw Dr. King was in a place where most whites continued to fight to maintain their racial privilege—the exclusive Detroit suburb of Grosse Pointe. On March 14, three weeks before his assassination, King came to speak at Grosse Pointe South High School, and Parks and a friend went out to hear him. The school board had debated for months whether to allow the event to be held there and relented only after organizers took out an extra $1 million insurance policy. "There was a horrible mess when he tried to speak out there," she explained. "They disrupted the meeting. . . . It was an all-white city." Fearing assassination, the police chief actually sat on King's lap as they drove up to the school. In the press conference afterward, King observed that it was the most disruption he ever faced in an indoor meeting. Parks was unsure, however, that King even knew she was there. "I got close enough to wave but I don't think he saw me. . . . It was just so crowded," she recalled.

King's speech, "The Other America," focused on the economic inequalities corroding American society. He put Detroit's recent uprising in the broader context of racial inequality in the city and throughout the nation.

> It is not enough for me to stand before you tonight and condemn riots. It would be morally irresponsible for me to do that without, at the same time, condemning the contingent, intolerable conditions that exist in our society. . . . A riot is the language of the unheard. And what is it America has failed to hear? It has failed to hear that the plight of the Negro poor has worsened over the last twelve or fifteen years. It has failed to hear that the promises of freedom and justice have not been met. And it has failed to hear that large segments of white society are more concerned about tranquility and the status quo than about justice and humanity.

Like Parks, King saw the roots of the riots lying in white indifference and intransigence to black demands for justice, equality, and real economic opportunity and challenged the blinders of Northern liberalism. Like King and many of her comrades in Detroit, Rosa Parks had grown increasingly frustrated with the lack of fundamental change. Fresh energy and strategies were needed—and Mrs. Parks welcomed a new generation of freedom fighters to the struggle.

CHAPTER SEVEN

"Any Move to Show We Are Dissatisfied"
Mrs. Parks in the Black Power Era

STANDING UP TO WHITE TERROR and intimidation from Scottsboro to the Montgomery bus
boycott, Rosa Parks "always felt it was my right
to defend myself if I could." Having long
believed in self-defense, she was a steadfast critic
of racism in the criminal justice system and a
proponent of the far-reaching social change
necessary to ensure real black equality. "I'm in
favor of any move to show that we are
dissatisfied," she told an interviewer in 1964.
"We still haven't received our rights as citizens."
To her, black demands often got mired in delay to
give the appearance of progress without
committing to actual change. "As long as we
formed little committees," Parks recalled, "and
went to the bus company and asked to be treated
like human beings and continued to travel on the
bus nothing happened." Increasingly frustrated
by the languid pace of change, she chafed under
the regular admonitions from white moderates
that black people were demanding too much. In
1967 she told an interviewer, "I don't believe in
gradualism or that whatever should be done for
the better should take forever to do."

Parks's lifetime of political work ran the gamut of approaches. A longtime admirer of Martin Luther King Jr., Ella Baker, Malcolm X, Septima Clark, *and* Robert F. Williams, she embraced multiple approaches, given the systematic and pervasive character of American racism. Working alongside the Left from the Scottsboro case to E. D. Nixon's Brotherhood of Sleeping Car Porters to the Highlander Folk School to her association with the National Negro Labor Council, Parks refused to be intimidated by the red-baiting of the era. She also knew that registering to vote and taking her youth group to see the Freedom Train exhibit—let alone galvanizing an organized bus boycott—were revolutionary acts in the postwar South. To her, a united front was key to black struggle. Rosa Parks's enduring commitment to racial justice and human rights formed a bridge between the civil rights struggle in Montgomery and black liberation in Detroit. Like many younger activists, Rosa Parks had grown frustrated with white intransigence toward black demands for equality in jobs, housing, schools, public services, and policing. Looking at her activities during this era provides a wider view of the Black Power era, its antecedents in past struggles, and the ways seasoned activists like Parks traversed its diverse currents.

In a 1970 interview, Parks sought to put the growing Black Power movement in context. She reminded the interviewer about the tremendous resistance and public criticism civil rights activists had faced in Montgomery and across the South from many white citizens and public officials, even though they were nonviolent.

> Dr. King was criticized because he tried to bring about change through the nonviolent movement. It didn't accomplish what it should have because the white Establishment would not accept his philosophy of nonviolence and respond to it positively. When the resistance grew, it created a hostility and bitterness among the younger people, who worked with him in the early days, when there was some hope that change could be accomplished through his means.

She contextualized rising black militancy as a response to the illegal and violent acts civil rights activists had endured at the hands of whites in the 1950s and early 1960s, observing, "And of course when it didn't [produce change], they gave up the philosophy of nonviolence and Christianity as the answer to the problems." Parks was quick to provide a broader historical view; even though Black Power advocates were criticized for not being like Reverend King, the minister himself had been similarly attacked for his militancy. The antagonism to Black Power was rooted in opposition to demands for substantive, systemic change and in many ways, Parks pointed out, similar to the attacks on King.

On numerous occasions, Parks explicitly observed that the increase in black militancy derived from white obstructionism. "If segregationists had realized . . . when the law had passed that there would be no more segregation, legally, because of race," she firmly explained, "if they had accepted it a bit more graciously instead of following this hard-core resistance and organizing White Citizen's Councils [and] all of these things they did to resist . . . , there wouldn't have been developed this new element that realized that with the nonviolent movement, what they had hoped had not been accomplished." Unending white resistance to racial equality, as Mrs. Parks was quick to note, had produced the terrain for black militancy to grow.

Time and again, she sought to show the roots— the legitimacy—of black rebellion. It galled her that black people were often told to wait, to be patient and not angry. She had long hated the ways black rebels were seen as freaks or demonized for their refusal to submit. Mrs. Parks was a kind, unassuming woman, raised in the church and in the Southern traditions of good manners and public dissemblance. She possessed a reserved demeanor, an enormously caring and gentle spirit, and a wealth of patience and forbearance. But that didn't mean she was not angry at the depth and breadth of American racism—and it did not mean she approved of the distinctions commentators now often tried to make between her "good" (though previously "dangerous") bus action and the "bad" and "dangerous" Black Power movement. As Septima Clark had noted more than a decade earlier, Mrs. Parks didn't broadcast her militancy, but she certainly had a steely determination and progressive politics at her core. Parks didn't appreciate attempts to try to divide the black community by demonizing its more militant elements. And like the younger people she described, Mrs. Parks's own frustration had heightened over the decades of white terror, obstruction, and indifference that greeted black protest.

Mrs. Parks's political activities and associations in 1960s and 1970s Detroit illustrate the continuities and connections between the civil rights and Black Power movements. Indeed, as she worked in Conyers's office attending to the socioeconomic needs of their Detroit con-stituents, Mrs. Parks continued her activities with the SCLC and NAACP *and* took part in a variety of Black Power events. Many underlying tenets of the Black Power movement were not new to her. A set of political commitments that had run through her work for decades—self-defense, demands for more black history in the curriculum, justice for black people within the criminal justice system, independent black political power, economic justice—intersected with key aspects of these new militancies.

Parks's beliefs and activities thus challenge the sharp line often drawn between the civil rights and Black Power struggles. The fable of Rosa Parks is so compelling because it exemplifies the heroic success of a grassroots struggle—a local boycott triggers a mass movement that ripples across the South and results in the passage of the Civil and Voting Rights acts, thereby correcting the legacy of racial discrimination in the South. Mrs. Parks herself had been invited to the White House on August 6, 1965, to watch President Johnson sign the Voting Rights Act into law to mark that victory. Seeing Parks at Black Power events in the late 1960s and 1970s demonstrates the limits of those successes and the larger goals of earlier struggles still unmet.

Moreover, the proper and quiet Rosa Parks is typically pictured in contrast to angry and violent black militants who ostensibly perverted the civil rights movement and sent the nation spiraling into the morass of 1960s rebellion. Conversely, within the emerging literature on Black Power, Mrs. Parks, like many other middle-aged black women, is implicitly treated as too proper, staid, and integrationist to have been compelled by—let alone helped nurture—Black Power. Thus, many people react uncomfortably with the idea of a Rosa Parks who stood with black radical trade unionists, cultural nationalists, antiwar activists, and prisoners' rights advocates. There is a tendency to see racial militants as hard or angry or filled with hate—and miss the love of humanity that undergirded many people's activism. Parks could love humanity and, through that love, be outraged by injustice and impatient with the lack of fundamental social change. That impatience was rooted in a tenderness toward people's suffering that made it impossible for her and many others in the Black Power movement to rest easy in the face of continuing injustice. To be thrilled by the growing assertion "Black Is Beautiful" and the increased emphasis on black culture and history was part of that love. It was not about hating other people, as Parks made clear; it was about loving yourself.

Parks continued to remind the nation that the struggle was not over. For her, carrying on the struggle in the late 1960s and 1970s meant supporting a new crop of black activists. Revolutionary Action Movement founder Max Stanford, now Muhammad Ahmad, described Mrs. Parks and a number of women elders as "more progressive than the men." According to Ahmad, Parks was a long-distance runner who "didn't let anything deter her." These elders might not have agreed with every direction the new activists took, but they saw the importance of supporting these young freedom fighters. Nonetheless, there is often a tendency, born in part from the sectarian impulses of the era, to try to pigeonhole Parks's ideology—was she a Communist? A nationalist? A revolutionary trade unionist? A peace activist? While she admired and consorted with many people who claimed these ideologies, there is little indication that she adopted one for herself. Mrs. Parks was a race woman. She possessed a deep activist sensibility, and like many others, particularly women of the era, she went where people were organizing. Similar to her mentor Ella Baker, Parks saw the point of radicalism as getting to the root of the problem. The bus boycott had not been an end in itself but part of an ongoing struggle. Refusing to cast the Black Power movement as a perversion of the civil rights movement, Parks was not afraid of ruining her reputation or getting in trouble, as some black leaders of her generation would feel about associating with these young militants.

Many revisionist histories of Rosa Parks and the bus boycott, which attempt to "set the story straight," detail her pre-boycott political activities, yet nearly all of these accounts end with the boycott and almost never show her ongoing political commitments in the Black Power era.

The fable of Parks is so powerful that even those who seek to challenge it often inadvertently hew to its contours. The focus on Parks's respectability has unconsciously made it easy not to investigate her activities in these later decades. People have assumed that there was not a story to tell in these later years, and indeed Mrs. Parks was not one to disrupt that assumption. As Julian Bond ruefully admitted, "I met her numerous times over her lifetime. . . . I just talked to her about innocuous things, never delved deeper. . . . I thought I knew everything there was to know about her."

Parks didn't tend to volunteer information, and interviewers rarely asked. Even with friends, she was often quiet about her political work. Her friend and physician William Anderson (who had taken part in the Albany Movement before moving to Detroit) explained that she would answer questions if asked directly but would never volunteer her ideas about political issues or events. "You would have to drag it out of her," journalist Herb Boyd recalled. Numerous friends and colleagues agreed with this assessment; Conyers's aides Larry Horwitz and Leon Atchison recalled that they would often read in the paper that Parks had attended some political event (many times "radical ones"), and often, neither knew she was going. Beginning with the Scottsboro case, Rosa Parks had learned to be discreet about her political activities. She kept her political opinions to herself and was never one to debate or recruit anybody. Indeed, part of her political philosophy flowed from the idea that people had to figure out the right direction for themselves: "It's very difficult for me to tell somebody else what they ought to do."

Reflecting her reserve about such details, her autobiography contains little information on these activities, perhaps because she wanted to keep them obscured. As Conyers noted, Parks was "a progressive but she did not wear her political philosophy on her sleeve." In addition, because Jim Haskins was less familiar with the Detroit political community, he asked fewer questions, shaping the arc of her autobiography. Perhaps, also, she did not believe people would approve.

Parks's unassuming personality stood in contrast to the brash manner of many radicals. As Chokwe Lumumba noted, "We were emulating really powerful people. King, Malcolm, Paul Robeson— those pan-Africanists, Kwame Nkrumah, Julius Nyerere, Sekou Toure. . . . [Many activists] were genuine, but had their own ego, and were high profile. Whereas Rosa was just unassuming. . . . Sometimes you would not notice she was there, or her contribution." In many ways, Rosa Parks was hidden in plain sight in the Black Power era. But as Northern Student Movement activist Frank

Joyce recalled, "Everybody knew that she did have radical politics."

Never one to seek public recognition, she had found her public fame around the boycott hard to bear. She chafed at the ways journalists continued to seek her out, telling an interviewer in 1973, "There are times when I'd like to get to be quiet and have some time to be like an ordinary person who nothing special ever happened to. I hope I won't be having to tell people that story for the rest of my life." In the late 1960s and 1970s, she still preferred to blend in—and often, in this era, she could. Many times she simply wanted to listen and participate, to do what she could and try not to attract attention. And if she used her stature, it would be for the promotion of the event or issue.

Conyers also attributed the omission of Parks's radicalism from the narrative of the civil rights era in part to the "discongruity" of it—"she had a heavy progressive streak about her that was uncharacteristic for a neat, religious, demure, churchgoing lady." Indeed, standard notions of Black Power leave little room for the quiet militant. In the popular imagination, black militants do not speak softly, dress conservatively, attend church regularly, get nervous, or work behind the scenes. Fundamentally, they are the opposite of a middle-aged seamstress who spoke softly and slowly. And yet there were many militants like Mrs. Parks who did just those things. As her cousin Carolyn Green explained, Parks made clear when she thought something was wrong or untruthful. "Her voice never went up. . . . But she would let you know."

She was "quiet and sweet," black nationalist Ed Vaughn explained, "but strong as acid." Friend Roberta Hughes Wright noted, "She's quiet—the way steel is quiet. . . . She seems almost meek, but we already know the truth of that, don't we?" "Fearless," Leon Atchison stated. Indeed, in interviews with her political associates from 1960s-era Detroit, even from some of the era's most prominent Black militants, numerous people attest to the gentleness of her spirit *and* her fearlessness—how unintimidated she was in her post-Montgomery political activities. This circumspect fearlessness was nothing new. In 1975, Vernon Jarrett, a black reporter for the *Chicago Tribune*, did a twenty-year retrospective series on the bus boycott. Jarrett had been warned by E. D. Nixon before he interviewed Mrs. Parks that she "ain't gonna talk much because she's a doer, not a bragger. But that woman is one of the most courageous citizens this country has ever known." Jarrett too was struck by this quality. "The contradictory personality that is Rosa Parks, that subdued thunder in her Southern country-woman's voice—did not prepare her listener for the little verbal bombs that she exploded."

Understanding Rosa Parks's militancy widens the lens on the work of radicalism more broadly. Part of what Mrs. Parks did in the years of Black Power was show up. She "spoke with her presence," as Conyers put it. And in the popular portrayals of Black Power, there has been a tendency to miss the saliency of this role. To understand Black Power as a constellation of movements means seeing the numbers of people who turned out for lectures, sold newspapers, attended rallies, built independent black cultural organizations, and joined defense committees for black political prisoners. Rosa Parks "was everywhere," according to bookstore owner Ed Vaughn. Able to keep herself above the ideological fray, she listened and learned, attending rallies and speeches and public mass meetings. She signed petitions, came out for lectures, and immersed herself in all the black history she could find. She protested police brutality, spoke out on behalf of black prisoners, let groups use her name, and helped found local prisoner-defense committees. She didn't necessarily join groups or agree with everything that was said, but it was important to take part. Above all, she wanted to be helpful—and if her presence allowed more people to see the issue, then by all means she would try to come. "She had a lot of guts to lend her name to left-wing causes," Conyers's aide Larry Horwitz explained, "things that people thought were scary." By the late 1960s, a new generation had come of age. She took heart in the pride and boldness of these young people, and they found sustenance in her support.

ROSA, MALCOLM, ROBERT, AND THE POLITICS OF SELF-DEFENSE

In the 1990s, Parks shocked black-nationalist lawyer Chokwe Lumumba when she told him that her hero was Malcolm X. Lumumba had assumed that her work and close personal relationship with King meant that he would be her personal inspiration. No, she clarified, she had certainly loved and admired King greatly, but Malcolm's boldness and clarity, his affirmation of what needed to be done for black people, made him her champion. Parks saw no contradiction in her deep admiration for both King and Malcolm X. Describing Malcolm as "a very brilliant man," she had read all she could on his ministry and political program by the mid-1960s. "Full of conviction and pride in his race," she noted, Malcolm X reminded Mrs. Parks of her own grandfather: "The way he stood up and voiced himself showed that he was a man to be respected." Having imbibed this tradition of self-defense from her grandfather, Rosa Parks had put it to use as a young person. "We always felt that if you talked violently and said what you would do if they did something to you," she explained in her autobiography, "that did more good than nonviolence."

Rosa and Raymond had been raised to be "proud" and learned they would have to speak up and act decisively for self-protection. "I just couldn't accept being pushed even at the cost of my life," she explained. Nonviolence on the individual level "could be mistaken for cowardice." Rosa's belief in self-defense and collective action stemmed as well from her Christian faith. "From my upbringing and the Bible I learned people should stand up for rights just as the children of Israel stood up to the Pharaoh."

Like many blacks and whites of that period, Mrs. Parks found the use of mass nonviolent action new and "refreshing," calling the boycott "more successful, I believe, than it would have been if violence had been used." Still, she found it "hard to say that she was completely converted to it." Her thinking coupled nonviolence with self-defense. For her, collective power could be found in organized nonviolence, while self-respect, at times, required self-defense: "As far back as I remember, I could never think in terms of accepting physical abuse without some form of retaliation if possible." Indeed, the Parks family, like many black Southerners, had long kept a gun in their home, even as they participated in the nonviolent movement.

Parks saw nonviolent direct action and self-defense as interlinked, both key to achieving black rights and maintaining black dignity. In regard to self-defense, she found herself closer in philosophy to Malcolm X than King. "Malcolm wasn't a supporter of nonviolence either," she noted. Still, she harbored tremendous respect for King's organized program and deeply held philosophy of nonviolence. Organized nonviolence in Montgomery during the bus boycott had offered a powerful rebuke to white city leaders and local citizens who thought black people too undisciplined and emotional not to resort to violence when provoked. Parks had delighted in the power of it. In 1962, at the SCLC's annual convention in Birmingham, a white man in the audience started hitting King, who did not defend himself. Instead King yelled, "Don't touch him! We have to pray for him." Parks witnessed the event, and saw this as "proof that Dr. King believed so completely in nonviolence that it was even stronger than his instinct to protect himself from attack." After the attack, knowing King must be in pain, Parks went and got him a bottle of Coca-Cola and some aspirin. She was extremely proud: "His restraint was more powerful than a hundred fists."

While Parks had a deep appreciation for nonviolent resistance, her resolute belief in self-defense continued amidst the growing momentum of the nonviolent movement. On a church program in 1964, she copied lines from Claude McKay's poem "If We Must Die":

If we must die—let it not be like hogs . . .
Though far outnumbered, let us still be
brave . . .
Like men we'll face the murderous,
cowardly pack,
Pressed to the wall, dying, but—fighting
back!

Parks encountered Malcolm X three times in the mid-1960s, and they became a bit friendly. In 1963, when the Northern Christian Leadership Conference and the Grassroots Leadership Conference were both held in Detroit, Parks attended both. Black radicals had come from across the country, including Harlem's Jesse Gray, Brooklyn's Milton Galamison, Freedom Now Party founder William Worthy, and Cambridge, Maryland, leader Gloria Richardson. Malcolm X wanted to meet Parks, and they had a warm greeting. At King Solomon Baptist Church on Detroit's near west side, Malcolm X preached his "Message to the Grassroots" to a crowd of three thousand. Linking black struggle in the United States to anticolonial movements internationally, he rebuked the civil rights movement: "The only kind of revolution that is nonviolent is the Negro revolution. The only revolution in which the goal is loving your enemy is the Negro revolution." Still he affirmed the importance of a black united front and of nonviolent disruption aimed at the federal government in Washington— a vision of independent political action that dovetailed with the emerging Freedom Now Party in Detroit. Just a couple weeks before Kennedy's assassination and Elijah Muhammad's silencing of Malcolm, the speech provided a preview of the post–Nation of Islam, politically independent Malcolm X.

Parks was also in the audience on April 12, 1964, when Malcolm X reprised his famous "Ballot or the Bullet" speech at a GOAL Legal Fund rally at King Solomon Church. Malcolm X extolled the power black people held, referring to the deciding role that black voters played in Kennedy's 1960 presidential election. Explaining that he was not an American but a "victim of Americanism," he called on black people to use the ballot independently and in unity: "A vote for a Democrat is a vote for a Dixiecrat. . . . It's time now for you and me to become more politically mature and realize what the ballot is for; what we're supposed to get when we cast a ballot; and that if we don't cast a ballot, it's going to end up in a situation where we're going to have to cast a bullet. It's either a ballot or a bullet."

This GOAL event helped to launch the Freedom

Now Party's 1964 campaign. Founded in October 1963 by Reverend Albert Cleage, Milton Henry, Luke Tripp, and others, the Freedom Now Party aimed to be an independent third party that protected the interests of black people. "We understand that a Democrat represents Democrats, a Republican represents Republicans but a freedom-now party candidate represents Negroes!" ran their slogan. The Freedom Now Party sought to build a party that put the interests of black people before partisan loyalty and backroom compromises with black leaders. In 1963, Cleage had urged a "no" vote—"No Taxation for Discrimination"—on a city millage referendum asking voters to increase revenue for Detroit's public schools. Though this stance put him at odds with some civil rights leaders, Cleage opposed the increase, believing that blacks should not give more money to a system that oppressed black children and refused to change its segregationist ways.

Rosa Parks had long seen the importance of independent black political power. Though she never put herself forward on the ballot of the Freedom Now Party, Mrs. Parks was a supporter, as were a number of her friends, including Mary Hays Carter. She began making appearances at Freedom Now Party rallies, read their newsletter, and followed their progress. In 1964, the Freedom Now Party ran a slate of candidates for

Congress, governor, and other state offices. All lost.

Parks had also been heartened by Malcolm X's reaching out to the civil rights movement and his journey to Selma in early 1965 at SNCC's invitation to support the movement there. United front politics, Parks thought, were the key. Right before Malcolm X was assassinated, she got the chance to have a longer conversation with him. On February 14, 1965, Mrs. Parks received a Dignity "Overdue Award" from the Afro-American Broadcasting Company. Milton and Richard Henry, who had helped create the Freedom Now Party, understood the emerging power of the mass media. Recognizing the negative images of black people portrayed in public culture (if black people were portrayed at all) and the limited ways the media covered black protest, they had founded this black broadcasting company in Detroit to put forth programming for "spiritually free black people." The Afro-American Broadcasting Company put out a two-hour radio show each Saturday on WGPR, which often featured Malcolm's speeches in the program. In 1965, they held their first awards ceremony. Along with Mrs. Parks, those honored that evening included the Motown Record Company, Marian Anderson, Sidney Poitier, and Jackie Gleason. Perhaps because Malcolm X was slated to give the evening's keynote, seven of the business honorees, including Hudson's Department Store and the Chrysler Corporation, refused to accept their awards.

There at Ford Auditorium in downtown Detroit, with Rosa Parks sitting in the front row, Malcolm X gave a powerful speech, often referred to as his "Last Message" because it occurred a week before his assassination. The week before, Parks had turned fifty-four. Malcolm X had reflected on his own birthday with Alex Haley. "A lot of water had gone under the bridge in those years. In some ways, I had had more experiences than a dozen men." As she sat in the audience that February evening, Rosa Parks too had had more experiences than a dozen men. She had gotten her political start with her grandfather's Garveyism and in her newlywed work with Raymond on the Scottsboro case. She found her own political footing in the lonely activism of the NAACP in the 1940s, encouraging youth activism, black voter registration, and legal challenges to white brutality. Her spirit was nourished in the interracial populism of Highlander Folk School. Used to all-black political organizing with the Brotherhood of Sleeping Car Porters and the Progressive Democratic League, she had helped spur and sustain a yearlong black bus boycott in Montgomery and had traveled the country raising money and attention for it. She watched the sea of humanity gather in DC for the March on Washington and had met many of the great civil rights luminaries of the twentieth century: A. Phillip Randolph, Ella Baker, Septima Clark, Eleanor Roosevelt, Thurgood Marshall—the list went on. She knew most of Motown's emerging black leadership, from Reverend Cleage to the Henry brothers, and had just been hired to work in John Conyers's Detroit office.

That February evening was a difficult one for Malcolm X. His Queens home had been fire-bombed that morning, but he came to Detroit anyway and was heavily protected that night. The crowd gathered that evening was sparse. In his speech, Malcolm X cautioned those gathered about the ways that the media was trying to determine the black agenda,

> I read in a poll taken by *Newsweek* magazine this week, saying that Negroes are satisfied. . . . When they think that an explosive era is coming up, then they grab their press again and begin to shower the Negro public, to make it appear that all Negroes are satisfied. Because if you know that you're dissatisfied all by yourself and ten others aren't, you play it cool; but you know if all ten of you are dissatisfied, you get with it.

Malcolm zeroed in on an issue that had troubled Parks for decades: the public perception that blacks were satisfied with their situation and the ways black people were induced constantly to affirm their contentment in American society.

He acknowledged the power of an organized black vote. Similar to the voter education and registration projects Parks had worked on in the 1940s and 1950s, Malcolm wanted black people to know "what a vote is supposed to produce . . . to utilize this united voting power so that you can control the politics of your own community, and the politicians that represent that community." Black self-determination required empowered and enfranchised black people, he explained that February evening, echoing what Mrs. Parks had told her NAACP youth a decade earlier. Like Malcolm, Parks had developed an increasingly international vision. She had always been an avid reader of the black press, which was covering anticolonial struggles across the globe. Back in 1960 at a Highlander meeting, Parks had linked discrimination at home to the increasing militarization of the Cold War. "As we eliminate legal segregation and discrimination . . . [we] should then begin working together for peace, world peace and disarmament and do away with war." By 1965, she was reading all she could on the antinuclear peace movement and on the geopolitical situation in Vietnam. Like Malcolm

X, she was an early opponent of U.S. involvement in Vietnam and watched the unfolding anticolonial movements across Africa and Asia with great interest.

Afterward Parks got Malcolm X to sign her program and spoke with him privately. Malcolm was likely as delighted as Mrs. Parks by this meeting. In his last years, as he began charting his own political and religious path, founding the Muslim Mosque and the Organization of Afro-American Unity, he took counsel from a number of black women leaders including Gloria Richardson, Maya Angelou, Vicki Garvin, and Queen Mother Moore, who had long histories of organizing experience to impart. OAAU member Peter Bailey recalled conversations where Malcolm praised courageous people in the civil rights movement, singling out both Fannie Lou Hamer and Rosa Parks. Parks would cherish that program and their conversation even more when the devastating news came seven days later that Malcolm X had been assassinated at the Audubon Ballroom in Harlem.

Self-defense to Rosa Parks was self-protection. This was a variation of Malcolm's argument in the "Ballot or the Bullet" speech when he explained, "I'm nonviolent with those who are nonviolent with me. But when you drop that violence on me, then you've made me go insane, and I'm not responsible for what I do." For both of them, nonviolence required a commitment to decency on both sides, and without that it could not be sustained indefinitely. In an interview in 1967, two months after the Detroit riot, Parks talked extensively about the power of nonviolence and the necessity of self-defense. Parks had grown increasingly disillusioned with the ways that nonviolent direct action over the past decade had repeatedly been met with white violence.

> If [nonviolence] had been received for what it was it would still work. But my belief is that if we are going to have non-violence and love and all that, it should be on both sides; it should not be met with violence because you actually can't remain nonviolent too long with the kind of treatment that would provoke violence. . . . If we can protect ourselves against violence it's not actually violence on our part. That's just self-protection, trying to keep from being victimized with violence.

Parks steadfastly put the onus of the problem—"the kind of treatment that would provoke violence"—on white action.

The virulence and persistence of racial inequality took its toll on her on many different levels. In 1965, Parks explained to George

Metcalf the trying situation black people were facing: "There is no longer the encouragement to endure it as it is. There is not enough strength to conquer it. Just the bitterness to lash out with whatever the impulse is to do." Discouraged by the vehemence of white resistance and the pace of change, Parks felt a kinship to the young people in the growing Black Power movement who "don't believe in absorbing this abuse, physically and otherwise; now that there are so many who are really in the belief that you have to meet violence with violence, it leaves me almost without any explanation of what is best, in a way."

Shortly after the devastating news of King's assassination, Parks told a reporter that she was unsure she could be "as strong, forgiving and Christian-like as Dr. King. Sometimes I think it's asking too much, in the face of all the oppression and abuse we have to bear. We shouldn't be expected not to react to violence. It's a human reaction and that's what we are, human beings." For Rosa Parks, who had long practiced Christian forbearance toward the endless harassment of her and her family, there still came a time when the abuse became too much to tolerate, when the assertion of one's humanity necessitated self-protection.

Parks had long admired Robert F. Williams's commitment to building a militant working-class NAACP chapter in Monroe, North Carolina, in the 1950s, and they may have met or spoken shortly after the boycott. Williams advocated "armed self reliance" alongside nonviolent direct action and, like Nixon and Parks in their work for the NAACP, took up a series of legal cases aimed at addressing white brutality and legal malfeasance. But his leadership drew attention from the FBI and the criticism of the national NAACP. He was ousted as Monroe NAACP president in 1959 for controversial remarks asserting the right of blacks to defend themselves. In 1961, following a riot in Monroe around the Freedom Rides, Williams gave a white couple shelter in his home, fearing the anger of the crowd. He was subsequently charged with kidnapping by the North Carolina police, and the FBI issued a "most wanted" warrant for his arrest. The Williamses chose to go into exile, first settling in Cuba and then China. While in Cuba, Williams published a pivotal book, *Negroes with Guns*, and broadcast a radio program called *Radio Free Dixie* that could be heard back in the United States.

When Robert and Mabel Williams returned from exile in China, they became friends with Rosa Parks and her young companion, Elaine Eason. Parks had met Eason in 1961 working at the Stockton Sewing Company sewing aprons. The sixteen-year-old Eason was a spirited young woman. While their days of sewing alongside each other were short-lived, their friendship spanned the next four decades. Eason, whose family also hailed from Alabama, had many questions for Mrs. Parks, eager to learn from this experienced activist. Later, after Parks began working for Conyers, Elaine worked in the same building downtown, and their friendship deepened. Having long delighted in the militancy of young people and looking to them to carry the movement forward, Rosa admired Elaine's passion and commitment. Over the decades Rosa and Elaine grew as close as family, and certainly part of that bond stemmed from a shared political spirit. Elaine's activism grew over the course of the 1960s, as she joined the Republic of New Afrika (RNA) and became romantically involved with Wesley Steele. Steele was one of the bodyguards protecting the Williams family upon their return to the United States.

It was through these RNA connections that the Williamses got to know Rosa Parks. Parks came to admire Robert and Mabel Williams even more "as we worked together," and they all gathered for Elaine's wedding to Wesley. Robert Williams came by Conyers's office, where Parks worked. During this period, an organized campaign emerged to prevent the extradition of Williams to North Carolina, which wanted him to stand trial. Parks joined the petition drive and the defense committee, and donations for Williams's extradition fight in 1969 were sent to Conyers's office. Conyers himself urged the Detroit NAACP to "express to the Governor its outrage at the prospect of Mr. Williams being extradited." Meanwhile, according to Mabel Williams, her husband was so disturbed by the ways Parks's contributions to the black struggle were overlooked that in the midst of fighting his extradition, Williams took time in his speeches to highlight the fact that Rosa Parks was living in Detroit, and yet people did not seem to understand her importance.

Three decades later, on October 22, 1996, Parks, in turn, mounted the pulpit in Monroe, North Carolina, to pay tribute to Williams following his passing. After seeing many comrades assassinated or die prematurely, she remarked on the good fortune of attending a funeral for a black leader who had lived a full life. She explained how she had "always admired Robert Williams for his courage and his commitment to freedom." In the long roster of her most treasured encounters and friendships, Mrs. Parks thus counted many of the period's most fearless black voices as friends and comrades.

KING'S ASSASSINATION:
ROSA PARKS MARCHES ON

Since he joined the movement in Montgomery in 1955, Martin Luther King's life had been repeatedly threatened. By 1968, he was routinely receiving multiple death threats. Lambasted for his stand against U.S. militarism abroad and for his attempts to build a movement for economic justice at home, King remained committed to these efforts. On April 3, he returned to Memphis, where he joined the struggle of striking sanitation workers and met with local leaders to prepare for an April 8 march. Just as the SCLC had faced in Albany, Birmingham, and Selma, the court issued an injunction to prevent the march. The organizers vowed to fight it. Angered, King told the crowd gathered that night, "All we say to America is: Be true to what you said on paper. . . . Somewhere I read that the greatness of America is the right to protest for right." That evening, King called home to arrange his upcoming Sunday sermon, entitling it "Why America Is Going to Hell."

On the evening of April 4, after a day of meetings, King walked out onto the balcony of his room at the Lorraine Motel and was shot by a single .30 caliber bullet. He was rushed to the hospital. Calls began to come in to the Parks home that King had been shot. "He can't die, I said to myself, he can't die," she said. King did not survive. According to the legal case, the sniper was James Earl Ray, who acted on his own. Ray died in prison in 1998 with significant questions (including from the King family itself) remaining about his guilt and the role of others in the assassination.

The news of King's death devastated the Parks family and ripped through the nation. Rosa "just went numb," playing Sam Cooke's "Long Time Coming" over and over. "I was lost. How else can I describe it?" Raymond could not eat for days. The day after the assassination, Stokely Carmichael declared, "White America made its biggest mistake because she killed the one man of our race that this country's older generations, the militants and the revolutionaries and the masses of black people would still listen to." Angry and disillusioned, people took to the streets. Riots broke out in 110 cities across the country.

Rosa Parks and Louise Tappes journeyed south. Parks first went to Memphis to join the march that King was to have led. But after speaking for a few hours with a number of the striking sanitation workers, she was overcome by grief and accepted Harry Belafonte's invitation to ride on his plane to Atlanta with the King and Abernathy families for the funeral. At the funeral, she was seated on the platform next to Ossie Davis, who began the memorial speeches.

The process of distorting King's legacy began even at his funeral. The funeral was packed with dignitaries and celebrities while many of the people who had worked alongside the civil rights leader in the movement did not get in.

Officials estimated that between thirty-five thousand and fifty thousand gathered in the streets around the church. Harry Belafonte recalled getting particularly angry at a prominent *New York Times* reporter standing next to him at the funeral. "I could not help but tell him that this grievous moment was in part the result of a climate of hate and distortion that the *New York Times* and other papers had helped create. . . . Just coming to grieve the loss was no cleansing of guilt." King's funeral would provide a preview of Parks's own fancier memorialization—the presence of dignitaries crowding out the people who should have been there, and the public desire to lionize the heroes of the movement apart from their actual goals and the movements they took part in.

The next month, Parks journeyed to Washington, DC, to join Coretta Scott King, Ralph Abernathy, and thousands of activists in carrying on the Poor People's Campaign that King had been organizing before his assassination. A cross between the Bonus Marches of the 1930s and the 1963 March on Washington, this poor people's movement aimed to organize a large contingent of poor people to descend on the nation's capital to engage in civil disobedience and force the government to address widespread economic inequality. As Reverend Abernathy—now head of the SCLC—explained: "We used to sing a song in our church—'Take Your Burdens to the Lord and Leave Them There.' We have decided that we are going to take all our problems, our bodies, our children, the rats and the roaches and everything to the White House and leave them with LBJ."

A month after King's assassination, poor people of all races from across the country set off for Washington in caravans, mule trains, buses, and on foot. They set up a tent city of plywood shanties on the Mall named Resurrection City. About 2,500 people stayed there, but heavy rain made the condition of the tent city hazardous, and Resurrection City was torn down by police on June 24. Perhaps the high point of the encampment came on June 19. Some 50,000 to 100,000 people who had joined the campaign gathered at the Lincoln Memorial for a Solidarity Day rally. Parks's first stop in DC was Resurrection City, and then she joined the rally at the Lincoln Memorial. Though not feeling well, she was determined to be there and play her part in continuing the campaign. She too wanted to connect their bus protest thirteen years earlier to this campaign for economic justice. Introduced to the crowd, who gave her a standing ovation, Mrs. Parks choked up, telling those gathered that she was glad to be there but wished that King could have been there with them. Still she affirmed, "Today everyone knows what we want. We don't plan to give up until freedom is attained for all persons, regardless of race." Coretta Scott King gave a powerful speech that day calling on American women to "unite and form a solid block of women power" to fight racism, poverty, and war.

It was an emotional and difficult trip for Parks. She told a *Washington Post* reporter, "My feelings are numb. I've been battered around too much." King's assassination had deepened her despair over the deep roots of racism in American society. The next year on July 3, 1969, bullhorn in hand, she returned to King's tomb to address a crowd there on his untimely death. In many ways, by the late 1960s, Parks had become an elder stateswoman in the vast and diverse black freedom struggle. She, Coretta Scott King, and Betty Shabazz, along with artists like Gwendolyn Brooks and Margaret Burroughs, all came to play this role in the ensuing years. Indeed, these women elders largely kept themselves above the ideological fray to support a broad range of mobilizations. Even if they did not see eye to eye about everything being done or said, they admired the interconnections between race and class, domestic and foreign policy fearlessly asserted by these young activists.

These relationships—and the importance that these elders held for young militants—have largely been overlooked. Ericka Huggins of the Black Panther Party criticized the "myth that people in the BPP had no high regard for people [like Rosa Parks]." Indeed, for many activists, to have movement stalwarts like Mrs. Parks on their side brought encouragement, protection, and a broader historical scope to their work. Such cross-generational solidarity was precious and cherished. "You can't minimize her validation," historian John Bracey observed. Her backing lent legitimacy. "If Mrs. Parks is there, it must be okay" was the message her presence signaled. "She never gave up," Bracey continued. "That's important to young people. 'Why are you tired? I'm not tired.' . . . She was an example. She could have retired, said 'I'm not in this, don't talk to me.' But she steadily kept coming out."

Parks often drove herself to events in a big old car; it had "the image of a tank," according to Conyers aide Larry Horwitz, which contrasted sharply with the physically diminutive Parks. Mrs. Parks was in demand by many sectors of the black freedom struggle, including organized labor. On May 6, 1969, Reverend Abernathy tele-grammed Parks about a strike of hospital workers seeking to form a union in Charleston that had been ongoing for six weeks; SCLC was issuing a national call for a Mother's Day march to express national outrage. Parks flew to Charleston to join the protest. A militant black labor movement took shape in 1968 in Detroit after a wildcat strike at Chrysler resulted in the disproportionate punishing of black strikers. Parks supported the efforts, supporting black labor candidates and occasionally joining the pickets.

Shirley Chisholm had been elected as the first black congresswoman in 1968 from a newly drawn district in Brooklyn. On June 28, 1969, the Women's Political Action Committee invited Chisholm for her first public appearance in Detroit. Parks gave the introduction, describing Chisholm as a "pepper pot." Highlighting Chisholm's family's roots in the Garvey movement, Parks celebrated Chisholm's "defiance and loyalty to her constituents . . . when she refused to sit on the assigned agriculture committee. Her aggressive and determined attitude landed her on the veteran's committee where she fought hard to end segregation in the military." Perhaps reflective of her own relationship with Raymond, Parks also highlighted the role Chisholm's husband, Conrad, played as "her closest friend and advisor." According to Fred Durhal, Parks also supported Chisholm's bid for the Democratic nomination for president in 1972.

Parks, like many of her civil rights comrades, had grown disillusioned with U.S. foreign policy and was an early opponent of America's intervention in Vietnam. According to Atchison, Parks was "passionate" in her opposition to the war, willing to oppose it early on when it was dangerous to do so. She met with veterans' groups and helped further the growing antiwar movement, attending numerous meetings, rallies, and teach-ins at Wayne State. According to Conyers, he and Parks had long been opposed to the war and wondered why King was taking so long to come out in opposition, later learning King had been warned to keep silent. Parks's intense focus on Vietnam was reflected in her mailbox, which filled with antiwar materials from the Fellowship of Reconciliation, the American Friend's Service Committee, the Wayne State's student newspaper, *South End*, the international Viet Nam Solidarity Committee (attached to the Women's International Democratic Federation), the Women's International League for Peace and Freedom (WILPF), and a number of socialist groups and mobilizations.

Sparked in part by revelations about the My Lai massacre, more than one hundred soldiers convened in Detroit from January 31 through February 2, 1971, to hold a hearing on the atrocities they had committed or witnessed in Vietnam. This event, sponsored by Vietnam Veterans Against the War (VVAW), came to be referred to as the Winter Soldier hearings—and was held in downtown Detroit. Parks strongly supported the VVAW, as did Conyers, and may have been involved with the hearings. On the second day, Conyers, along with Senator George McGovern, called for full congressional hearings into the issues raised by the soldiers' testimonies. Along with Coretta Scott King, Ella Baker, and Virginia Durr, Parks had been affiliated with the Women's International League for Peace and Freedom for many years. With Scott King, she was listed as one of the sponsors of the Jeanette Rankin Brigade antiwar protest held in Washington, DC, on January 15, 1968, marching under the banner "We Oppose the Vietnam War and Racism and Poverty at Home."

Parks's understated feistiness came through in June 1968 when she received the Capitol Press Club's first Martin Luther King Jr. award. Accepting the honor, she sought to set the record straight, referring to the notion that her bus stand stemmed from tired feet as "something of a joke" and carefully explaining to the reporters gathered, "I didn't move because I was tired of being pushed around." Parks sometimes found all the fuss about her bus stand puzzling. To her, resistance was natural, as she reminded an interviewer following her Press Club award. "It's always amazing to me that people thought it was [startling]. It seems to me it's natural to want to be treated as a human being."

BLACK POWER: A NATIONAL MOVEMENT, A LOCAL STRUGGLE

Parks was keenly interested in building a movement to strengthen black voting and economic power nationally, provide support for local community mobilizations, and build black cultural institutions. Given her experience and influence, various activists and groups sought her involvement. While some civil rights leaders viewed the emerging Black Power movement with trepidation, Parks saw a number of continuities with previous political movements she had worked with.

Her political approach in many ways resembled her skills as a quilter. "Any good woman my age from Alabama definitely knows how to quilt," she observed. Her respect for ancestry and her appreciation for conserving a black past—"the use of small scraps by making quilts"—resonated with strands of Black Power and cultural nationalism in this period. Moreover, the faith that from small pieces would emerge a majestic whole, the ability to sew pieces from many places and to see the value in new materials for the color and texture of the quilt, informed her political life. Black Power did not, for Mrs. Parks, ruin the quilt of black protest. It enriched it. Nor did it require scrapping the previous pieces or reveal their irrelevance. This new swatch would be sewn into the existing whole because she could see how it came out of other designs and helped give added dimension to the emerging pattern. Above all, the need for people to work together and not be divided, for people to pitch in to assist the actions of others, was key to her philosophy: "In quilting maybe somebody would come in to visit, it might be a friend and would just join in and help."

Parks continued to read voraciously, keeping up with a number of newspapers and magazines each day and assiduously following local, national, and international issues. Arthur Featherstone, who worked alongside her at Conyers's office, described Parks as "always reading" and having "collected thousands of newspaper clippings." Subscribing to various black newspapers, including the *Birmingham World* and *Michigan Chronicle*, and militant publications from SCEF's *Southern Patriot* and *Now!*, the Freedom Now paper, to Wayne State's student newspaper, the *South End*, she kept abreast of racial politics in Alabama long after she left and closely followed local political struggles in Detroit. She saved scores of papers, from the *Detroit Community Voice* to *The Ghetto Speaks* to the *Southern Patriot* to *Now!* Vonzie Whitlow recalled the Parks's living room stacked with piles of newspapers and magazines. Parks didn't talk much about politics, her cousin Barbara Alexander remembered, but she kept all sorts of articles.

Possessing an archivist sensibility, Parks kept an extensive clipping file which—along with many of the periodicals she received—is now preserved in her papers at Wayne State University. Many articles she kept for more than a decade were stories of black radicalism and Black Power. Looking through those files, which predominantly cover the mid-1960s through the mid-1970s, reveals the scope of Mrs. Parks's intellectual and political worldview. The issues that captured her attention were wide-ranging: reparations and the meanings of Black Power, emerging militant groups like the Black Panthers and the Republic of New Afrika, events like the Attica uprising and the Angela Davis case, the war in Vietnam, and free speech at home all sparked Mrs. Parks's interest. She was affiliated with the work of dozens of Detroit groups, and her mailbox filled with announcements of antiwar rallies, black history symposia, Afrocentric programs, and community organizing meetings.

According to the *Pittsburgh Courier*, Rosa Parks was part of a "militant group" of blacks at the 1968 Democratic Convention in Chicago that refused to back any presidential candidate. They held a meeting at the YMCA in downtown Chicago spearheaded by delegates Richard Hatcher, John Conyers, and Yvonne Braithwaite. Like Harry Belafonte and Lerone Bennett, Parks was not an official delegate but took an active part in the meeting. Named the National Committee of Inquiry, the group had formed in the months leading up to the Democratic

Convention because many felt the Democratic Party wasn't sufficiently committed to prioritizing black issues or encouraging black leadership. Finding the process of selecting delegates in both major parties "undemocratic . . . and a mockery of representative government," they sought to nurture an independent black power base in national politics. Endorsed by Coretta Scott King, along with Belafonte, Bennett, Hatcher, and Conyers, this mobilization formed the seed that grew into the 1972 Gary Convention.

Rosa Parks attended the third national conference on Black Power in Philadelphia on August 29, 1968. Many of the leading Black Power advocates, like Amiri Baraka, Ron Karenga, Max Stanford (later Muhammad Ahmad), Richard Henry, Stokely Carmichael, and H. Rap Brown, were there along with nearly two thousand participants. Mrs. Parks kept her customary low profile and had no speaking role. As she would at many events, she sat, listened, and did her knitting (or some sort of handwork), according to Nathan Hare, who recalled her mingling with people, talking particularly with Queen Mother Moore. The conference—with its theme "Black Self-Determination and Black Unity through Direct Action"—garnered national attention from the media, the Philadelphia police, and the FBI. As Max Stanford was leaving, Hare pulled him aside to introduce him to someone he needed to meet.

That person was Mrs. Parks. Stanford was "blown away. Here was the mother of the civil rights movement."

Continuing to work with activists throughout the country, Parks journeyed to Gary, Indiana, in March 1972 to attend the National Black Political Convention. That convention, convened by Amiri Baraka, Ron Karenga, and Richard Hatcher, brought together ten thousand black people from across the nation to outline an independent black political agenda during this presidential election year. Independent black politics was not new to Parks. She had been involved in independent black organizing two decades earlier with E. D. Nixon's Progressive Democratic Party and had long been convinced of the power of an organized black vote—and she was not about to miss this historic gathering. Gwen Patton recalled Parks giving a short greeting at the Convention, conveying her "blessings" of the event.

Asserting that both parties "had betrayed us" and protected white political interests, the Gary convention agenda focused on creating a black united front in order to harness black power nationally and support local initiatives. While some of the Michigan delegation, led by Coleman Young, who were more loyal to the Democratic Party and UAW, walked out partway through the convention, Parks did not. Perusing the book tables at the convention, Parks was captured on film by black photographer LeRoy Henderson. Henderson, who photographed numerous Black Power demonstrations and black caucuses in the 1960s and 1970s, spotted Mrs. Parks gazing admiringly at a poster of Malcolm X. "I was there with my camera watching, recognizing people, and grabbing candid shots of them . . . capturing this stuff for future generations. . . . Standing at this poster table was a lady nobody even seemed to know who she was. . . . I knew it was Rosa Parks."

Parks also found herself part of a growing, diverse Black Power scene back home in Detroit. "Honest to God, almost every meeting I went to, she was always there," Ed Vaughn recalled. "She was so regular." She began wearing "colorful African-inspired garb," according to Brinkley, and took pleasure in new opportunities to learn about African cultural influences. The dissemination of black history to young people had long been one of her priorities, and in Detroit she supported after-school programs, independent black schools, Afrocentric educational initiatives, and black history curricula. Close to home, the Afrikan History Club at McFarlane Elementary School made Mrs. Parks its honorary secretary.

As much as her health and schedule allowed, she turned out for black events in the city. "Dang, that's Rosa again," Vaughn would note. Indeed, her schedule was so busy in the late 1960s that she convinced her brother, Sylvester, and his wife, Daisy, to allow her niece, fifteen-year-old Rhea, to come live with the Parkses to help look after her mother and Raymond. There were many meetings, functions, and out-of-town events that Rosa wanted to attend, and she wanted someone else at home because neither her mother nor Raymond was in good health. "She was always going somewhere," cousin Carolyn Green recalled.

But she was not always widely noticed. The combination of her unassuming presence and that her stature in the 1960s and 1970s was not what it would become by the 1990s meant that Parks's political activities sometimes escaped broader attention. But the fact that she came out was important to many younger activists. While Mrs. Parks was not a street activist, if asked to do something, according to Dan Aldridge, she would. "People would be surprised at how she would come out," he explained. "She was so ladylike and genteel. But she had a depth of political sensibilities."

Parks was in the midst of a growing black cultural and political nationalism in the city. With roots before the 1967 uprising, a Black Arts Movement emerged in the city. Long interested in black history, art and literature, Parks came to some of the Thursday evening biweekly forums at Vaughn's bookstore and attended the Black

Arts Convention in 1966, which brought Stokely Carmichael, H. Rap Brown, Don Lee, and Nikki Giovanni and a host of young black writers and other nationalists to Cleage's church. She tuned in to a new black radio station, WCHB, and saw shows at the Concept East Theater, a theater company founded to increase the opportunities for black artists to write, direct, produce, and act in Detroit's fairly small theater scene.

Other activists—including Rosa Parks's friends Richard and Milton Henry—took up the call for reparations, believing that slavery and its legacies had fundamentally shaped the American political economy and required economic and political redress. The Henry brothers helped convene a five-hundred-person gathering on March 29, 1968, in Detroit to discuss the need for justice, reparations, and black autonomy—and the potential for creating a black nation within the United States. Two days later, one hundred people signed a document forming the Provisional Government of the Republic of New Afrika (RNA), outlining a doctrine for the black nation and naming a provisional leadership. Queen Mother Moore was the first to sign. Robert F. Williams was named president in absentia; Betty Shabazz was named the second vice president. The RNA advocated a separate state for African Americans to be formed in the five "black belt" states of Mississippi, Alabama, Louisiana, Georgia, and South Carolina as land due black people as reparations for the legacy of slavery. Parks closely followed and occasionally participated in the RNA's activities, though it is difficult to document which events she attended. Many of her friends were deeply involved, and she was called on for help at key moments.

By most accounts, Parks did not attend the RNA's second annual convention on March 29, 1969, which resulted in a historic confrontation between black radicals and the Detroit police. Three hundred people gathered at Reverend Franklin's New Bethel Church. As the meeting finished, a shooting occurred outside the church. In response, the police broke down the doors of the church, poured hundreds of rounds into the church, and brutally arrested all the men, women, and children gathered. Police claimed self-defense, but an article in the *Michigan Chronicle* later revealed that members of the FBI, the CIA, and the Detroit police department's "subversive squad" were in attendance who could have prevented the melee outside and identified who actually shot the officer, but instead, they stood by. Several convention members were wounded. One young policeman was killed and another wounded. The entire convention remaining at that point, 140 people, was arrested en masse.

Reverend Franklin (the pastor of the church) notified black judge George Crockett of the mass arrests. Parks, alongside a number of friends, had worked hard to see Crockett elected to Recorder's Court in 1966. A bold legal advocate, Crockett had defended the eleven members of the Communist Party charged with violation of the Smith Act; represented Coleman Young and others before the House Committee on Un-American Activities (HUAC); and worked with the National Lawyers Guild in Mississippi. As a judge in Recorder's Court, Crockett had been devoted to rooting out police misconduct and establishing firmer judicial oversight.

In the middle of the night, Judge Crockett proceeded to the police station, where he found legal disarray. The 140 people from the RNA convention were being held incommunicado. No one had been formally arrested, and in disregard of customary procedure, everyone was being treated as suspects—fingerprinted and given nitrate tests to determine if they had fired guns. An indignant Crockett set up court right in the station house, demanding the police either press charges or release people. He had handled about fifty cases, releasing most of the men, women, and children, when the Wayne County prosecutor, who had been called in by the police, interceded and promised a return to normal procedures.

Crockett came under tremendous criticism for this intervention. White politicians and citizens called for his impeachment; 200,000 people signed a petition spearheaded by the Detroit police officers' association accusing Crockett of "gross misconduct." In response, a Black United Front of nearly sixty organizations ranging from the NAACP to the RNA coalesced to support Judge Crockett. On April 3, 1969, they called for demonstrations in support of Crockett, and some three thousand people responded. Greatly disturbed by the police action at New Bethel, Parks was active in the campaign to defend Crockett. On a slip of paper for a speech for Detroit's Alabama Club, she highlighted the similarities between police brutality in Montgomery and Detroit and then noted "my experiences with Judge Crockett," perhaps suggesting some personal tie to the events at New Bethel or Crockett's actions at the police station.

Police brutality continued to escalate in Detroit. In 1971, the police department created a special undercover unit, "Stop the Robberies, Enjoy Safe Streets" (STRESS). Using a decoy officer and usually two to three other officers, STRESS, in its first nine months, made 1,400 arrests and killed ten suspects (nine of whom were black). This tiny unit was responsible for 39 percent of Detroit Police Department deaths in its first year—and DPD topped the nation for civilian deaths. By September 1973, the number of STRESS fatalities had risen to twenty-two. Parks supported Coleman Young's bid to be

Detroit's first black mayor in 1973; one key promise he made—and ultimately delivered on—was to end STRESS.

After the police roundup at New Bethel Church, a section of the RNA decided to move its operations to Mississippi. Richard Henry, now known as Imari Obadele, led a group south to begin acquiring land, settling on a farm in Jackson, Mississippi; Milton Henry, now Gaidi Obadele, stayed behind in Detroit. Following the New Bethel incident, the FBI stepped up its monitoring of the group. The Mississippi farm was threatened and raided, and in August 1971 RNA members engaged in a showdown with police. On that day, the FBI and the Jackson Police Department attacked the RNA farm with arms, tear gas, and a tank. A shoot-out between the RNA and the police ensued. One Jackson police officer was killed, and another patrolmen and an FBI agent were wounded. Eleven RNA members, including President Imari Obadele (who was not at the farm during the shootout), were arrested, and the police began to brutalize the suspects, including one of the women who was pregnant. The defendants were paraded half-clothed through downtown Jackson.

A neighbor phoned RNA Minister of Justice Chokwe Lumumba back in Detroit. Fearing what would be done to the people in custody, Lumumba frantically called Representative

Conyers's office to ask the congressman to intervene. According to Lumumba, Conyers's office "got back to us immediately" that they had gotten the assurances from the Justice Department that the suspects would be humanely treated. Lumumba found out later that it was Rosa Parks who had acted so quickly. "She intervened and really saved their lives. If they had gone on unabated, some people would have killed. That was her intervention. . . . She saved the lives of my comrades."

Conyers's version of the story corresponds to Lumumba's. When Obadele died, Conyers "vividly recall[ed] Dr. Obadele working with Rosa Parks from my Detroit office, in 1971, to secure his safety in the Jackson, Mississippi jail following the RNA's confrontation with the police. He often told me that the actions of Rosa Parks saved his life in that Mississippi jail." Eight members of the RNA were convicted of murder; a year later, Obadele was convicted of conspiracy and served more than five years of a twelve-year sentence. Detroit city councilwoman JoAnn Watson remembered Obadele saying that during his five years in prison Parks would periodically call the prison to check on his well-being, being clear that this was "Rosa Parks calling" and informing prison officials they were being watched.

Mrs. Parks had long been critical of the ways black defendants were treated within the criminal justice system. The 1970s and 1980s saw a number of black activists face criminal prosecution. Parks joined the efforts to draw public attention to this political persecution. In 1971, Reverend Ben Chavis had been sent to Wilmington, North Carolina, by the United Church of Christ to help engage students in a boycott of city schools. Seen as militant troublemakers, he and nine others would be subsequently charged with arson and conspiracy in the firebombing of a white grocery. All were convicted. Outraged, defense committees were started across the country to press for their sentences to be overturned. Detroiters founded a local Wilmington 10 Defense Committee—its honorary chairpersons in 1976 included John Conyers, Judge Crockett, and Rosa Parks—which called for an appeal in the case and fund raising to support it. Parks followed the case closely from her home in Detroit, as she did with the case of UCLA professor Angela Davis. (Involved in the Free the Soledad Brothers campaign, Davis had been placed on the FBI's 10 Most Wanted list and charged with murder and kidnapping in connection with the death of Judge Harold Haley but was ultimately acquitted of all charges.) Davis came to Detroit two weeks after her acquittal for an SCLC event at the Coliseum. Parks introduced her to the crowd of twelve thousand as a "dear sister who has suffered so much persecution."

Long committed to criminal justice regarding sexual violence against women, Parks was one of the founders of the Joanne Little Defense Committee in Detroit. Little was charged with murder when she defended herself against the sexual advances of her jailer, Clarence Alligood. Little had been in jail for burglary and Alligood threatened her with an ice pick and forced her to perform oral sex. Little managed to grab the ice pick, stabbed Alligood, and escaped, turning herself in to police days later. Her case brought gender issues to the forefront of many Black Power groups—and a broad-based grassroots movement to defend Little grew across the country. The mission statement of the Detroit group affirmed the right of women to defend themselves against their sexual attackers and raised the interlocking issues of poverty and criminal defense—and the ways poor people could often not afford to mount an adequate defense. Parks was one of the people put in charge of soliciting help from other organizations. Little was eventually acquitted.

Parks also campaigned vigorously on behalf of Gary Tyler, a sixteen-year-old black teenager who had been wrongfully convicted for the killing of a thirteen-year-old white boy. As schools were desegregated in Louisiana, Tyler was riding a school bus attacked by a white mob angered by integration. Police boarded the bus and pulled

Tyler off for allegedly shooting a boy outside the bus, even though no gun was found on the bus. In a five-day trial, after police pressured some of Tyler's classmates (who would later recant) to testify, Tyler was sentenced to death. Parks gave the keynote at a packed meeting and rally of over three hundred people in Detroit on June 13, 1976, on behalf of Tyler. She attended meetings and continued to work to see his conviction overturned. In July 1976, the Supreme Court ruled Louisiana's death penalty unconstitutional. However, Tyler, imprisoned at the notorious Angola prison, was never freed.

Throughout these years drawing attention to the political nature of these prosecutions remained a key priority for Parks. In 1981, a broad swath of activists from the Black Liberation Army, the RNA, the Weather Underground, and the May 19th Coalition were arrested in connection with the $1.6 million robbery of a Brink's truck in Nanuet, New York. During the robbery and apprehension of the suspects, a security guard was killed, and a shoot-out between the activists and police left two Nyack officers dead. More than twenty people would be arrested in connection to the robbery—many of whom were known revolutionaries, though not all were part of the plot. (Members of these groups had also successfully helped Assata Shakur escape from prison in 1979, and law enforcement had become increasingly suspicious of these groups.) Chokwe Lumumba was defending RNA leaders Fulani Sunni Ali and Bilal Sunni Ali on conspiracy charges. Worried about radical high jinks and a politicized trial, the judge barred Lumumba from representing Fulani Sunni Ali, citing Lumumba's behavior in the courtroom. Unwilling to acquiesce to this assault on civil liberties, Lumumba and others fought back and ultimately won back the right for Lumumba to represent the Alis in the case.

In the midst of the case, Lumumba returned home to Detroit to find a small note in the mail. The writer thanked Lumumba for all his efforts "standing up for your people. . . . For standing strong and not flinching." Lumumba read the letter and thought, "This is a nice person who decided to write me. Really sweet. Then I put the letter down. A day later, I thought, 'Rosa?!' I went back and looked. The letter was from Rosa Parks." At the age of seventy, Mrs. Parks, always the dedicated correspondent, had taken the time to write another letter—to tell one of the most prominent black nationalists in the city (whom she had not met in person at that point) that she was proud of his efforts.

NEW DIRECTIONS, CONTINUING STRUGGLE
Continuing her varied activism, Parks campaigned vigorously for George McGovern in 1972 and

actively called for the impeachment of Richard Nixon. She addressed an overflowing crowd of fifteen thousand at the first Michigan Black Expo, sponsored by the Southern Christian Leadership Conference's Operation Breadbasket in July 1972, paying tribute to both King and Angela Davis. She appeared on a program with Reverend Charles Koen of the Cairo (Illinois) United Front. Formed in 1969 to counter white-vigilante and police violence in Cairo, the Cairo United Front led a years-long boycott of white businesses; Parks praised the "unity created by the new black awareness."

Feeling there was still much work to be done, she told Studs Terkel in 1973, "Even with much of what has happened to our dismay and to our unhappiness . . . I'll continue to be hopeful that there will be a way for us to eventually know freedom, with all of its meaning." In another interview from 1973, she expressed a similar sentiment: "A lot of things have happened and are still happening, that I wish would not have taken place. But you have to remain optimistic. When things get bad, you have to keep telling yourself that maybe it's just a phase, one more thing we have to go through. Nothing comes easily. We have to keep on trying, as long as we are alive."

In 1975, Parks returned to Montgomery to commemorate the twentieth anniversary of the boycott, telling the cheering crowd: "I'm very proud we've come from a voteless and a hopeless and a helpless people to a people who can and should hold the balance of the power politically." From the pulpit at Holt Street (where the first mass meeting had taken place), Parks was firm in her belief that the struggle was not finished. "Don't stop," she insisted. "Keep on. Keep on keeping on."

During the 1979/1980 school year, Parks paid a visit to the Black Panther Party's Oakland Community School, an independent black elementary school started to address the deficits in Oakland's public education system and the Panthers' longest-running survival program. The students performed a play they had written in her honor, which included a reenactment of her bus stand, and then she answered questions. "It didn't matter if they asked the question again and again, she answered them," according to the school's director, Ericka Huggins, who recalled how much Parks loved it. "She just kept thanking me and the instructors and the Black Panther Party for doing what we were doing." The students and entire staff were "touched," according to Huggins that Parks "came all the way" and talked about it for weeks afterward. Huggins recalled her own delight at Parks's visit. "I consider Rosa Parks a radical woman, a revolutionary woman, showing up in real time at an elementary school run by the Black Panther Party."

The late 1970s were a difficult time for Parks personally. Her ulcers continued to plague her, and she developed heart trouble. The family still struggled economically. Even more upsetting, Raymond, her mother, and Sylvester all developed cancer. "There was a time," Parks recalled, "when I was traveling every day to three hospitals to visit them." This took a lot out of her. She cut her work at Conyers's office to part-time. In 1977, after a five-year battle with throat cancer, Raymond died at the age of seventy-four, devastating the sixty-four-year-old Rosa. Three months later, Sylvester died. "My health wasn't too good at that time either, but I kept on working," she explained. "I couldn't do every-thing I wanted to, but I did what I could." And two years later, her mother passed away at the age of ninety-two. Within two years, Mrs. Parks's closest family—and foundation of her support— had all passed away. This was an aching loss.

The emotional toll was accompanied by economic insecurity. Various friends stepped in to try to raise money again. In 1976, a six-hundred-person fund-raiser was held to build a "shrine" for her in Detroit, a museum-residence where she would live and people could visit and learn the history of her life in the struggle. Articles ran in the black press about these fund-raising efforts. At the same time, Durr, Horton, and Terkel hoped to raise money for a home and steady income for

Parks to move back to Alabama. Durr wrote to Horton in 1979, "She tells me she has no money, that she wants to come back to Alabama where it is warm and I have no idea what her Federal pension will be. . . . When Congressman Conyers was here last spring I tried to talk to him about it, but he evidently misconstrued my remarks and got on the defensive and said he had done his best for Mrs. Parks and very abruptly ended the conversation." None of these efforts came to fruition.

BLACK POLITICS IN THE REAGAN ERA
Even the depths of her personal loss did not stop her political activities. As she regained her physical and mental strength, Mrs. Parks carried on her political commitments. "I don't plan as long as any effort is being made to be discouraged," she told a reporter in 1983. Like many of her civil rights comrades, Parks had long followed the movement to oppose apartheid in South Africa and joined efforts to challenge U.S. support of South Africa's all-white government. Alongside other activists in the Free South Africa Movement, she walked the picket lines in Washington, DC. On December 10, 1984, the seventy-one-year-old Parks made headlines, carrying a sign that read, "Freedom Yes Apartheid No!" She told the crowd how grateful she was to be there with them. Mrs. Parks patiently

explained to one reporter who seemed incredulous as to why she had come out, "I am concerned about that [South Africa's apartheid], and I am concerned about any discrimination or denial of any people regardless of their race." Arthur Featherstone, who worked alongside Parks on Conyers's staff, described Parks's "special concern for what's going on in South Africa . . . it really hurts her to see people being killed, as they were in Alabama, Mississippi and other states in the 1950s and '60s." In April 1985, she flew to Berkeley as part of coordinated anti-apartheid demonstrations to mark the anniversary of King's assassination. And in January 1986, she journeyed back to Ebenezer Baptist Church for the National Conference Against Apartheid, where Bishop Desmond Tutu gave the keynote.

Parks had difficulty saying no to causes she found important. She helped lead a march in Philadelphia in 1976 to prevent the closure of Philadelphia General Hospital, which served many black and poor residents. Concerned with the U.S. military role in Central America and the Caribbean, in 1984 she served as a judge, along with Judge Bruce Wright, Reverend William Sloan Coffin, and Ben Chavis, in a war-crimes tribunal sponsored by the National Lawyers Guild, the Center for Constitutional Rights, the National Conference of Black Lawyers, and La Raza Legal Alliance. The tribunal sought to examine and expose U.S. military activities and covert operations in Central America and the Caribbean and help spur antiwar activism against U.S. military interventions across the Americas.

She supported Jesse Jackson's bid for the Democratic nomination for president, headlining a fund-raiser for Jackson at Howard University in April 1984. In 1988, she came to the Democratic Convention in Atlanta to support him. Called onstage to cheers of "Rosa, Rosa, Rosa," the seventy-five-year-old Parks joined Jackson at the podium. Honored in Philadelphia, Parks explained to the thousand people gathered, "At some point we should step aside and let the younger ones take over. But we first must take care of our young people to make sure that they have the rights of first-class citizens. . . . And when we see so little done by so many, we just will not give up."

Closer to home was the nearly all-white suburb of Dearborn, home of the Ford Motor Company. The mayor had pledged to keep "Detroit's trash out," and in 1978 only a few blacks lived in Dearborn—many of those women serving as live-in domestics. The city then passed an ordinance forbidding "nonresidents" from using its parks. "Its mayor said the ordinance would keep the city clean. That was a metaphor for keeping it all white," NAACP activist Joseph Madison explained. In 1985, he and Parks began to make plans for a boycott of the entire city. To Parks, the Dearborn ordinance "was like many of the intimidating tactics we had to fight against in the civil rights movement. . . . I could not bear to see it happening again." The slogan for the boycott became "If you can't play, don't pay." On the eve of the boycott, the city rescinded the ordinance.

Madison and Parks continued working together. "People have a difficult time thinking of Rosa Parks as a fighter," Madison explained. But fight she did. In August of 1987, Madison and Parks joined forces to call for a boycott of a local retail chain they saw discriminating against black employees. As Madison explained in 1988, "If there's anything you write about Rosa Parks, you ought to try to dispel the myth that she is an old, frail woman. She is active, very forceful in a gentle way and extremely committed to the progress of young people." Madison decided to run for president and asked Parks to run for vice president of the Detroit NAACP in 1985. "We were basically battling against the old guard," explained Madison, "reaching out to the young people, becoming more active." The slate lost.

At a gala celebrating Parks's seventy-seventh birthday at the Kennedy Center in Washington, DC, in 1990, Lou Rawls, Dick Gregory, Sister Sledge, Dionne Warwick, Cicely Tyson, and Melissa Manchester performed tributes to Parks.

While always gracious, Parks did not seem to be in a love-song sort of mood and was one of the few on the program to highlight contemporary political issues, telling the star-studded crowd to "fight for the freedom of Nelson Mandela and those in South Africa." In her brief speech she told those gathered "not to give in or give up our struggle to peace, justice, goodwill, and freedom for all oppressed people," ending with the reminder that "many of us are oppressed today."

Four months after Nelson Mandela was released from Robben Island prison, he came to Detroit as part of a U.S. trip to promote sanctions against the South African government. Somehow Parks had initially not been invited to meet him, but Judge Damon Keith insisted on getting her a place in the receiving line, despite Parks's embarrassment. Mandela came off the plane amidst the cheering crowd of dignitaries and well-wishers, and froze when he saw Mrs. Parks. Slowly he began walking toward her, chanting "RO-SA PARKS! RO-SA PARKS!" The two seasoned freedom fighters embraced.

Conyers, Dick Gregory, and Rosa Parks all were supporters of reparations. By the late 1980s, calls for reparations had coalesced into the founding of N'COBRA, the National Coalition of Blacks for Reparations in America. According to its founding statements, three centuries of chattel slavery and another century of government-sanctioned segregation and inequality meant both the American government and businesses owed black people reparations. In 1994, N'COBRA held its annual meeting in Detroit. Both Rosa Parks and Jesse Jackson attended, Parks sitting in the front row next to Queen Mother Moore.

The next year, on October 16, 1995, Mrs. Parks and Queen Mother Moore journeyed to Washington to take part in the Million Man March, along with Dorothy Height, Maya Angelou, and Betty Shabazz. Parks received many calls from friends, particularly women friends, urging her not to go. Despite the "criticism and controversy [that] have been focused on in the media," Parks felt it was a "new day in America." As she had for decades, Mrs. Parks went where people were committed to doing good work; whether she supported the entire message or how it might look to other people were not her primary consideration. And so at the age of eighty-two, she accepted Louis Farrakhan's invitation to come to Washington, DC, to address the march. Greeted with an extraordinary ovation from the crowd, she spoke about Raymond's role in the struggle and how she was "honored that young men respect me and have invited me as an elder."

CONCLUSION

"Racism Is Still Alive"
Negotiating the Politics of Being a Symbol

ROSA PARKS'S MOST HISTORIC HOUR may have occurred on the bus in December 1955, but a moment that perhaps revealed more of her strength of character came forty years later. On August 30, 1994, at the age of eighty-one, Parks was mugged in her own home by a young black man, Joseph Skipper. Skipper broke down her back door and then claimed he had chased away an intruder. He asked for a tip. When Parks went upstairs to get her pocketbook, he followed her. She gave him the three dollars he initially asked for, but he demanded more. When she refused, he proceeded to hit her. "I tried to defend myself and grabbed his shirt," she explained. "Even at eighty-one years of age, I felt it was my right to defend myself." He hit her again, punching her in the face and shaking her hard, and threatened to hurt her further. She relented and gave him all her money—$103. Hurt and badly shaken, she called Elaine Steele, who lived across the street and had become a key source of support. Steele called the police, who took fifty minutes to arrive. Meanwhile, the word went out that someone had mugged Parks. "All of the thugs on the west side went looking for him," Ed Vaughn recalled, "and they beat the hell out of him."

Commentators seized on the news of Parks's assault to bemoan the decline of a new generation of black youth. "Things are not likely to get much worse," lamented liberal *New York Times* columnist Bob Herbert. "We are in the dark night of the post-civil rights era. The wars against segregation have been won, but we are lost. With the violence and degradation into which so many of our people have fallen, we have disgraced the legacy of Rosa Parks." The editors of the *Detroit Free Press* similarly intoned, "It is impossible to escape the cruel irony of the attack on Rosa Parks, beaten and robbed in her Detroit home Tuesday night by an assailant described as an African-American male. How could the woman credited with sparking the nation's civil rights movement to obtain equality for black people be assaulted by a black man?" With the nation eagerly consuming news of a black underclass, Parks's mugging served as a convenient metaphor for the degraded values of a new generation.

While saddened by the attack, Mrs. Parks did not see it as a sign of community dysfunction, rejecting the idea that the biggest problem facing the black community was now black people themselves. Rather, she urged people not to read too much into it. "Many gains have been made. . . . But as you can see, at this time we still have a long way to go." Rejecting the media's characterization of Skipper as representative of a new, degenerate cohort of black youth (a view held by many black people of her generation), she prayed for him "and the conditions that have made him this way." Her approach at eighty drew from her lifelong commitment to young people. "I hope to someday see an end to the conditions in our country that would make people want to hurt others." Mrs. Parks still believed, as she had with regard to the 1967 riot, that the way to stanch individual acts of violence was to transform the structures of inequity that provided the ground in which they grew. Even as she regularly reminded young people of the importance of good character, hard work, and motivation, Parks remained concentrated on changing the conditions that limited their ability to flourish. "She adored kids," her cousin Carolyn Green, who became one of her caretakers, noted. "Worst child in the world and [she] always saw some good in everybody. That's her philosophy."

To the end, Parks placed her hope in cultivating youth leadership. Worried that adults had become "too complacent," Parks founded the Rosa and Raymond Parks Institute for Self Development with Elaine Eason Steele in 1987, seeking also to honor Raymond and his political commitment. According to Steele, "It always bothered her that he was kicked to the curb and never thought of.

He, in fact, was her rock." The institute, like the youth wing of the Montgomery NAACP she had founded four decades earlier, sought to develop leadership skills in young people to bring them into the struggle for civil rights. A cross between Miss White's and Highlander, the institute stressed the importance of self-respect, comportment, and education for liberation to Detroit students. Black history for Rosa Parks had been one of the great transforming discoveries of her life, so the institute focused on exposing young people to African American history and encouraging them recover their own family's past. "When students come to class and demand to be educated," Parks observed, "education will take place." The institute sent young people both south and north through its "Pathways to Freedom" program to engage students in field research and immerse them in black history, including the opportunity to retrace the path of the Underground Railroad. Raymond had always regretted the lack of opportunity to get an education, so one key aspect of the institute's work was to provide college assistance. Parks saw a curriculum that stressed black pride and self-knowledge as a way to address the dropout problem affecting many black youth.

Parks was clear that the movement was not over, nor was it limited to the public's narrow view of civil rights as color-blindness or the end of legalized segregation. "Our struggle will never go away so I just have to keep on going on," she told a reporter in 1985. Critical of Reagan's policies and his "watering-down" of the U.S. Commission on Civil Rights, Parks asserted that Reagan "didn't understand the struggle" because he "never had to struggle." She well understood the "forces at work to destroy what gains have been made" and warned of "taking too much time out to just sit down and not do anything, [or] that'll soon be reversed." And she remained steadfast about the need to "rededicate and reunite ourselves into a movement. I don't think it's time to stop or slow down or become complacent of what may be ahead." Throughout the 1990s, even as her health waned, Parks spoke against many forms of social and racial injustice. She condemned Governor George W. Bush's use of the death penalty in Texas. And, on September 19, 2001, a week after the terrorist attacks on the World Trade Center, she joined with Danny Glover, Harry Belafonte, Gloria Steinem, and other human rights leaders to speak out against a "military response" to the attacks and to call on the United States to act "cooperatively as part of a community of nations within the framework of international law." Refusing the terms of post–civil rights racial politics, Parks continued to see the struggle for racial justice as urgent and ongoing.

"I UNDERSTAND THAT I AM A SYMBOL": BEING ROSA PARKS

> As time has gone by, people have made my place in the history of the civil-rights movement bigger and bigger. They call me the Mother of the Civil Rights Movement. . . . Interviewers still only want to talk about that one evening in 1955 when I refused to give up my seat on the bus. Organizations still want to give me awards for that one act more than thirty years ago . . . I understand that I am a symbol.
>
> —Rosa Parks

In 1980, an episode of the television game show *To Tell the Truth* featured three "Rosa Parkses." The weekly show presented three contestants who played the same person and attempted to fool a celebrity panel. Contestants earned prize money for each vote they received. That week, the real Parks, Contestant Number 3, tried to convince the celebrity judges that she was the person who had refused to give up her seat on the bus. She spoke characteristically thoughtfully and in great detail about the events of 1955. Yet two of the three celebrity judges voting chose Contestant Number 2, a demure lady wearing a lovely church hat and pearls who claimed she spontaneously decided one day just to make a stand, and who was actually Lois Alexander, director of the Harlem Institute of Fashion and the Black Fashion Museum. One judge explained her choice of Contestant Number 2 by citing the "gentleness" about her. The symbol of Rosa Parks had become more compelling than the reality.

As the years went by, Parks noted, people still "only want[ed] to talk about that one evening in 1955." In an interview in the late 1960s, she chafed at the detail interviewers wanted—"It just seems so much." In 1973, she told an interviewer, "I hope I won't be having to tell people that story for the rest of my life." In a 1978 interview, she explained that she was "somewhat resigned to whatever contribution I can make." She believed her public role and appearances were necessary to preserve the history of the struggle and help young people carry it forward, but she wished for personal space.

> I always have to refer to something Dr. King once said. . . . He asked the question, "Why should I expect personal happiness when so much depends on any contribution that I can make?" But I find myself asking myself, "Why should I expect personal happiness, if people want to find out what, who I am or what I am or what I have done. . . . There are times when I

feel I can hardly get up and go, and once I get there and see their [young people's] reaction, I feel somewhat rewarded."

Though Parks had not been included in the local commemorations of the Montgomery bus boycott in the first years, she returned to Montgomery for the twentieth anniversary commemoration in 1975. This time, Mrs. Parks spoke from the pulpit at Holt Street, where she reminded those gathered to "keep on" the struggle for justice and equality. However, it wouldn't be until the twenty-fifth anniversary of the boycott—and particularly the thirtieth and thirty-fifth—that these commemorations garnered significant national attention.

Reporters descended on her in 1980. A *Detroit Free Press* reporter described Parks as "weary of telling the story, weary of the reporters, weary of the questions." She informed him, "It's very difficult, very painful, to go over the same things all the time." She told the *Los Angeles Times* that she did "very well" left alone and didn't "like being overinflated." The reporter stressed how often Mrs. Parks "slips in and out of rooms almost soundlessly and prays not to be noticed." Her friend Louise Tappes explained, "Rosa would rather just forget the whole thing." Still faced with requests for interviews and appearances to talk about her actions twenty-five years earlier, Parks found it "difficult going back to that time.

I don't keep it in my mind if I can avoid it. I know that good came out of it for a lot of people, but it wasn't the most pleasant experience I ever had." In 1995, on the fortieth anniversary of the boycott, she embarked on a 381-day tour throughout the United States. An *Ebony* article noted that she had "logged more frequent flyer miles than a busy business executive. Perpetually on the go, she keeps up with a numbing schedule of events that would be daunting to a person half her age."

Parks saw black history as an activist tool to challenge injustice in the present and continued to do events, large and small. "My problem," she told Myles Horton in a 1981 oral history interview, "is—I don't particularly enjoy talking about anything." And yet over and over she talked about her bus stand, feeling she had a responsibility to do so. Throughout her life, if she was asked to do something for the good of the race—even if she might have preferred not to—she usually did it. Parks told another reporter in 1988, "I've always tried to be helpful to people in need but I could live without the publicity." Indeed many interviews Parks did in the 1960s, 1970s, and 1980s expressed her discomfort with how she had become a symbol—both because of what it had done to her private life but also because of the limited ways that people had come to understand her action and the movement more broadly. While her own notions of decorum and race work made it impossible for her to refuse these interviews or lash out at the questions, she noted, "it has been very taxing on me physically and mentally."

Increasingly in her older age, Parks seemed to come to some peace with her public role. In 1988 she explained to an *Ebony* reporter, "There was a time when it bothered me that I was always identified with that one incidence." She achieved this partly by focusing on what still needed to be done. "I find that if I'm thinking too much of my own problems and the fact that at times things are not just like I want them to be, I don't make any progress at all. But if I look around and see what I can do, and go on with that, then I move on." Perpetually committed to advancing the struggle, Parks accepted the role of "mother of the civil rights movement" in order to carry its history to students. In an interview in 1990, she lamented the fact that so many young people weren't familiar with key civil rights activists like Fred Gray or Fannie Lou Hamer and hadn't been "taught of the suffering we have went through." But that was changing; she was "encouraged that many young people . . . are interested in what happened." To her, the teaching of black history had to begin "as early as they can learn anything else." And so she answered thousands of letters and attended hundreds of school and youth programs held in her honor.

With the help of Jim Haskins, she wrote an autobiography geared for young people. Mrs. Parks had grown tired of public versions of her story that bore little relationship to her own life and wanted to set the record straight: "I cannot reach everybody personally . . . I think the story would give them much information that they may not get just reading what other people have written. Many people have written their own versions of my life and how they view it. But when I tell my own story, then I know that is my own life."

Parks drew pleasure from young people's performances of her 1955 arrest. "They have their own interpretation of what it was like. Sometimes it can be quite interesting, and sometimes amusing," she observed. Yet she often became trapped as symbol of a movement long since over. "They equate me along with Harriet Tubman and Sojourner Truth and ask if I knew them." Though Parks often participated in public events as a way to keep the struggle going, these commemorations increasingly confined the movement to the past. Regardless of her intentions, her iconic image began to take on a life of its own. Contrary to Parks's own philosophy, the process of Parks's iconization, Rosa Parks Museum director Georgette Norman observed, often had the effect of distancing young people, leaving them feeling "you cannot be an icon . . . [you're] nothing like me."

"PUTTING YOUR BAD IMAGES IN A MUSEUM"

Committed to honoring the history of the movement, Parks had labored with Coretta Scott King, John Conyers, and many of King's other associates since the assassination to get a holiday in his honor. Resistance ran high, and Parks traveled throughout the country to support various statewide efforts for the holiday. In 1983, that fifteen-year effort paid off, and President Reagan reluctantly signed the King holiday into law. But one of the paradoxes of the holiday was that almost as soon as it was institutionalized it began to get coopted by those who saw the civil rights struggle as a thing of the past. The King honored on the third Monday of January was a pale version of the friend and comrade that Parks had known. Having worked hard to get this national holiday, Parks was critical of the ways King was now being whitewashed. "He was more than a dreamer. He was an activist who believed in acting as well as speaking out against oppression." The King who had decried U.S. militarism, the structures of economic inequality, and the complacency of American liberalism was hardly to be found in the public celebrations.

At the same time, in the decades after the boycott, outcry grew among black activists and the black press that Parks hadn't received her due. An article on the tenth anniversary of her bus stand quoted friends and supporters who hoped "some national organization will have the genius, with some planning to give this woman the acclaim she deserves for what she means to America." Time and again, articles would be written about the "forgotten" Rosa Parks, many noting how "most Americans don't know her name." In 1978, *Los Angeles Sentinel* writer Jim Cleaver noted, "It is rather strange that her name cannot be found in the *Encyclopedia Britannica* or even the *Ebony Handbook.* Yet she stands head and shoulders above the so-called leaders of this century, whose names grace the various reference books."

Many black leaders and citizens looked for ways to give Parks her due. As she grew older, the honors flowed in. Streets were named after her, stained-glass windows made in her honor. In 1991, a bust of Parks was unveiled at the Smithsonian. Coretta Scott King, Joseph Lowery, Dorothy Height, John Conyers, and John Lewis all attended the unveiling. Parks called it "the high point of my life."

This national attention amplified in the wake of her mugging; Parks now was the right kind of black person to be honoring, implicitly contrasted with angry black activists and nihilist black youths. In 1999, Parks received the nation's highest recognition, a Congressional Gold Medal. Representative Julia Carson of Indiana spearheaded the effort and explained the importance of Parks receiving the honor "while she can still feel it." Carson enlisted Tavis Smiley's help to win support for the bill. Tavis put out the word to his listeners to "call, fax, email, carrier pigeon" their representatives about Parks getting the Congressional Gold Medal. Giving Parks this tribute became a cause in and of itself. All but one congressman, Texas Republican Ron Paul, ultimately voted to bestow the award on Parks; the Senate vote was unanimous.

On June 15, 1999, President Clinton presented Parks with the medal. Calling Parks's action and the resulting movement "the quintessential story of the 20th Century . . . the triumph of freedom," President Clinton honored Parks as a "living American hero" and compared Parks's bus stand to the battle for freedom waged on the beaches of Normandy and behind the Iron Curtain. "For us what has always been at stake is whether we could keep moving on that stony road, closer to the ideals of our Founders—whether we really could be a country where we are all equal." In a curious rewriting of the Founding Fathers, Clinton conceded that "people who have no position or money and have only the power of their courage and character are always there before the political leaders."

Brinkley noted the irony of these tributes. "Now that Rosa Parks's body was too feeble to march and her voice had faded to a whisper, politicians lauded her as a patriotic icon. She had grown . . . harmless and safe to exalt." One headline in the *Los Angeles Sentinel* tellingly proclaimed, "Rosa Parks Inspires Without Speaking at Museum Dedication, 45 Years Later." Historian Mike Marquesee has written about a similar process of turning Muhammad Ali into an icon exactly at the moment when Ali was silenced by Parkinson's. "The man who had defied the American establishment was taken into its bosom. There he was lavished with an affection which had been strikingly absent thirty years earlier." The tributes to Parks evidenced a "patronizing attitude towards older people," according to nonagenarian activist Esther Cooper Jackson, "the way the whole movement is erased, the heroes are just names without relating it to society and the significance of their lives." Increasingly, civil rights activists were honored to show America as a beacon of opportunity, by people who believed the United States had become a postracial society.

With the increasing popularity of heritage tourism, civil rights memorials and other movement-related tributes have gathered increasing cachet. At least fifteen museums have opened since 1990 commemorating civil rights activism—the King memorial on the Mall in Washington, DC, opened in 2011, and more are in the works across the South. "The civil rights movement is the new World War II," according to Doug Shipman, CEO for the National Center for Civil and Human Rights set to open in Atlanta in 2014. Civil rights tourism is the product of an unusual marriage between movement veterans and their allies who seek to preserve the history of the civil rights struggles, and political and corporate interests that see heritage tourism as a lucrative way to attract state and federal resources and tourism dollars. According to historian Glenn Eskew, these new civil rights museums have ushered in a "new civic religion that celebrates the triumph of racial tolerance and the assimilation of blacks into the existing political and capitalist world system." Explained former Birmingham mayor David Vann, "the best way to put your bad images to rest is to declare them history and put them in a museum."

At the very site of Parks's bus stand stands Troy University's Rosa Parks Museum. Dedicated in 2000, the three-story, fifty-five-thousand-square-foot state-of-the-art museum and library surprised Parks, who commented at the opening festivities, "In 1955, when I was arrested . . . I certainly never thought I would be remembered in such a grand manner." Buses have been indispensable to the historical memory of Parks and the boycott. The Troy Museum boasts a high-tech bus that reenacts the scene that December evening. Dearborn's

Henry Ford Museum boasts the "actual bus" where it all began. The National Civil Rights Museum features a bus visitors can board with a recording telling them to "move to the back . . . If you don't move out of that seat, I'll have you arrested." Viewers often leave convinced that today is nothing like the bad old days of segregation.

Georgette Norman, the director of the Rosa Parks Museum, worries that the ways that Parks has been memorialized "distracts" from the ongoing task of social justice that Parks herself was committed to. Curiously, even though brass plaques grace the former homes of many bus boycott activists in Montgomery, at the Cleveland Courts projects where Parks actually lived, there is a less auspicious green sign. The Parkses' apartment is no longer rented and has been placed on the National Register of Historic Places. But there has not been sufficient political will to upgrade the Cleveland Courts projects, where hundreds of working poor people still reside, which may explain the rather shabby sign there for one of Montgomery's famous. The less pretty parts of history and enduring social inequity are not as amenable to profit and thus easier to cast aside. The reality of Parks's class background sits at odds with the ways her image and legacy have been stripped of working-class markers—yet such reference might make her more identifiable for a younger generation.

> She wasn't a symbol, she was the real thing. . . . I think that most people were not interested in knowing the full story of Mrs. Parks's life . . . the concept that there are among us people who dedicate their lives to racial and economic justice gets completely lost.
>
> —Martha Norman Noonan

This depoliticized exaltation held tenfold when Parks died. An avalanche of congressmen, senators, and presidents rushed to honor Parks, hoping perhaps that "a tired old woman" lying in the Capitol building would cover up the federal travesty of inaction around Hurricane Katrina two months earlier. Her funeral provided a political opportunity for a new set of images to paper over those unsettling ones. By casting her as the nonthreatening heroine of a movement that had run its course, the memorialization of Rosa Parks proved useful in constructing a view of America as a postracial society. "Everyone wanted to speak," explained longtime friend Judge Damon Keith, who helped coordinate the funeral.

By honoring Parks apart from her life history of struggle, by celebrating the movement but consigning it to the past of the old South, by reducing it to buses, soft voices, and accidental acts and by feting the dignitaries over the grassroots people who sought to honor her, Parks's public memorial exposed the saliency of this narrow, gendered vision of movement history in American public life. The fable of the "not-angry" Parks would be used to place the movement firmly in the past, celebrating Parks as a proper heroine with a legitimate grievance, compared with the demands of others, which could then be marginalized. Overlooked were the forces and people who had long kept Rosa Parks quiet and the reality of Parks's long-standing anger at social injustice.

Rosa Parks may be the most widely known American woman of the twentieth century. In 2004, high school students were asked to name their top ten "most famous Americans in history" (excluding presidents) from "Columbus to the present day." Sixty percent listed Rosa Parks, who was second in frequency only to King. Parks's iconization thus provides an important window onto public investment in particular histories of the civil rights movement.

Scholars such as David Blight, John Hope Franklin, and Eric Foner have examined the political investments in the distorted histories of slavery and Reconstruction that emerged at the turn of the twentieth century. A popular history arose during that period that took a benign view of slavery and cast Reconstruction as a despotic and debauched period in American history. Serving political interests that sought to entrench segregation and economic inequity, decimate black voting power, and solidify national economic interests in cotton production, this history proved crucial to the task of Southern redemption and national unification. By legitimizing the various forms of segregation and exclusion that took root throughout the country at the opening of the twentieth century, these "histories" proved useful in framing the problem not as how to undo the legacies of slavery and Northern exclusion but on the task of national reconciliation and the need to control black people.

Looking at Parks's funeral reveals the "memory wars," to use Blight's terminology, now at play around the civil rights movement. As with the history of Reconstruction, a mythic history of the civil rights movement developed at the turn of the twenty-first century to serve contemporary political needs. According to this new popular story—and essential to the framing of Parks's memorial—the civil rights movement demonstrated the resiliency and redemptive power of American democracy. This nonviolent revolution proved the power of American dissent and self-correction. Parks's funeral communicated a lesson on the history of American progress and the end of racism, proclaiming a once and final end to the Second Reconstruction. In this narrative, racism was cast as an aberrant flaw rather than a constitutive element of American democracy—that, once recognized, had been eliminated.

National histories give comfort; they promote civic pride and communicate national values. They explain—and thereby justify—present-day action *and* inaction. Promoting reconciliation and national unity, those turn-of-the-century histories of Reconstruction explained why further federal government intervention was no longer needed. By portraying former slaves as angry, sexually promiscuous and reckless individuals who illegitimately sought special rights, these mis-histories cast black people as responsible for their own problems and undeserving of full rights.

The other side of the same coin, the celebration of the quiet Rosa Parks and the distorted popular histories of the civil rights movement at play today are also used to demonstrate how America cured itself of its previous history of discrimination. With the legacy of racial discrimination now vanquished, the problems people of color face can once again be cast as the product of their own values and poor character. Images of a debauched and violent black underclass, similar to those that had peopled the old histories of Reconstruction, were the backdrop of the Parks fable.

Of course, those histories are different. Woodrow

Wilson's showing of *Birth of a Nation* at the White House is, in key respects, a world apart from Rosa Parks lying in honor in the Capitol. Yet aspects of these mythologies operate similarly. Just as early histories of Reconstruction explained why no further action from the federal government was needed and allowed for the criminalization of black people and a cheapened labor supply, so too does the fable of Rosa Parks and the successful end to the Second Reconstruction. Just as turn-of-the-century Reconstruction histories held up good black people as deferential and happy, so too does the incessant celebration of Parks as "quiet" and "not angry." A tribute to a quiet national heroine proves that good values and individual acts are rewarded—that once revealed, real injustice is eradicated in a democracy like America without people having to get aggressive about it. The national honor for Rosa Parks also became a way to mark the death of racism, a form of national self-congratulation that Parks spent her life fighting against. Persistent educational inequality, widening economic disparities, skyrocketing incarceration rates for people of color, unending wars, and rampant racial and religious profiling— these contemporary injustices were implicitly rendered as so very different from the clear wrong that Parks had protested, despite the fact that the actual Rosa Parks and many of her colleagues had spent a lifetime trying to address them.

While many of the eulogies sought to put Parks's protest firmly in the past, Parks herself had continued to insist on the enduring need for racial justice in the present. Parks had kept on speaking her mind on the ways "racism is still alive"—reminding Americans "not [to] become comfortable with the gains we have made in the last forty years." Indeed, she ended her auto-biography observing, "Sometimes I do feel pretty sad about some of the events that have taken place recently. I try to keep hope alive anyway, but that's not always the easiest thing to do."

As King had before his death, Rosa Parks spoke in 1995 about how she wanted to be remembered. "I'd like people to say I'm a person who always wanted to be free and wanted it not only for myself." A full accounting of Parks's life and politics thus offers a different set of reasons for the nation to honor her. Laboring for decades in relative obscurity, Parks and her colleagues faced white terror to challenge racial injustice and till the ground for a movement, determined at the very least to register their dissent, even if they could deal no significant blow to white supremacy. When her courageous stand galvanized a mass movement, she did what she could to cultivate and sustain it. And when it gained certain success, despite the considerable sacrifice it had entailed for her and her family, she did not rest but joined with new and old comrades in the late 1960s and 1970s and onward to keep fighting for social justice and racial equality. That combination of steadfastness and outrage, tenacity and courage is what deserves national veneration.

Doing justice to Parks's legacy requires something much harder for the nation than a simple casket lying in the Capitol. It means acknowledging that the roots of racial and social injustice in American society are deep and manifest. It entails a profound recommitment to the goals she had spent her lifetime fighting for— real justice under the law, community empowerment and voting rights, educational access and equity, economic justice, and black history in all parts of the curriculum. It calls for dedicated, persistent action, year after year, decade after decade, as she did, to create systemic social change. Finally, it means heeding her advice to Spelman College students: "Don't give up and don't say the movement is dead."

ACKNOWLEDGMENTS

THERE IS NO WAY TO write a book like this without the help of a community of people. My first thanks goes to Julian Bond. When I was an undergraduate and then subsequently as his teaching fellow, Julian Bond taught me how to tell this story. More recently, he has been steadfast in his efforts to get the Rosa Parks Archive opened to scholars and in his support of this research.

A host of friends and colleagues made this book possible. Irva Adams, Gaston Alonso, Caroline Arnold, Beth Bates, Jennifer Bernstein, Chris Bonastia, Herb Boyd, John Bracey, Naomi Braine, Doug Brinkley, Brenda Cardenas, Julie Cooper, Matthew Countryman, Emilye Crosby, Paisley Currah, Angela Dillard, Tilla Durr, Jason Elias, Johanna Fernandez, Melissa Harris-Perry, David Garrow, Henry Louis Gates, Brenna Greer, David Goldberg, Stephanie Melnick Goldstein, Laurie Green, Joshua Guild, Gwendolyn Hall, Roderick Harrison, Wes Hogan, Hasan Jeffries, Amy Schmidt Jones, Peniel Joseph, Ira Katznelson, Robin Kelley, Steve Lang, Chana Kai Lee, Laura Liu, Eric McDuffie, Mojúbàolú Okome, Annelise Orleck, Kimberly Phillips, John Ramirez, Barbara Ransby, Russell Rickford, Dinky Romilly, James Smethurst, Irene Sosa,

Robyn Spencer, Kelly Stupple, Celina Su, Patricia Sullivan, Heather Thompson, Patricia Turner, Stephen Ward, Jocelyn Wills, Barbara Winslow, Craig Wilder, and Gary Younge all provided key assistance, inspiration, and support. There would be no book without them.

Numerous archivists assisted with this endeavor. I am particularly grateful to the research staffs at the Library of Congress; Wayne State's Reuther Library; the Amistad Center at Tulane; the State Historical Society of Wisconsin; Boston University, the Schlesinger Library at Radcliffe; the University of Wisconsin, Milwaukee; and Alabama State College. An AAUW American Fellowship helped fund my research sabbatical, and a Tow Travel Grant enabled me to visit various archives. The Center for Place, Culture, and Politics seminar and a PSC-CUNY grant helped me finish.

In Detroit and Montgomery, many people enabled me to do this research. Thanks go to Dorothy Aldridge, David Ashenfelter, Eleanor Blackwell, Carol Carter, John Entenman, Sherrie Farrell, Alfonzo Hunter, Judge Damon Keith, Keenan Keller, Georgette Norman, Gregory Reed, Howard Robinson, Elaine Steele, Mills Thornton, Penny Weaver, and Danton Wilson. My aunt Susan Artinian provided wonderful support and hospitality.

Numerous people gave generously in interviews,

committed to the belief that the political life of the great Rosa Parks merits substantive, scholarly research. I am immeasurably grateful to Barbara Alexander, Leon Atchison, Muhammad Ahmad, William Anderson, Dan Aldridge, Dorothy Dewberry Aldridge, Peter Bailey, General Baker, Julian Bond, Herb Boyd, John Bracey, Jamila Brathwaite, Candie Carawan, John Conyers, Doris Crenshaw, Fred Durhal, Willis Edwards, Nikki Giovanni, Robert and Jean Graetz, Carolyn Green, Nathan Hare, Larry Horwitz, Ericka Huggins, Alfonzo Hunter, Esther Cooper Jackson, Frank Joyce, Judge Damon Keith, Roslyn King, Marian Kramer, Chokwe Lumumba, Rhea McCauley, Martha Prescott Norman Noonan, Jack O'Dell, Gwendolyn Patton, Quill Pettway, Judy Richardson, Howard Robinson, Mildred Roxborough, Adam Shakoor, Sue Thrasher, Ed Vaughn, JoAnn Watson, Loretta White, Vonzie Whitlow, Mabel Williams, and Thomas Williamson.

My students at Brooklyn College supplied tremendous enthusiasm for this project and remind me continually of the importance of this research. A number of student research assistants provided key assistance over the course of the project: Alexander Perkins, Dane Peters, Khalina Houston, Darryl Barney, and Marwa Amer. It is hard to imagine this book without Marwa Amer, who was unstinting in energy, unflagging in insight, and the best research companion a scholar could hope for.

My editor, Gayatri Patnaik, is the definition of excellence—committed to the political biography I wanted to write and to the grace of its prose, and with a font of enthusiasm for this project. This book is vastly better for her efforts, those of the amazing Rachael Marks, Rosalie Wieder, Susan Lumenello, Marcy Barnes, and the careful work of the rest of the staff at Beacon, as well as my wonderful indexer Tara James and proofreaders Athan and Nancy Theoharis.

During the writing of this book, I have been engaged in a contemporary struggle for justice, which began with the case of my former student Fahad Hashmi, challenging the rights violations occurring in the federal judicial system post-9/11. Like Mrs. Parks, my friends and comrades in that struggle demonstrate what it means to be steadfast and undaunted in speaking truth to power. I am particularly grateful to—and thankful for—the Hashmi family, Sally Eberhardt, Laura Rovner, Pardiss Kebriaei, Rawad Guneid, Brian Pickett, Shane Kadidal, Suzanne Hayes, Saadia Toor, Leili Kashani, Sean Maher, Farah Khan, Bill Quigley, Amna Akbar, Vikki Law, and the people who attended the vigils outside the Metropolitan Correctional Center in New York for their work for justice. That struggle profoundly shaped how I would see and reflect the history I tell here.

I am blessed by the remarkable gift of friendship—of friends who read chapters, reminded me time and again of the importance of telling a new history of Rosa Parks, carried on about the world with me, and sustained me over the years this book took. Prudence Cumberbatch, Dayo Gore, Karen Miller, and Brian Purnell discussed each twist and turn of this research, and cared tremendously about me and this project. Komozi Woodard was immeasurably supportive from this project's inception and unwavering in his belief that the bigger story of the radical Rosa needed to be told. Arnold Franklin endured endless conversations about the book and my spirits. Alejandra Marchevsky is a "friend of my mind."

And finally, like for Mrs. Parks, this all begins with my family, who taught me to love justice and practice kindness—and inspire me with theirs—and to whom this work is dedicated.

ADDITIONAL COPYRIGHT INFORMATION

Excerpts from the poems "Harvest" and "Nikki Rosa" by Nikki Giovanni and from the Claude McKays poem "If We Must Die" are reprinted here with permission.

Earlier versions of portions of some chapters were previously published: " 'A Life History of Being Rebellious': The Radicalism of Rosa Parks," in *Want to Start a Revolution? Radical Women in the Black Freedom Struggle*, Dayo Gore, Jeanne Theoharis, and Komozi Woodard, eds. (New York: New York University Press, 2009); "Accidental Matriarchs and Beautiful Helpmates: Gender and the Memorialization of the Civil Rights Movement," in *Civil Rights History from the Ground Up: Local Studies, a National Movement*, Emilye Crosby, ed. (Athens: University of Georgia Press, 2011); " 'The Northern Promised Land That Wasn't': Rosa Parks and the Black Freedom Struggle in Detroit," *OAH Magazine of History* 26, no. 1 (January 2012).

Center Point Large Print
600 Brooks Road / PO Box 1
Thorndike ME 04986-0001 USA

(207) 568-3717

US & Canada:
1 800 929-9108
www.centerpointlargeprint.com